God Gave the Growth

Dear Lisa,

Thank you so much for your dedicated service on the Commission on Ministry, and for your love for Christ's mission in our church! You are greatly appreciated!

+ Snow Brown Snell

Nov. 2019

God Gave the Growth

Church Planting in the Episcopal Church

Susan Brown Snook

Morehouse Publishing
NEW YORK

Unless otherwise noted, the Scripture quotations contained herein are from the New Revised Standard Version Bible, copyright © 1989 by the Division of Christian Education of the National Council of Churches of Christ in the U.S.A. Used by permission. All rights reserved.

Morehouse Publishing, 19 East 34th Street, New York, NY 10016

Morehouse Publishing is an imprint of Church Publishing Incorporated.
www.churchpublishing.org

Library of Congress Cataloging-in-Publication Data
Brown Snook, Susan.
 God gave the growth : church planting in the Episcopal Church / Susan Brown Snook.
   pages cm
 Includes bibliographical references and index.
 ISBN 978-0-8192-2997-7 (pbk.) — ISBN 978-0-8192-2998-4 (ebook) 1. Church development,
New—Episcopal Church. I. Title.
 BV652.24.B766 2015
 254'.108828373—dc23
                          2014050181

Cover design by Laurie Klein Westhafer
Typeset by PerfecType, Nashville, TN

Printed in the United States of America

This book is dedicated to the first four pioneers at Nativity,
four intrepid souls who dreamed of a church and helped it come to birth:
Mark and Jennie Dobbins
Alastair and Mary Longley-Cook

And to my husband, Tom, and daughters, Sarah and Julia,
without whose support none of this could have happened.

Well done, good and faithful servants.

I planted, Apollos watered, but God gave the growth.
1 Corinthians 3:6

Contents

Acknowledgments

I am not an expert on church planting—merely a practitioner. On my own, I would only be able to tell you the story of Church of the Nativity in Scottsdale, Arizona, which a team of lay people and I planted in 2006, and which I now serve as rector. This book is possible, however, because many other wise and gracious people agreed to let me interview them and learn their stories. I am grateful to those I have spoken with, not only for their time, but for the courage, perseverance, prayer, and sheer hard work it takes to plant a congregation, or to support others who are planting. Without their wisdom, this book would have been much diminished. My thanks go out to these interviewees: Jimmy Bartz, Tom Brackett, Christopher Carlisle, Andy Doyle, Carmen Guerrero, Anthony Guillén, Kellie Hudlow, Clay Lein, Frank Logue, Lang Lowrey, Mary MacGregor, Katie Nakamura Rengers, Ema Rosero-Nordalm, Kirk Smith, and Daniel Velez Rivera. I am also tremendously grateful to The Episcopal Church's Director of Research, C. Kirk Hadaway, for invaluable help in supplying important statistics related to the church.

I am grateful also to the team of intrepid pioneers who have shared this journey with me, from 2006 to the present. Church planting is never an individual endeavor; it's a team project. The folks who formed a committed team to plant Nativity, populate its many ministries, and transform lives with the love of God in Jesus Christ have much to be proud of, and they have earned my eternal gratitude. They are too many to name, but their names are written in the book of life. Thank you to all who have created a labor of love at Nativity.

And of course, I am grateful to my family for putting up with my hard work for lo, these many years. Thanks to my dear daughters, Sarah and Julia, for being the first members of Nativity's youth group and Sunday school, and for helping pioneer a new Christian community. And most of all, thanks to my husband, Tom Snook. Without his love and support in so many ways, none of this would have been possible.   ❧

Foreword

That same day Jesus went out of the house and sat beside the lake. Such great crowds gathered around him that he got into a boat and sat there, while the whole crowd stood on the beach. And he told them many things in parables, saying: "Listen! A sower went out to sow. And as he sowed, some seeds fell on the path, and the birds came and ate them up. Other seeds fell on rocky ground, where they did not have much soil, and they sprang up quickly, since they had no depth of soil. But when the sun rose, they were scorched; and since they had no root, they withered away. Other seeds fell among thorns, and the thorns grew up and choked them. Other seeds fell on good soil and brought forth grain, some a hundredfold, some sixty, some thirty. Let anyone with ears listen!"
Matthew 13:1–9

How many times have you heard the story of the sower of seeds? How many times have you heard it in terms of church planting or the good news? We are the sower, our preachers and teachers interpret. Or, are we the ground? Either way we often turn the parable into a lesson where we are at the center and we are either a good or a bad sower; or, we are good or bad soil.

What if Jesus offers us a different picture of the reign of God with the parable of the sower? What if God is the Sower? God the Creator flings the seed far and wide. God the Father indiscriminately sows the seed—even doing so without the earth's or our own authorization.[1] Furthermore, God is sowing Jesus. Theologian and priest Robert Farrar Capon says that we typically read this as if the living Word, Jesus, is not in the world until we get there.[2] The Most Rev. Rowan Williams once said we tend to lead the baby Jesus by the hand into the world; however, God is *already* present in the world.[3] We are not the ones bringing Jesus to the world.

The living Word of God is present in many kinds of soil, working mysteriously in the world, and we may be witnesses or not. Moreover, the power of the seed is not "undone by its placement."[4]

If the Episcopal Church is to experience the fullness of God, we must leave familiar soil and go out into God's world where God is present. We must bear witness to the mysterious and wonderful things that God is doing in the life of God's creatures. Surely we will see that some of the ground is harsh indeed. The Word of God is found among the rocks, weeds, and thorns, and may be in need of some tending there. We are faithful when we seek out these new (and sometimes uncomfortable) places to look for the living Word.

The Episcopal Church is not afraid of a little gardening. We are the kind of church that tends the soil so seeds can take root; that pushes back the thorns so the seed has room for light and water.

We are the inheritors of a tradition that has found the living God out in the world and has courageously followed him away from the safety of home and hearth to build altars in the wilderness. Will we leave the same legacy as Abraham and Sarah?

In every era the church has had to figure out its unique context. In every time and in every place for more than twenty centuries, the church has fearlessly, tirelessly, faithfully walked out into the world, found a plot of earth and set up a table and there made communion.

This time is no different. We may be in need of courage. We may be in need of new economies. We may have to restructure. We will most definitely

---

1. Robert Farrar Capon, *Kingdom, Grace, Judgment: Paradox, Outrage, and Vindication in the Parables of Jesus* (Grand Rapids: Eerdmans: 2002), 61.
2. Ibid.
3. Rowan Williams, Compass Rose Forum, Lambeth Palace, 2010.
4. Capon, 68.

need to leave the building. All in all, this time is no different than the time that has come before.

It is our responsibility to build the church for and of the future, to fund it, and to nurture it into life abundant. We are the vine tenders and the vine growers. We are the harvesters and we are the laborers. We are the ones to whom a new generation of Christians, who call themselves Episcopalians, will look upon and give thanks to for such faithfulness.

The Rev. Susan Brown Snook has offered us a unique and energetic template for our commitment to build these new communities in the world—grown from the seeds of God's living Word. Our church, with its great tradition of evangelism and mission, has in recent years looked to other denominations for guidebooks to map our new context and to discern how we could raise up new missional communities. Snook gives us a resource from our own tradition using our vocabulary and the depth of our own theology to show us exactly how we might begin to see God working in the world.

I believe that the Episcopal Church is being remade, reformed, and rebirthed in this era. It is not dead, nor is it dying. It is alive. We have not seen such a great opportunity for mission since the very first years of the Christian church. There has never been a greater time than this to be a Christian and to share our faith with others. I would not choose another place or context in which to work. We have been chosen for just such a time as this. Even now God is praying for laborers to be sent out.

With courage, commitment, and faithfulness in one hand and Snook's book in the other, we have the tools to nurture and harvest what God so graciously has sown in the world about us. That being said, books do not plant churches—people do. How will you see the path, the rocks, or the weeds where we find God already at work? How will you tend the soil in your particular context? Where will God's Word begin to take root with your help? What will be the parable you write today that will be your legacy for the church and for future generations?

The Rt. Reverend C. Andrew Doyle
Episcopal Diocese of Texas
December 2014

Introduction: The Leap of Faith

A few years ago, my family took a vacation to Hawaii, the land of sapphire blue ocean, soft breezes, green mountains, and kind and friendly people. One day, on the island of Kauai, my family talked me into going with them on a zip line. I had never been on a zip line before.

Well, if you've never been on a zip line, here's how it works. You climb up five or six flights of stairs and stand on a platform big enough to hold about ten people, looking down on a canopy of treetops. The platform sways gently in the ocean breeze. The leaders hook each person into an elaborate helmet and harness, carefully explaining that the whole getup has been thoroughly tested and will hold up to three thousand pounds. The harness gets hooked to a thick wire running from the swaying platform to a second platform in a tree about half a football field away and somewhat downhill. You stand in your harness, take a step off the platform into the air, give a wild yell, and as the harness takes hold of the wire, you take a swinging, joyous ride down the wire to the platform in the tree.

My husband went first, shouting in glee, and then my two daughters took the plunge, laughing and hollering. Then it was my turn. I got all hooked up, I stood on the edge of the platform ready to go—and I just couldn't do it. I looked at the ground, five or six stories below, and froze in fear. It looked awfully far down. I knew that the harness was supposed to hold me—I had seen it work perfectly for my husband and daughters—but I couldn't take that first step. Why, I thought, would anyone want to leave this perfectly good platform and step out into the air? This platform might be small and swaying, it might not be terribly comfortable, it might get awfully cold if I stayed here all night—but still, why shouldn't I just stay right here?

The leader started urging me, "Go on the count of three! One! Two! Three!"

I simply could not make myself take the first step. My family started yelling encouragement from far away; encouragement that sounded suspiciously like, "You're being really stupid, Mom!" The family in line behind me sighed in disgust and leaned against the rail to wait impatiently. I stood on that platform, frozen.

Finally, I looked at my family, I looked at the leader, I looked at the group behind me, and I said to myself, "What's the worst that could happen? I could die, and I'm prepared for that." I closed my eyes, counted to three, and stepped off the platform.

And that's when I discovered why people do zip lines. You step off the platform and there's a split second of free fall—and then your harness goes to work. You find yourself caught, and held, and as you shout in triumph, you find that you are being taken for the wild, joyous, careening ride of your life.

Planting a church feels a little bit like riding a zip line. All the preparation, prayer, and training you have done throughout your ministry are ready to be tested. Will the equipment hold? Should you step off that platform? Should you take a risk with your career and your reputation? Should you maybe just stay in a nice established church, where things are safe and predictable? Or should you take a step of faith, trusting that God will be there to catch you and carry you on a joyous ride?

I became the founding priest of Episcopal Church of the Nativity, Scottsdale, Arizona, in 2006. Arizona's bishop, Kirk Smith, had declared his goal to plant ten new churches in ten years. I had been ordained as a priest for three years, after a career as a certified public accountant and then a stint as a director of Christian education. I was ready for a new challenge, so I went to the bishop and asked him to let me plant a church. He agreed and assigned me a growing suburban area of north Phoenix and Scottsdale. With a team of active and committed lay people, we officially launched worship in an elementary school in Advent 2006 with 106 people in attendance. Nativity has grown since then by ten to fifteen percent each year and is now a program-size congregation. In 2012 we became a parish of the Diocese of Arizona and built and moved into our permanent church building.

Nativity represents a traditional Episcopal church plant, located in a growing suburban area. Our worship is both traditional and lively. We worship using Rite II according to the rubrics, occasionally using elements from *Enriching Our Worship*; our music comes from traditional Episcopal hymnals as well as from chant, classical, jazz, and gospel traditions. We project our liturgy and music on a screen to make it easy for non-Episcopalians to follow, while also making hymnals and prayer books available for those who prefer to use them. We have strong children's and youth programs, and we engage in a number of community outreach and service ministries, including partnerships with other churches in Phoenix, Navajoland[1], and Mexico. Many of our current members were not attending a church when they found Nativity, though a number of them had church backgrounds in the distant past. Nativity is an example of how a newly planted traditional church can reach many new people in a community. A traditional church plant, intentionally located in a growing area, demonstrates that the Episcopal Church's classic ways of creating liturgy and forming community are still effective in the twenty-first century.

Historically, the Episcopal Church has planted many churches like Nativity, in growing areas of towns and cities. The wave of church planting that enlivened the church in the 1950s and 1960s generally followed this traditional model, and resulted in many of the vibrant churches that Episcopalians attend today. But American society is changing, and while I believe traditional church planting is still a vital ministry for the church, new models are essential too. Many dioceses are located in areas of the country that are not blessed with population growth like Arizona is. Many have declining financial resources and overbuilt inventories of church buildings that are too large for their current congregations. Is church planting even relevant to dioceses in this situation? Are there other models of church planting that we should be trying, even in places with declining populations and tight financial resources? As long as there are significant, and growing, numbers

---

1. Navajoland was created out of the Episcopal dioceses of Utah, New Mexico, and Arizona during a transitional period of 1977 to 1987 to better unify the area in respect to Navajo language, culture, families, and area events.

of people who have not heard the gospel and are not part of a community of faith, I believe that there are. The traditional model of planting a new congregation that will buy land and build a building may not be relevant—but there are other creative possibilities.

Across town from Nativity, in western Phoenix, the Rev. Carmen Guerrero is planting another kind of church—Iglesia Santa Maria, one of Nativity's partner congregations. Santa Maria shares space with St. Mary's Episcopal Church, an older Episcopal congregation worshiping in an Anglo-Catholic style. The neighborhood around St. Mary's has grown to include increasing numbers of Latinos, mostly first-generation immigrants and their children, and Santa Maria is responding to this population shift while St. Mary's continues to minister to its own members. Santa Maria has been in existence for about a year, providing Spanish-language worship, music, and education programs for around one hundred people each week. Santa Maria also coordinates a bimonthly food distribution to people in need in its community, one of the projects that Nativity helps with. Santa Maria is an example of a Latino or other ethnically focused church plant, which reaches out to new folks by worshiping in languages other than English, using music and worship that is relevant to the group, and often, providing help the community needs. And it was started without any need for capital investment, because it uses a physical asset, a church building that was already strategically located for mission with a new population.

Meanwhile, in a storefront in Birmingham, Alabama, the Rev. Katie Nakamura Rengers, a twenty-eight-year-old priest, and the Rev. Kellie Hudlow, a thirty-five-year-old vocational deacon, are gearing up for a new ministry concept. They are creating The Abbey, a coffeehouse that will welcome any passer-by who wants to come in to buy coffee. A professional manager will run the coffeehouse, but a priest or deacon, in collar, will always be behind the bar, serving and chatting. Another clergy person from the diocese (including, at times, the diocesan bishop, the Rt. Rev. Kee Sloan) will be sitting at a table, welcoming people for conversation or counseling. The coffeehouse will host Bible studies, discussion groups, and eventually, prayer services, beginning with the daily office and later on, the Eucharist. While anyone will be welcome, Rengers and Hudlow see their ministry as responding particularly to the Millennial generation's alienation from institutional Christianity, desire to form community and explore important issues, and attraction to ancient spiritual practices. It will operate under a completely different financial model than an ordinary church, because it will be partly or fully supported financially by the coffeehouse revenues. The Abbey is an example of a nontraditional church plant, which I will call a "Fresh Expressions" plant. A Fresh Expressions community strives to reach populations such as young adults or other groups who are not interested in traditional models of church.

Each of these types of church plants is reaching new people, in very different ways, and each is responding to important demographic changes. In the U.S. today, Episcopal membership is declining sharply while the total population continues to rise steeply. Within that total increase in population, important shifts are occurring. The population of some areas is shrinking while others grow, yet churches too often become mired in anxiety about the declining churches while failing to respond to the opportunities presented by growth. Some people are leaving urban centers, while others, who may speak different languages or be from other parts of the world, move in. Increasing numbers of people, including many young people, have never been exposed to the gospel in any meaningful way, and are therefore unlikely to enter even the most welcoming traditional church.

All of these changes impact the way the Episcopal Church does ministry. Too often, the impact means decline and even closure of once-vital churches. But change represents not simply danger, but also opportunity. God still has a mission in our communities full of shifting realities. As Christians, we believe that that Holy Spirit is always at work, healing and renewing creation and calling people into relationship with Christ. Jesus called the church to answer the Great Commission[2] in all times and places. Cultures and populations may change, but God's mission among us remains constant. And God's mission has a church: a catholic church of which the Episcopal Church is one branch. God still calls Episcopalians, like other Christians, to join in the divine mission of love and reconciliation.

One way the Episcopal Church can join in God's mission in a changing world is to plant new churches that respond to our shifting context in vital and creative ways. Yet the Episcopal Church is far behind in responding to this gospel call. You could say that Episcopalians are standing on a swaying

---

2. Matthew 28:16–20.

platform looking down. The place we are standing is not particularly stable, but it is all we know. Many of us are finding it very difficult to take a step into the unknown territory of church planting—though we have seen other churches succeed at this adventure, and though we have a long history of successfully planting churches ourselves in the not-so-distant past. We could stay where we are, and ignore the voice of the Holy Spirit calling us into a new reality. Or we could trust God to guide us in taking the next step. Is the gospel that we have discovered in the Episcopal Church worth sharing with others?

I believe it is. Following Christ was never meant to be risk-free. Jesus himself came into a risky world as a vulnerable human being in order to bring God's kingdom to earth, and he gave his life to do it. Jesus sent his disciples out without a staff or any possessions, to rely on local hospitality and tell the good news of his arrival. The Episcopal Church can go out into the world to preach this good news too.

I believe that it is time for our church to take a risky, scary leap, and to start planting new churches all over this country. Church planting is not the only way to do the ministry God calls Episcopalians to—we should also be revitalizing some of our existing congregations. But this book is about planting new congregations. Why should we do it, how can we do it well, and what changes should we make in order to make this ministry successful? With God, all things are possible, and it is possible to plant new churches, to reach new people, and to change lives through the power of Christ. When we do take that leap of faith, I believe the Holy Spirit will be there waiting for us, and we will find ourselves caught, and held, and carried along for a wild, joyous, careening ride of faith.

PART ONE

Planting Churches to Join in God's Mission

Why plant churches? In an era of overall declining attendance at Episcopal and mainline churches, why spend time and money to plant new congregations? We plant churches to join in God's mission, to reach new populations, and to answer God's call. In this section, we will explore the church's mission in a new era, discuss the most important reasons for planting new churches, and talk about the different kinds of church planting that will be essential in the years to come.

God's Mission Has a Church

When my family moved to Austin, Texas, in the mid-1970s, one of the first things my parents did was look for a church. There was not much question about which church to attend; they were Episcopalians, so they looked for an Episcopal church. There was not even much question about which Episcopal church to attend; one attended the church closest to one's home. The first Sunday we were in town, that's what we did. Without much discussion, we joined the church and became faithful members. I attended Sunday school and youth group there; that church sent me to summer camp and awoke in me a sense of calling to the priesthood (which, I didn't answer till many years later, but that's another story). My parents have now been faithful members of that church for forty years.

Back in the mid-1970s, that's what people did. Wherever you lived, you looked for the correct religious congregation to join according to your particular brand loyalty: Baptist, Methodist, Episcopal, Roman Catholic, Jewish, and so on. Outside of Christian and Jewish options, there weren't many; a few people didn't attend any particular church but still were able to name some sort of family affiliation. Whatever church you joined assumed that you had been a member of another church somewhere, and asked you to hand over your transfer papers so they could account for you properly. In my cousins' Baptist church, they had regular altar calls and tracked who was "saved," but in the Episcopal church, people were baptized as infants, confirmed in the sixth grade, and assumed to be decent Christians thereafter. It was all very logical and orderly.

I don't have to tell you that's not how things work any more. A number of faithful Episcopalians still maintain their brand loyalty, but there are many more religious options than there used to be. One of the most popular options is "None," a preference adopted by increasing numbers of people, especially younger people. Gen-Xers and Millennials whose Boomer parents did not raise them in a church have little background in scriptural or religious knowledge, except what they read in the news—and that news is too often negative. What reason would they have for seeking out a church to add to their busy lives? School, sports, and scouting activities are ever more frequently scheduled on Sunday mornings, and parents gamely commit to them. People juggle frenetically busy schedules, and their spiritual lives fall into insignificance behind all the other priorities they try to meet. Faith, if they have it, often becomes distant background noise, recalled in times of trouble.

In the meantime, the world has gotten ever more confusing and complex. Futurist Bob Johansen says that we now live in VUCA world: a world of Volatility, Uncertainty, Complexity, and Ambiguity.[1] Americans are no longer sure that they can count on the institutions of nation, religion, and society that once upheld our culture. Distrust of authority, conflicts over social issues, and scandals in some denominations have led many people to flee the churches they once filled. A church can no longer assume that it will have a certain market share of the population in any one place due to brand loyalty, nor can it assume that any Episcopalians who move into a neighborhood will join the closest Episcopal church. Episcopal churches once built their appeal on an "attractional" model that, in the worlds of the classic movie *Field of Dreams,* assumed that "If you build it, they will come." Those same churches are finding that the attractional model no longer brings people inside the church doors. They no longer come.

---

1. Bob Johansen, *Leaders Make the Future: Ten New Leadership Skills for an Uncertain World* (San Francisco: Berrett-Koehler, 2012), 1.

God's Mission Has a Church

Yet God surely is still moving in our communities. Christ certainly still loves the religiously unaffiliated people who bustle down the streets, fill the coffee shops, beg on the street corners, crowd into the schools, and work in the restaurants, shops, and high-rise office buildings of our communities. The Holy Spirit without doubt is still at work to bring God's love to those who have no knowledge of it. God still has a mission in our land.

Like any organization, the church talks a lot about mission: What is the mission of the church? What is the mission of each congregation? It is essential for church planters and diocesan and denominational leaders to think and pray about the mission of new churches. Yet there is a growing understanding in the Christian world that the church doesn't have a mission—God has a mission, and God calls the church to join in what God is already doing. Darrell Guder says:

> The ecclesiocentric understanding of mission has been replaced during this century by a profoundly theocentric reconceptualization of Christian mission. We have come to see that mission is not merely an activity of the church. Rather, mission is the result of God's initiative, rooted in God's purposes to restore and heal creation. "Mission" means "sending" and it is the central biblical theme describing the purposes of God's action in human history.[2]

It is because God has sent us that we gather in communities of faith where the gospel is preached, the sacraments are celebrated, and people are sent out to join in God's mission in our daily lives. The activities we do in church glorify God, strengthen Christians in discipleship, and nourish God's people, but true mission happens outside the church, and every Christian is a minister. The mission of the church is no longer "attractional"—seeking to bring people in, but "incarnational"—seeking to send people out.

This realization that God's mission happens in every part of life, not just in church, and certainly not just in the Episcopal Church, begs the question: Does God care about the number of people who attend worship each Sunday,

---

2. Darrell L. Guder, ed., *Missional Church: A Vision for the Sending of the Church in North America* (Grand Rapids, MI: Eerdmans, 1998), 4.

and how large our churches grow? Are growth and evangelism integral to the church's mission, or is our mission limited to social outreach work, or faithful worship, or serving the people we have already? Are attendance and membership numbers important at all?

Well, if not, the New Testament is curiously full of attendance and membership numbers. A quick perusal of the Acts of the Apostles shows the church growing by well-enumerated leaps and bounds, with large numbers of people responding to the apostles' proclamation of the good news of Christ. Luke, the author of Acts, eagerly counts the crowds who join in the apostles' teaching and fellowship. In fact, God's mission to reach many new people with Christ's love, and Christ's call to the church to join him in that mission, and the Holy Spirit's activity in empowering the church to do it, could not be any clearer than it is in the New Testament. God is on a mission to reconcile the world to God's self, and God calls the church to join in doing it. That is why the church exists, to do the things God is already working in the world to accomplish.

According to the Book of Common Prayer, "The mission of the church is to restore all people to unity with God and each other in Christ."[3] This mission is very ambitious, to say the least—but if you're following the Son of God, miracles do happen. I believe this mission encompasses many aspects of church activity: from the forgiveness of sins (John 20:19–23), to proclaiming the year of the Lord's favor (Luke 4:16–20), to helping the "least of these" (Matthew 25:40), to working with Christ for a new creation (2 Corinthians 5:17), to praying that the will of God be done on earth as it is in heaven (Matthew 6:10).

And surely this mission of reconciliation encompasses evangelism as well. In fact, I would argue that evangelism is what makes all these other missions possible, because committed disciples are the ones who do Christ's work in the world. In the gospel of Matthew, Jesus's last words to his disciples are his command to go and make disciples:

> And Jesus came and said to them, "All authority in heaven and on earth has been given to me. Go therefore and make disciples of all nations, baptizing them in the name of the Father and of the Son

---

3. Book of Common Prayer, 855.

*and of the Holy Spirit, and teaching them to obey everything that
I have commanded you. And remember, I am with you always, to
the end of the age."* Matthew 28:18–20

And in Acts 1:8, Luke describes what Jesus said to his disciples just
before he ascended to heaven, commanding the disciples to share the good
news: "You will be my witnesses in Jerusalem, in all Judea and Samaria, and
to the ends of the earth."

Our existing churches are beautiful, faithful congregations of people.
But that does not mean they are the only congregations Jesus wants us to create. Jesus told us clearly that we should not be satisfied in whatever comfortable Jerusalem we find ourselves in, but that we need to go out—to Judea,
Samaria, and the ends of the earth—to make disciples of all nations. The
disciples we make do not have to be in foreign lands. They can be our neighbors, "Samaritans" who have never entered a church, but who are hungry for
deeper spirituality, for the knowledge of Christ's love.

In the Episcopal Church, many of us concentrate admirably on social
justice and on bringing the kingdom of God to earth. I believe that this work
is one good thing, but not the only thing we should be doing. Social justice
work is entirely compatible with answering Jesus's call to make new disciples. Helping people come to know Christ and grow in relationship with him
gives them the gift of abundant, eternal life. Welcoming them into a community of faith that nourishes them with the sacraments, teaches them about
Christ, and inspires them to live in Christ-like ways makes the kingdom of
God a lived reality. Gathering them into churches helps marshal resources to
help people in need. In fact, the church *must* make new disciples if we plan
to do social justice work, help the poor, or transform unjust structures of
society. This is long-term work, and it will require generations of disciples
to do it.

Evangelism is what makes the mission of the church possible, and planting new churches is one important way to reach new people who will do
this mission. Some of these new Christians will concentrate on social justice,
and some will concentrate on teaching, or worshiping, or making new disciples. This is how it should be. The Holy Spirit gives all these gifts so that
the church can accomplish its God-given mission of reconciling all people to
unity with God and each other in Christ.

Leadership Skills for a New Era

Bob Johansen, in his book, *Leaders Make the Future: Ten New Leadership Skills for an Uncertain World,*[4] names ten leadership skills that he believes will be necessary to navigate a new VUCA world. The first three skills he names are the Maker Instinct, Clarity, and Dilemma Flipping.

The Maker Instinct, Johansen says, is something we all share—it is the desire to create new things. A Maker can be anyone from a woman creating beautiful quilts in the same way her grandmother used to do, to a digital native creating applications for the iPhone. But the leadership skill required for the future is not just the desire to create alone, but the ability to create in concert with others: to bring people into networks that build and grow things together. The process of building a team that in turn creates a new congregation is a vital skill in church planting, as we will discuss. I believe that not just individual Episcopal leaders, but also the Episcopal Church as a whole, must begin to recognize its divine calling to use the Maker Instinct to create new congregations of faith across the country. We must come together as an organization that recognizes its calling to join God in the divine mission of touching all people with God's love, and we must build the organizational structures and equip the leaders to make it possible.

Johansen defines the second leadership skill, Clarity, as the ability to

- see through messes and contradictions;
- make things as clear as they can be and communicate that clarity;
- see futures that others cannot yet see;
- find a viable direction in the midst of confusion;
- see hope on the other side of trouble.[5]

A church planter is a person who can look at a community and begin to dream, pray, and discern about what God is doing there and how a congregation might join God in that mission. A church planter sees clearly through confusion and ambiguity, to envision something that does not yet exist, and can communicate that vision to others so compellingly that others are inspired to join in making that vision a reality. This is a skill that the

---

4. Bob Johansen, *Leaders Make the Future: Ten New Leadership Skills for an Uncertain World*, 2nd ed. (San Francisco: Berrett-Koehler, 2012).
5. Ibid., 45.

Episcopal Church as a whole needs to cultivate. We need to discern where God is working in our communities and how we can join in that mission. We must begin to see clearly through all the confusion and ambiguity of church decline, to the mission that underlies everything the church does, and we must join together as a church-wide team to make God's vision a reality.

Dilemma Flipping may be the most important skill for us to cultivate in the Episcopal Church. The future, says Johansen, will be filled with dilemmas, which unlike problems, cannot be solved—only navigated in creative ways. He writes:

> The dilemmas of the future will be more grating, more gnawing, and more likely to induce feelings of hopelessness. Leaders must be able to flip dilemmas around and find the hidden opportunities. Leaders must avoid oversimplifying or pretending that dilemmas are problems that can be solved. Dilemma flipping is a skill that leaders will need in order to win in a world dominated by problems that nobody can solve. . . . Dilemmas are often embedded with hope, even if the hope is hidden.
>
> Dilemma flipping is reimagining an unsolvable challenge as an opportunity, or perhaps as both a threat and an opportunity. Dilemma flipping is the ability to put together a viable strategy when faced with a challenge that cannot be solved in traditional ways.[6]

I am not sure that any concept so clearly describes what we are facing in the Episcopal Church. Faced with declining numbers, we must decide whether decline is a problem or a dilemma. If it is a problem, we can solve it. However, I think it is a dilemma, and we need to navigate it. Our traditional ways of reaching people are no longer working as effectively, because the culture around us has shifted. We are not going to be able to manage the culture into a box that suits our traditional institutions. And we are not going to be able to solve the problem of shifting culture by doing what we are already doing, only working harder and better at it. Problem solving will not make the dilemma go away.

The challenge that faces the church is to begin to see the shifting culture not as a danger, but as an opportunity. We live in a post-Christendom world, which means that we must envision church mission in post-Christendom

---

6. Ibid., 57, 59.

ways. If we can cultivate this fresh vision, if we can join the Spirit in the ongoing work of renewal, we can begin to navigate the church's dilemmas anew. Planting new churches is one way we can turn our dilemma into opportunity in the Episcopal Church. Some of the new churches will look quite traditional, though the very fact of newness requires them to "ask the key missional questions of identity and purpose that existing congregations often take for granted."[7] Some new churches may look so different from the traditional model that other Episcopalians will look at them askance and wonder whether they are really Episcopal churches. Some of them will sing unfamiliar music and worship in new languages and minister to populations that are unprecedented in our church. All of them will be joining in a vital mission to live out Christ's reign on earth, through imperfect but lovely and faithful congregations of the Episcopal Church.   ❧

---

7. Craig Van Gelder and Dwight J. Zscheile, *The Missional Church in Perspective: Mapping Trends and Shaping the Conversation* (Grand Rapids, MI: Baker Academic, 2011), 161.

2

Why Plant Churches?
Let's Do the Numbers

The kindly, retired priest sitting next to me at the clergy gathering asked me what I was doing these days. Enthusiastically, I told him that the bishop had called me to become a church planter, and started telling him about my plans. My companion's enthusiasm didn't match mine. His brow furrowed, his head tilted, he interrupted me. "Why should we plant new churches," he asked, "when the ones we have aren't full?"

Why, indeed? In a denomination where the average congregation has fewer than seventy people on Sunday, often scattered in a sanctuary built for a much larger crowd, why should we plant new churches? Why not work harder to fill the ones we have? While revitalization of existing churches is certainly important, planting new churches is also an essential strategy for reaching new people with the gospel of Jesus Christ. This should not be an either-or question.

There are many good reasons to plant new churches, and I'll address six of them in chapter 3. But here's an absolutely essential one: planting new churches—whether traditional stand-alone churches or innovative new expressions of ministry—is one of the best ways to reach new people with the good news of the gospel.

New churches grow faster, on average, than established ones.

David T. Olson, in *The American Church in Crisis*,[1] discusses population trends in the U.S. and attendance trends in American churches of all denominations. According to his research, in 2004, 52 million Americans attended church in a typical week—17.7% of the American population.[2] That means, of course, that 82.3% of the U.S. population does not attend a church in a typical week. Jesus said that he would teach us to "fish for people"—well, there are plenty of fish in the sea.

That 17.7% figure is strikingly low, and it represents a sharp decline from 1990, when 20.4% of Americans attended church in a typical week, an alarming 14% attendance drop in fifteen years. Yet the real shock comes when we look at the American population. During that same period, 1990 to 2005, the population of the U.S. *grew* by 52 million people. The church in America is nowhere close to keeping up with population growth.[3]

Olson goes on to look at the American church's decline in three categories: evangelical, Roman Catholic, and mainline Protestant churches. Attendance across mainline churches, he discovers, is dropping sharply. Part of this decline can be attributed to the human sexuality discussion (accounting for about one-third of the decline in the Episcopal Church's case, according to Director of Research Kirk Hadaway[4]), but Olson identifies several other reasons, all pointing directly to the imperative to plant new churches. For instance, mainline churches are made up primarily of older congregations, started before 1965, and a high percentage of older churches are declining. Mainline denominations face a corresponding shortage of new churches, he continues, stating flatly, "The only possible tactic available to recoup the attendance losses occurring in established churches and through closures is to start new congregations." He points out that for the Evangelical Lutheran Church in America simply to maintain its present size (though it would still be declining as a percentage of the total U.S. population), it would have to

---

1. David T. Olson, *The American Church in Crisis* (Grand Rapids, MI: Zondervan, 2008).

2. Ibid., 28. Even if one looks at "regular participants" in a church (those who attend on a consistent basis, though not every week), the percentage of Americans who attend church expands only to 23%. If we argue that the higher figure is more accurate in these days of Sunday morning soccer games, this still leaves 77% of Americans without any meaningful connection to a church community.

3. Ibid., 35.

4. Ibid., 38.

plant eight times as many churches as it currently does. The ELCA is declining by 26,500 attendees per year and its new churches add only 3,100 new attendees per year.[5]

Olson compares the Christian church in America to a species threatened with extinction:

> Why does extinction occur? It is a complex question. Extinction occurs most often when a species faces a crisis or change in its environment and is unable to adapt. Predators, often human, invade and take over a niche, bringing disease and destruction. As a species begins to be threatened, these changes combine to produce a low fertility rate. Survival comes down to simple math: the number of births must outnumber the deaths for a species to survive. When deaths outnumber births, the species goes extinct. . . . The long-term survival of the church can be evaluated by the number of new churches born each year that survive and prosper, by the health and reproductive rate of established or "adult" churches, and by the number of churches that close each year.[6]

Unfortunately, the Episcopal Church is in full decline—possibly on the way to extinction, if Olson's argument is correct—along with the other mainline denominations. Our membership and attendance has fallen steadily from a height of 3.1 million active baptized members in 1965 to about 1.9 million in 2012,[7] at a time when the total U.S. population increased from 194 million to 314 million.[8] Take a look at those figures again. During a forty-seven-year period, the U.S. population *increased* by a whopping 62%, and the numerical membership of the Episcopal Church *decreased* by a shocking 39%. As a percentage of the U.S. population, the picture is even worse. The Episcopal Church fell from 1.6% to a minuscule 0.6%, a 63% decline, over the same period of time.

---

5. Ibid., 56.
6. Ibid., 118.
7. Figures provided by C. Kirk Hadaway, Director of Research, The Episcopal Church. Please note that actual membership figures in 1965 were about 3.4 million, but in 1986 the church changed the definition of members to include only "active baptized members," excluding members in name only. Hadaway was kind enough to provide the adjusted totals for 1965 including only "active baptized members" so that we are able to compare consistent numbers in 1965 and 2012.
8. http://www.multpl.com/united-states-population/table.

The Episcopal Church is utterly failing at fishing for people.

Does the demise of the Episcopal Church as we once knew it really matter? I think it does. It's not that Jesus died so that America would be plastered with Episcopal churches far and wide. But Jesus did form a community of disciples, and commanded them to go out and make more disciples. The church has done exactly that ever since. If the Episcopal Church is declining, it is either because we have lost our will to make new disciples (which Jesus commanded us to do), we haven't figured out how to reach people in present day culture (as opposed to the culture of fifty years ago), we have decided that we only care about ourselves (despite Jesus' command to love our neighbors), or we simply have fallen into a deep depression about our ability to speak Christ's good news to a world starving for good news (although we are people of the resurrection). The numbers themselves may not matter, but the people do. Jesus did not die so that we could be comfortable inside our existing churches; Jesus called his disciples to risk great things for the gospel. We need to be risking great things too.

So how are we doing with planting new churches, the one strategy that Olson believes can help the mainline denominations reverse their decline? From 2003 to 2012, across the church, Episcopalians closed 432 churches. During that same period of time, across the church, we planted only 129 churches, the vast majority during the 2003 to 2009 period. Only nineteen churches were planted from 2010 to 2012. During one year, 2012, across the entire church, only three new congregations began.[9] In a church whose founder left, as his final words to his disciples, a command to go forth into all nations and make disciples, the Episcopal Church seems to have given up hope of obeying, opting instead to stay right here and wait for extinction.

But is church planting really a good strategy for us? Is it true that new churches grow faster than older ones in our Episcopal context? Is there a real reason to make church planting a cornerstone of a strategy to reverse our decline? Or is church planting simply another risky proposition offering low return on investment? Is it true, as some say, that four out of five church plants fail?

To help find the answer to this question, Hadaway provided me with survival and attendance statistics for Episcopal congregations started between

---

9. Figures provided by C. Kirk Hadaway, based on congregations filing parochial reports.

2000 and 2008. During those years, 118 new congregations were formed; however, 19 of these were either formed due to conflict over sexuality (such as those remainder congregations formed after their majorities had left the Episcopal Church), or were closed due to the sexuality conflict. I believe these nineteen congregations should be considered separately; therefore, to analyze the success of regular church plants, I will look at the other ninety-nine new congregations.

Of the ninety-nine new congregations formed between 2000 and 2008, sixty-nine were still open in 2012, a 70% success rate over four or more years. It is definitely *not* true in the Episcopal context that four out of five new congregations fail. In fact, Episcopal congregations have a much greater chance for success than many non-denominational church plants, precisely because of our Episcopal context. Most Episcopal churches are started deliberately and strategically, with financial and clergy support from a diocese. This is a very different context than a single non-denominational minister who decides to start a church on his or her own.

How is the attendance in new church plants? Across the sixty-nine church plants that remained open in 2012, the average Sunday attendance was ninety-five people. This compares to average attendance of sixty-four people across the whole church during that same year. In other words, the newer churches were 48% larger, despite having much less time in which to grow, and in many cases, far fewer financial, building, and staff resources. The ten largest church plants from 2000 to 2008 (including my own church plant, Church of the Nativity) had 2012 average attendance of 359 people. The largest, St. Philip's Frisco (Diocese of Dallas) was formed in 2002 and had 2012 average attendance of 712. The second largest, La Iglesia de Santa Maria in Falls Church, Virginia, a Latino congregation, was formed in 2008 and already averaged seven hundred people by 2012.

In a publication on the Episcopal Church's website,[10] Hadaway discussed factors associated with growth in churches during the 2000 to 2005 time period. One of the most important findings was that newer churches are more likely to be growing churches. The graph below shows the striking difference in growth between older and newer congregations; newer congregations were roughly twice as likely to be growing as older ones.

---

10. http://www.episcopalchurch.org/sites/default/files/facts_on_episcopal_church_growth1.pdf

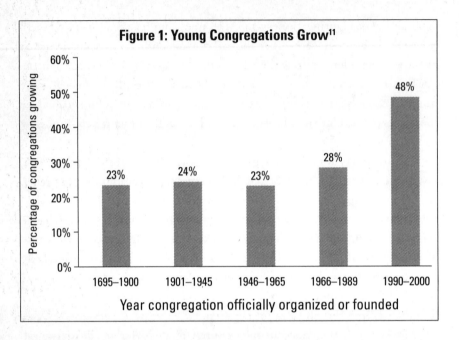

Figure 1: Young Congregations Grow[11]

The potential for growth in new churches is very impressive.

In fact, I believe that the potential for growth is even greater than these statistics indicate. I believe we can improve on the attendance, growth, and survival numbers shown above. That's why I'm writing this book—to help us think together about how to plant churches, and how to do it successfully, to touch as many people with Christ's love as we can. The Episcopal Church has something worth sharing, and I believe it is up to us, with the power of faith, to share it.

What is it that prevents the Episcopal Church from taking a step off the somewhat shaky platform where we find ourselves in the early twenty-first century? Are we afraid of failure? Are we unsure we have enough money? Do we lack courageous leaders who are willing to risk their careers and reputations? Are we simply resigned to growing smaller and less significant each year? Do we not believe that new disciples of Jesus, committed to their faith and to ministries of loving God and loving our neighbors, can truly help transform this hurt and broken world? Have we lost faith that the Holy Spirit is present and active, and calling us to take a leap of faith? ❧

---

11. Facts on Episcopal Church Growth, www.episcopalchurch.org/files/facts_on_episcopal_church_growth1.pdf, p. 2.

~ 3

Why Plant New Churches?
Six More Good Reasons

I n the school cafeteria, Church of the Nativity's worship service will begin in an hour. The Ford Explorer that holds the entire church setup has just pulled up to the back door. Twenty ministry leaders are already on hand to begin setting up the altar, banners, credence table, candles, and chairs, and twenty more helpers will arrive within the next half hour. The energy and excitement are palpable. At the welcome table, the greeters' brigade is already talking and laughing, laying out the newcomer gifts and brochures they brought in shopping bags from home. In the nursery, the caregivers are spreading out blankets and toys they store in their garages during the week, preparing to welcome and love infants and toddlers. In the Sunday school room, two teachers spread out materials for a Godly Play lesson that will engage the children even though the full Godly Play setup is not available. In the worship area, the altar has been unfolded and dressed, the altar guild is busy setting up, and the priest is on the lookout for the couple that is bringing the baptismal font for the baptisms that day. The choir, which practiced at a member's home last Wednesday, is warming up to the music played on a portable keyboard. In the corner, a few people are discussing how to get the news out about the new church to more folks in the community. In the hallway, the outreach team is deciding which of several proposed community service projects to concentrate on next. Every person knows his or her ministry, and every person is excited about the prospect of welcoming new folks, teaching new children, recruiting new help for outreach projects, and engaging more people in worship. And every person is working very hard to make it happen.

Should the Episcopal Church be planting new churches? I discussed one reason in the previous chapter: new churches are more likely to grow, and to grow larger and faster. Here are six more good reasons why we should be planting new churches.

A New Church is Mission Focused

People who join a new church—especially on a launch team—don't do it because the building is beautiful (it's not) or because their grandparents went to that church (they didn't). They join because they have a real sense that God is calling them to ministry in that community, and because they have felt God's presence in this congregation in a way they have not felt it before. Everyone there knows that this church is there to join in God's mission. They will invite their friends, they will talk to others about their faith and the miracles they see happening, they will labor in ministry, and they will pray and give and lead in that church because of that mission focus. For these mission leaders, the experience of helping to plant this church will be life changing, growing their faith and their relationship with God as they watch miracles begin to happen in their congregation.

Craig van Gelder and Dwight Zscheile write about this tangible sense of mission in a startup congregation:

> It is often observed that starting new congregations with a missional imagination and posture is easier than reorienting existing ones. This is so in part because the process of planting a new church is inherently missiological and open ended. Leaders of new congregations must ask the key missional questions of identity and purpose that existing congregations often take for granted. These congregations must engage with those outside their doors in order to grow and thrive. . . . New missional congregations keep at the forefront of their minds and hearts the question of how they can give the gospel as well as their gifts to the community. They resist the tendency to make their own institutional stability and survival the primary end. Rather, they recognize that their

primary end—indeed, the very reason for their existence—is participation in the Triune God's mission in the world.[1]

That sense of mission is among the factors that C. Kirk Hadaway associates with growing churches in the publication "Facts on Episcopal Church Growth."[2] Congregations that have a clear sense of mission and purpose, something that is absolutely necessary in a church plant, are more likely to grow.

Any church can cultivate a sense of mission, but in a well-led church plant, that sense is inescapable. There are no consumers in a church that meets in a cafeteria, a storefront, an office building, or a bar. Every person present knows that she is a part of God's mission in the community, and that God is doing something new, exciting, and life-transforming through this church. It is that palpable, widely shared sense of mission and enthusiasm that I discovered for the first time at Nativity, and it is that sense of mission and enthusiasm that I would like to see spread throughout the Episcopal Church. Yes, established churches can, and should, discover that mission focus too.

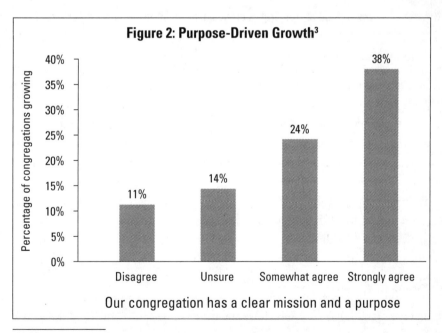

Figure 2: Purpose-Driven Growth[3]

---

1. Van Gelder and Zscheile, 161–62.
2. http://www.episcopalchurch.org/sites/default/files/facts_on_episcopal_church_growth1.pdf
3. Ibid., 6.

But you just can't avoid it in a new church. That, I think, is one reason new churches tend to grow faster than established ones. In fact, Hadaway showed enthusiasm to be one of the most important factors in growing churches.[4]

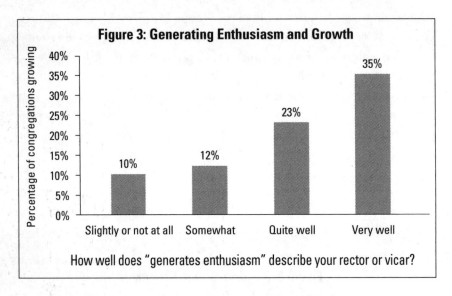

Figure 3: Generating Enthusiasm and Growth

Percentage of congregations growing

- 10% — Slightly or not at all
- 12% — Somewhat
- 23% — Quite well
- 35% — Very well

How well does "generates enthusiasm" describe your rector or vicar?

A New Church Can Respond to Population Shifts

In 2003, Stephen C. Compton, an executive with the United Methodist Church in North Carolina, wrote *Rekindling the Mainline: New Life Through New Churches,* arguing that mainline denominations should make church planting the "permanent, primary strategy for extending the reach of God's church into the hearts of people who do not yet know the joy and wholeness of life that comes from a relationship with God."[5] He narrated the rise and decline of the mainline churches, pointing out that their major growth spurts came during the 1950s and 1960s, the very time when mainline denominations were responding to population shifts by planting new churches in the areas being built to accommodate a nation on the move. As people moved from rural communities to urban and suburban ones following World War II, he says, the large denominations proactively planted new churches in the newly populated areas—which is why they grew rapidly during those years.

---

4. Ibid., 16.

5. Stephen C. Compton, *Rekindling the Mainline: New Life Through New Churches* (Herndon, VA: The Alban Institute, 2003), xii.

In contrast, Compton points out, the mainline denominations' current period of decline is marked (and quite possibly caused) by many fewer church starts, even as the population continues to shift. One of the best reasons to plant new churches is that we can do it strategically, carefully placing churches in areas of population growth and positioning them to reach new generations of people. New suburbs are being built today, especially in southern and western cities, but the Episcopal Church is not keeping up with the growing population in newly built areas. In these growing suburbs and other new developments, we should start traditional church plants, which will eventually build church buildings and be self-supporting parishes. Churches located in growing, newer areas are more likely to grow, according to statistics provided by Hadaway.[6]

In the meantime, the ethnic and demographic character of many older neighborhoods is changing, and churches in those older areas risk significant decline if they are not able to find ways to reach their new neighbors. This situation calls for intentional and strategic action. Too many existing churches

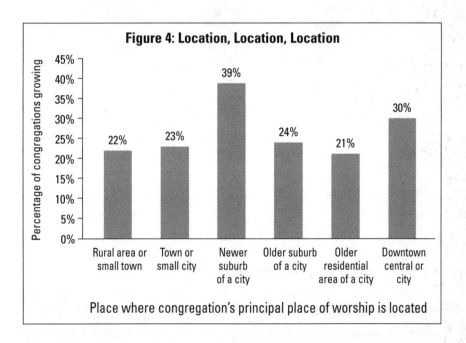

Figure 4: Location, Location, Location

6. http://www.episcopalchurch.org/sites/default/files/facts_on_episcopal_church_growth1.pdf

find it difficult or undesirable to make the changes required to reach out to the new people they find surrounding them. Yet surely the gospel compels us to speak Christ's words clearly to unfamiliar neighbors as well as to those like ourselves. In changing neighborhoods, older congregations can continue to worship while reaching out to new demographic groups, allowing their facilities to be used for worship in styles or languages appropriate to their changed context, and also remaining true to the heart of the Episcopal tradition. These multi-cultural congregations are more likely to grow, according to Hadaway.[7]

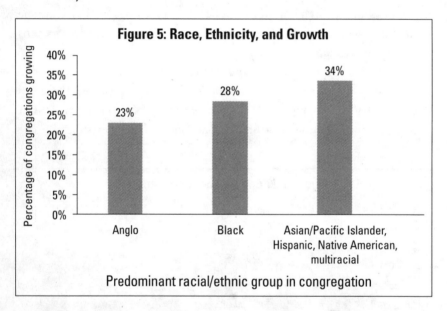

Changing our congregations in order to reach changing neighborhoods might require bringing new leaders on board who are bilingual and bicultural, either to start a second congregation meeting in the same location, or to shift to an intentionally multicultural style of worship.

A New Church Can Respond to Generational Shifts

New and changing neighborhoods are not the only important shifts our church should be responding to. A generational shift is occurring in U.S. culture as well. Baby Boomers and Gen-Xers raised their children in church much less

---

7. Ibid.

consistently than their Builder and Silent generation parents, meaning that Millennial generation members have much lower rates of church participation than their parents did at a similar age. Yet studies show that Millennials are nevertheless interested in spirituality; many have the same questions and spiritual yearnings their parents had, yet are wary and skeptical of the institutional church. Instead of abandoning the Millennial field to more proactive evangelical denominations, the Episcopal Church should be actively looking for new ways to connect to this large and increasingly vital generation. Connecting with young adults does not necessarily mean what it meant in the 1980s and 1990s (providing rock bands and video screens in mega-churches). Many young adults are drawn to smaller, more intimate communities who engage in ancient practices and sing traditional hymns and chants. Fresh Expressions worshiping communities with a less institutional, more invitational, more interactive feel than our traditional parishes may help these young adults develop a life-changing relationship with Christ.

A New Church Can Try New Things

Change is hard in an established church. After all, the church is filled with people who are there because they like it the way it is. A new church has more freedom to dream, to experiment, and to do things in different ways. New churches can focus on nontraditional populations, or on people who prefer to hear jazz music in worship, or on young adults who want to meet at night rather than in the morning, or on people who speak Mandarin. A new church may be more open to new types of people than an established congregation that has become accustomed to a group of people that are like themselves. A new church should, in fact, do a careful study of its neighborhood and make a special effort to reach people no one else is reaching.

Hadaway showed that congregations that are willing to change and try new things are more likely to grow:[8]

> Change is the name of the game in a new church; things never stand still. There are few congregational traditions to rest on—you make the traditions up as you go along. Everything is an experiment. This willingness to change is strongly associated with growth.

---

8. Ibid.

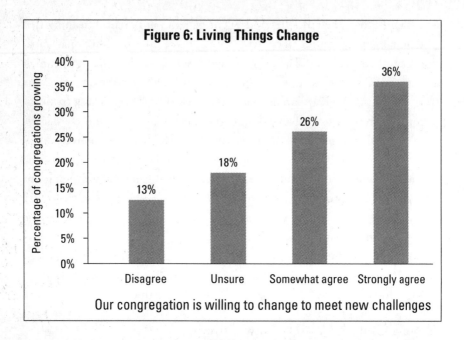

Figure 6: Living Things Change

Our congregation is willing to change to meet new challenges

Newness and innovation is essential to the growth of Christianity, within boundaries. One of the strengths of Anglicanism, I believe, is our form of worship, passed down from the apostles through the ages. I do not believe that our worship is irrelevant or outdated, and I do not advocate that Episcopal churches should unthinkingly adopt worship styles that have been successful in evangelical churches. In fact, the worship style of my own church plant is traditional, and I believe traditional worship helps many people connect to God very deeply. But I do think that churches need to look carefully at the different contexts in which we find ourselves, and ask how to speak God's truth into those contexts.

Tom Brackett, the Officer for Church Planting and Redevelopment for the Episcopal Church, says that he would like to see:

. . . fresh gatherings of people ready to engage with what God is doing out in the world around them, with a compelling expression of the good news that is accessible to the context they're called to serve. Church planting is really important for mainline Christianity simply because when we start a new ministry we don't have the old momentum or inertia to borrow from, so we have to re-examine all the old assumptions of a legacy church and ask, how do we make these gifts accessible to the people that God already loves so much? So for instance, we think our ritual is really meaningful, so the question in a new church start is, how do we make that ritual accessible in a meaningful way to people who have no prior exposure to either ritual or to being in community? So [church planting] asks us to make fresh and new the gifts we've had with us all along. . . . Typically people who start new ministries tend to be more readily engaged with the surrounding world, so their posture tends to be on the edge of the institution looking outward. Their primary passion is for what God is already doing in the world around them.[9]

New Churches Benefit Existing Churches

One of the biggest barriers to church planting in many dioceses is, sadly, the opposition of established churches. Yet existing churches can benefit from the presence of new churches. In many cases, churches oppose a new plant nearby because they are afraid of losing members to it. But the world does not have a predetermined, limited number of Episcopalians, who are traded from one church to another. New churches reach new people. People who do not attend any church are more likely to attend a new church than an established one, possibly because the new church is more open and receptive to new people. Studies have shown that a new church in a community does not harm existing churches, even when the new church grows rapidly to become a mega-church.[10]

In fact, new churches actually can benefit existing churches. Consider a new church, trying new forms of worship, attempting to reach different kinds of people in innovative ways, and letting others hear its stories of success and failure. A new church is able to try things an established church might be much more hesitant to try, but established churches can pay attention and learn from what new churches are doing. New forms of worship,

9. Tom Brackett, telephone interview with the author, June 24, 2014.
10. Penny Long Marler and C. Kirk Hadaway, "New Church Development and Denominational Growth (1950–1988): Symptom or Cause?" in *Church and Denominational Growth: What Does (and Does Not) Create Growth or Decline,* David A. Roozen and C. Kirk Hadaway, ed. (Nashville: Abingdon, 1995), 83, cited in Compton, 45.

innovative ways of gathering people, fresh models of leadership, all can be experimented with in church plants. Church plants can, in fact, become the research and development department of a denomination.

New Churches Are in a Different Part of the Church Life Cycle

Stephen C. Compton notes that a number of scholars have described the similar life cycles of human beings and congregations. Both are born, they grow, they reach adulthood, they begin to decline, and they die. In the case of congregations, the process may not be linear; churches may go through different cycles of regeneration and rebirth and they may tenaciously cling to life for a very long time. Yet the natural progression mimics the human life cycle.[11]

The Birth stage, Compton says, is brief, almost momentary, but it is chiefly responsible for establishing the DNA of the congregation. In the exciting birth stage, the church's mission is established, its core values are determined, and a group of leaders is assembled for whom starting the new church will be a life-changing experience. Because the church is eager to grow, it will begin intentionally looking for ways to impact its community and get the word out about the church to new people. The leadership group researches its community and designs worship that will speak deeply to the spirituality of the people in its area. Every leader is committed to praying for the church, and every member is clear about its purpose, mission, and values.

In the second stage, the Vitality stage, Compton says that the church enjoys an extended period of growth. Its ministries, membership, discipleship opportunities, and community outreach activities are all growing. Its financial stability is growing as well, often along with increasing professional staff and expanding permanent facilities. The church's values are refined and applied to new situations.

In the Equilibrium stage, a congregation's growth slows and traditions become more set. The congregation begins to focus on maintaining the status quo. Members are satisfied with their congregation, and important ministries are maintained. The new members entering the congregation each year about equal those who die, move away, or fall away. The congregation finds ways to maintain its stability by avoiding changes, including the changes that might lead to growth. Membership may fluctuate within a range because

---

11. Compton, 14–25.

of leadership transitions or other factors, but in general, over a long period of time, the membership remains relatively stable. Compton compares this stage to a high, wide mesa. The ground seems flat and comfortable, but the risk of sudden drop-off is high. Congregations in this stage of life find it difficult to change and adapt to new circumstances, but as long as their environment is stable, they can continue in this stage for a long time.

Decline begins in the fourth stage. The number of new members each year no longer equals the numbers who depart. Attendance, finances, and ministries begin to languish. Congregational conflict increases as people grow more anxious about the changes they are experiencing. The church begins to acknowledge that it will not be able to sustain itself indefinitely. Though churches may linger in this stage for a long time, if concerted action is not taken to change the focus of the church's ministries, then the fifth stage, Death, is not far off. Some churches inevitably will die, even after long and productive lives.

Compton says that the first two stages of the congregational life cycle, the Birth and Vitality stages, account for most of the growth the congregation will experience during its history. He cites Hadaway, suggesting that

> ... young churches have a "window of opportunity" for significant growth that may last for ten or fifteen years. Why do new churches tend to grow more rapidly than older churches? It could be, Hadaway notes, that new churches are more flexible and open to change; growth-producing ideas can be put into practice; leaders are able to lead; rapid adjustments can still be made to changing circumstances; and friendship networks have not yet solidified, allowing for easy acceptance of new members.[12]

If a church's greatest opportunity for growth occurs during its first ten to fifteen years, then perhaps a big part of the reason for mainline stagnation and decline, says Compton, is the failure of mainline denominations to plant many new churches. If the average Episcopal church is forty years old or older, then at best most are in the "Equilibrium" stage; at worst, many are declining or dying. "When denominations cut their levels of new church development, as many did in the late 1960s, they not only lose the potential growth of those new churches, they are also saddled with a progressively

---

12. Compton, 19, citing C. Kirk Hadaway, "The Impact of New Church Development on Southern Baptist Growth," *Review of Religious Research* 31, no. 4 (June 1990), 377–78.

higher proportion of slower-growing older congregations," says Compton.[13] The effect of planting few congregations now will last for years to come.

Why Plant New Churches?

"I planted, Apollos watered," says the Apostle Paul, "but God gave the growth."[14] If Paul had not taken arduous journeys all over the eastern Mediterranean, if he had not taken a perilous leap of faith, risking his reputation, his health, and finally his life, would any of us even know about Jesus Christ today? Can Jesus Christ still make a difference to this wounded world? Could it be time for us in the Episcopal Church to take our cue from Paul, and trust God to lead us in reaching new people? We risk far less than Paul did—we sacrifice not our lives, but merely some time, some money, and some talent. But for us, as for Paul, much work lies ahead. There is a world out there that hasn't heard of Christ's love in any meaningful way, and lives by a far different set of rules than those Christ taught. Do we believe that God still has a mission to the people around us? Is loving God and loving our neighbors a mission worth staking our ministries on? Is making new disciples who will carry that love to a world in aching need of transformation a worthy goal for a venerable mainline church? Does the Episcopal Church have something unique to give in the world of the twenty-first century?

I believe that planting new faith communities is vital to God's mission through our church. Through the Episcopal Church, the Holy Spirit has something special to offer a world that is increasingly disengaged from any faith. Our way of following Jesus, our engagement with the questions of scripture and the issues of life, our particular way of loving God through our worship and loving our neighbor through our teaching, fellowship, and social service ministries, opens up a relationship with Christ for people who are desperately hungry for those things. In a world that often assumes that shrill, anti-science, fundamentalist voices represent all Christianity has to offer, the Episcopal Church offers a fresh, vital way of following Jesus. I believe the Episcopal Church is a precious gift, entrusted to us by God. But like all of God's gifts, it is not to be hoarded, but to be shared, generously, like the treasure it is. ❧

---

13. Ibid., 36.
14. 1 Corinthians 3:6.

∾ 4

What Kind of Churches
Shall We Plant?

In January 1882, a young Episcopal seminarian named Endicott Peabody, the scion of a prominent New England family, arrived by stagecoach in the frontier town of Tombstone, Arizona. A few months before, the town had achieved notoriety as the site of the shootout at the OK Corral, featuring Marshal Wyatt Earp, his two brothers, and his friend Doc Holliday. Endicott Peabody came to the frontier with the express purpose of planting the first non-Roman Catholic church in the Arizona territory. Undeterred by the Wild West atmosphere in the town, Peabody set to work. He formed a baseball team, visited every house in town, and persuaded the townspeople to give money and labor to build St. Paul's Episcopal Church, which is still a parish of the Episcopal Diocese of Arizona. He left Tombstone after only six months, but his name endures as a patron saint of the Diocese of Arizona and the founder of St. Paul's Tombstone.

(As an amusing side note, the altar rail at St. Paul's Tombstone was dedicated by the Wyatt Earp family, at the urging of Earp's friend "Bignose Kate," the common-law wife of Doc Holliday. One hundred thirty years later, in remembrance of this event, the altar rail at my parish, Church of the Nativity, Scottsdale, was dedicated in Endicott Peabody's honor by his great-grandson, Endicott Peabody IV, a member of Nativity.)

The St. Paul's Tombstone story, with all its frontier color, highlights familiar elements of traditional church planting. A clergy person is sent by a bishop to start a church in an identified territory with a growing population. On his/her own, or with a group of interested lay people, the clergy person gathers a congregation and inspires them to achieve a high goal: starting a church that will worship through the ages and act as an important center of community life. The worship it offers is more or less traditional, Episcopal-style. The congregation is expected to support the church building, its ministries, and its clergy with financial contributions, becoming a parish after a period of diocesan support. Endicott Peabody achieved these goals in a remarkably short time.

Endicott Peabody's church plant is what I would call a "traditional church plant," a way of planting churches that is still relevant today. My own parish, Church of the Nativity, is a traditional church plant. But while most of our Episcopal churches were planted this way, a new era in the church calls for new ways of doing things—not instead of, but in addition to, our traditional models. I will be highlighting three basic kinds of church plants:

- traditional church plants
- ethnic-focused church plants
- "Fresh Expressions" church plants

Traditional Church Plants

I have heard it argued that traditional church planting is no longer viable in the twenty-first century: that the financial resources don't exist, that not enough people are interested in our ancient style of worship and our standard church structures, that society is changing too fast to accommodate more local churches, that churches should not have buildings, that we should not plant traditional new churches when we already have many older churches that are dwindling. I disagree. Though we should be starting alternative kinds of churches as well, I believe that over a century after Endicott Peabody's time, planting traditional churches is still an important way to reach new people, and an important Episcopal growth strategy, especially in areas of the country with growing populations. It should not be the only growth and evangelism strategy and it is not the only vital and necessary way to plant churches, but it is an important one in the right context. The local church has been the center of church life in almost every denomination for well over a thousand years. The church's major ministries happen through its local congregations, in which people connect with each other, gather for worship, and go out into their communities to do Christ's work in the world. The local church serves as the center of worship, of inspiration, and of community life. Traditional churches contribute huge amounts of money and labor to charitable causes of all kinds. The institution of the church, with its buildings and governance structures, helps ensure long life and continuity through the years. And the institutional church, with all the bad press it gets, is the bedrock that makes it possible for church leaders to plant new, nontraditional forms of community that reach different populations. Without the leadership and financial support of our traditional churches, new nontraditional plants would not be possible.

What is the right situation for a traditional new church start? Generally these plants are founded in growing suburbs or other new or redeveloping neighborhoods, where the economic base of the surrounding area can reasonably be expected eventually to support a church financially. Planting new churches in the places where people now live, as opposed to where they lived twenty or fifty years ago, is absolutely at the core of the church's mission. The fact that we may have dwindling churches in older neighborhoods and rural areas should not prevent us from starting growing churches in newer neighborhoods. Our failure to do so over the last thirty or forty years is probably one major reason why the church is declining rather than continuing to grow, as Stephen Compton points out.[1] The people in the growing areas generally will not travel far to find a church, so we need to make the effort to meet them where they are. The first word of the Great Commission, after all, is "Go."

Those who argue that the financial resources don't exist to start traditional churches are forgetting that the majority of the necessary resources will come from the joyful contributions of the people who join the new church. A diocese that plans to start new traditional churches should indeed plan to give significant financial support in the beginning. On a strict cost-benefit analysis, however, a diocese can expect to begin receiving returns on

---

1. Compton, 36.

its investment in the form of assessment payments within a few years if the church is successful.[2]

Those who argue that a church is not a building are correct, but that does not mean that a building is not important for many congregations. Congregations need a place to gather and to worship. A congregation that does not have a dependable place to gather (whether rented, borrowed, or owned) is likely to remain small—which is a fine result for some churches, but not for all. A building provides opportunities for growth, discipleship programs, worship, evangelism, and neighborhood outreach that might not otherwise exist; a building grounds a church in the community and makes it visible. At Nativity, for instance, our building (dedicated in December 2012) allows us to offer after-school programs and a place for tutoring children from the elementary school down the street. Having a building allows us to hold Vacation Bible School and other summer programs for children and youth. We can host twelve-step and neighborhood meetings; we can hold our own meetings and discipleship programs in a dependable location. These advantages are hard to appreciate if you have never been part of a church that didn't have a building.

The advantage of planting traditional churches is that they have great potential for achieving self-sustainability, for reaching new people and helping them grow in relationship with Christ, and for changing lives and making a difference in their communities. Wherever a diocese is seeing significant population growth, it should be considering how to plant new worshiping congregations. St. Philip's, Frisco (Diocese of Dallas), planted in a growing suburb, and St. Benedict's, Smyrna (Diocese of Atlanta), planted in a redeveloping part of the central city, are examples of resource-size congregations that started recently according to a traditional model and grew very fast. Like Church of the Nativity, these churches offer traditional Episcopal worship and have traditional buildings and leadership structures. I believe there is a vitally important role for planting growing Episcopal churches with traditional worship and education programs for all ages—even in the twenty-first century.

---

2. For instance, by my calculations, the Diocese of Arizona invested approximately $150,000 in the startup of Nativity, and Nativity now pays over $90,000 a year in diocesan assessment. More on the finances of church planting will be discussed in chapter 13.

Ethnic Church Plants

The traditional church plant is not the only important initiative the Episcopal Church should be emphasizing, however. A second, and I would argue, probably the most vital kind of church plant for us in the coming years is the ethnic plant: one that reaches out to a growing ethnic group in a particular area. Taking purposeful steps to reach the rapidly growing non-Anglo populations in the U.S. should be a cornerstone of the Episcopal Church's mission and evangelism strategy in the coming decades.

According to a study done of Episcopal congregations in 2010 and available on the Episcopal Church website,[3] the racial and ethnic composition of the Episcopal Church in the United States is as follows:

White / European American	86.7%
African American or Black	6.4%
Latino	3.5%
Asian / Pacific Islander	1.4%
Multi-Racial	1.2%
Native American	0.8%

Meanwhile, what is the ethnic composition of the U.S. as a whole? According to statistics released by the U.S. Census Department in 2011[4], the area of the Episcopal Church's greatest strength, the white/not Hispanic group, is the one group that is declining, rather rapidly, as a percentage of the whole U.S. population (though it is continuing to grow, slowly, in terms of total numbers of people). From 2000 to 2010, the white/not Hispanic group declined from 69.1% to 63.7% of the total U.S. population. Meanwhile, two groups that are quite small in the Episcopal Church, the Latino and Asian groups, are growing by leaps and bounds in the population as a whole. From 2000 to 2010, the Latino or Hispanic group grew from 12.5% to 16.3% of the total U.S. population, while the Asian population grew from 3.6% to 4.8% of the population. And, while the Asian increase is very impressive on a percentage basis, the most important story here is the increase in the Latino/Hispanic population. In sheer numbers, the Latino/Hispanic group grew by an incredible 43% in

---

3. http://www.episcopalchurch.org/sites/default/files/episcopal_overview_fact_2010.pdfm page 2, Figure 3.
4. http://www.census.gov/prod/cen2010/briefs/c2010br-02.pdf

one decade. And that's not the end of the story: the Pew Research Center projected in 2008[5] that by 2050, Hispanics will grow to comprise 29% of the total population of the U.S. (nearly doubling in size), while the non-Hispanic white population will become a minority, at 47% of the U.S. population. The Pew Research Center issued another report in 2014[6] that predicted that in 2014, Hispanics would become the majority population in California and New Mexico, and that Texas may not be far behind.

It should be evident that the Episcopal Church has not done nearly enough to reach non-white/non-European ethnic groups, not if we want to live into God's dream of a church that represents the diversity of our country. Planting churches to reach growing non-Anglo populations, especially the Latino population, should be the single most important growth priority for our church. Jesus commanded his disciples to go to all nations and make disciples; in the U.S. we have all nations coming right here. There is no excuse for letting our church remain an overwhelmingly Anglo enclave when there are so many other people in our cities we could be reaching.

Ministering with fast-growing Latino and other populations certainly will require some deep thought and some intentional, strategic change in our church. And it will involve a substantial commitment of resources. Some Latino and other newly arrived immigrants do not have the economic resources to sustain a church on their own. Reaching these populations will mean that dioceses, and the Episcopal Church itself, will have to devote money to paying clergy and other expenses, knowing that it may be a long time before some of these churches can reach sustainability.

The Rev. Carmen Guerrero, who has planted several Latino churches, tells the story of the genesis of La Trinidad, which meets at Trinity Cathedral, Phoenix. She was supplying at Iglesia San Pablo, a Latino congregation in Phoenix, one Holy Week, when she discovered that the county sheriff, in an anti-immigrant move, had sent sheriff's deputies to park outside the church on Good Friday, hoping to catch undocumented immigrants on their way into church. She recounts:

---

5. http://www.pewhispanic.org/2008/02/11/us-population-projections-2005-2050/
6. http://www.pewresearch.org/fact-tank/2014/01/24/in-2014-latinos-will-surpass-whites-as-largest -racialethnic-group-in-california/

People were parking far away and slipping in through the back door, that's how faithful they were. They wanted to be in church on Good Friday. I thought then that there was plenty of room at Trinity for a Latino congregation, and the sheriff wouldn't come park outside Trinity where many powerful people come to church. So I went to the bishop and the dean and suggested it, and we put up a sign announcing our Spanish services. People are looking for a church, a place that will welcome them.[7]

There is a crying need for churches that will welcome Latino people in the name of Jesus, even if many of them are outcast in the rest of our society. Unfortunately, though many Latinos have church backgrounds, they have not always been welcomed in American churches. According to Anthony Guillén, the Missioner for Latino/Hispanic Ministries for the Episcopal Church:

[Often Latinos] don't go [to church] because their experience has been so negative. They've experienced a church that talks down to them, belittles them, says that it's wrong to ask questions or challenge the church's teachings, or reminds them they are sinners not worthy of sacraments. Or just doesn't want them . . . [and] won't do anything in Spanish. A lot of Latinos go to church and find they're really not welcome in lots of ways. They're looking for community. . . . That's why evangelical, Pentecostal, and Jehovah's Witnesses churches are growing—they invite people. People are willing to go because they are being welcomed. We [the Episcopal Church] may be an obvious choice for them because we're a catholic community, but if we don't invite them they won't come.[8]

Clearly, one reason the Episcopal Church has not done well with Latinos on a large scale is that we have failed to devote resources to reaching this important population. The idea that Latino ministries will be expensive and may not ever be self-sustaining is surely an issue for many dioceses. There are several factors that might mitigate the expense of ethnic churches, however. First, a number of our declining majority-Anglo churches are located in areas with shrinking Anglo populations but rapidly growing Latino and

---

7. Carmen Guerrero, interview with the author, June 26, 2014.
8. Anthony Guillén, telephone interview with the author, July 10, 2014.

other ethnic populations. That means that we already have buildings and other assets in good locations to meet this growing mission opportunity. These older congregations could make the changes necessary to start welcoming the people who now live in their neighborhood, rather than give up and accept inevitable decline and eventual death as their current members age and move away. Alternatively, a diocese could call a church planter to start a Latino congregation that shares the building of an older church, as Guerrero is now doing with her current church plant in Phoenix, Iglesia Santa Maria, which shares the building of the older congregation of St. Mary's. It is a clear strategic use of a valuable church asset to leverage a building we already have to reach the under-served population in its neighborhood. Isn't that what a church is supposed to do?

We should also emphasize that Latinos can and do give to support their churches. Iglesia San Mateo, Houston, had average attendance in 2012 of almost 1,200 people, with plate and pledge income of approximately $260,000. While newer immigrants tend to have low incomes, Guillén notes that:

> The census tells us clearly that two-thirds of Latinos here were born in the U.S. About the same number speak English at home. This is an important factor in thinking about Latinos. The group [called] New Generation Latinos is bilingual and bicultural. They are not first-generation immigrants in the last ten to fifteen years. In schools, colleges, and the workforce, they are English dominant. There are twenty-one million of them. That group is an up-and-coming group, very tech savvy and goal-oriented. . . . There are also many third- and fourth-generation Latinos who are professors, nurses, mayors, politicians, business owners, lawyers—a large group of professional Latinos.[9]

I asked Guillén why, other than the obvious demographic growth, it is vitally important to reach Latino people, and why the Episcopal Church has a terrific mission opportunity with them now. He replied:

> The Latino population generally today is still very connected to traditions back home. Most of them involve faith, church, family, respect, community, those kinds of things the church could capitalize on.

9. Guillén, interview.

We have probably two generations for the young people, the New Generation Latinos, before those young people become so enculturated in the American mainstream that they will have lost some of that. Now, many young adults do not have to be . . . convinced about the need to believe, the existence of God, the benefits of church attendance, belonging to Christian community, giving back to God, or being thankful to God. Those things are inherent in Latino culture. It's a no-brainer to reach out and talk about their faith; they're more than willing to talk about faith. . . . That group is still connected to. . . and value their parents and grandparents, their faith, and traditions. They are easy to bring into the church. . . . We [in the Episcopal Church] have a lot of strengths we can build on. I think today if you were to ask most Latinos in our churches about why they're there, most would not tell you because it's a catholic church or because of the liturgy. They would tell you that what they found, what attracted them, was preaching that seemed directed to them. Many people have said, "I heard the gospel for the very first time when I came to the Episcopal Church after going to church all my life.". . . We acknowledge their intelligence; we want them to participate. That's a big message to them, that they're important and valuable. They notice the role of women in the church and they like it. The liturgy speaks to them, but the number one thing is inclusivity. . . . We are a people who are thoughtful. Latinos find that they come and ask questions and people are willing to answer. It's okay to ask.[10]

Latinos, and other ethnic and racial groups, are not easily categorized. It is clear, however, that the Episcopal Church must be doing far more than it is already doing to reach growing non-Anglo populations.

Perhaps the most difficult obstacle for us to overcome in the area of ethnic church planting, however, is not the lack of financial resources, but the lack of leadership resources. We have a critical shortage in the Episcopal Church of bilingual and bicultural priests and lay leaders to plant new congregations, especially given the specialized set of skills that a church planting team should have. Guillén describes his dream for starting a training institute for Latino church leaders:

---

10. Ibid.

There should be a school or academy or seminary institution teaching courses in Latino culture, history, and spirituality. There's something like that in the Roman church (the Mexican American Catholic College in San Antonio) that teaches who Latinos are and also teaches Spanish. We need a center like that. I was on a plane from Houston to Tulsa in February, and the plane was two-thirds full of college-age kids just out of language school in Salt Lake City; they were LDS missionaries going to evangelize in Tulsa. I can almost guarantee they had some success. We need a training school, not just for Latinos. We need to learn about Asians too, the second fastest-growing group. Someone has to take seriously the need to form people to be missionaries—bishops, clergy, and lay people.[11]

Such an institute to equip people to minister with ethnic communities could be combined with a training institute for church planters to create a cadre of well-equipped entrepreneurial clergy leaders. We should emphasize that lay leadership is just as important, however. The Episcopal system depends heavily, and appropriately, on the leadership of all the baptized. A very serious priority for the Episcopal Church should be to provide Christian education and leadership training to the lay people in our ethnic congregations. Some will grow to be important lay leaders in our church, and some may become ordained leaders. Both kinds of leadership are vital if we are to reach new populations in the Episcopal Church.

Natalia Derritt is a lay Latina community leader in Leesburg, Virginia, who is working with the Rev. Daniel Velez Rivera to help start a Latino congregation at St. Gabriel's Episcopal Church. I will give her the last words about what Latinos are looking for in a church:

I cannot say honestly in the Episcopal Church it's going to be the perfect place, because I don't believe there are any perfect places, but this is about faith. It's about a safe place. It's about [feeling] grounded that you have a place that people can love you. It's about a place that says we have faith. And it's not about a place of beauty; it's about the structure of the faith, the strength of the faith that is spiritual. I believe everyone has that. The difference between the Anglo and the Latino, I don't believe

---

11. Ibid.

that is [a difference]. Faith is faith. Physically a big difference, yes; God made a rainbow. We can be different persons; that is the beauty of the rainbow. That is the beauty of the physical structures, the colors, the forms, the figures, and everything that is physical. But when we talk about faith, it is beyond physical. In the community, what you need when you come to a place, you feel you can call it a community. We are made, human beings, to be in a community. When you see a place that is community, that loves you, that accepts you, that you can share happiness, you can share sadness, those are what make a community a place where we all can come to. That is the faith and that is the connection with God.[12]

Fresh Expressions Church Plants

In 2012, the Pew Forum famously released a report called "Nones on the Rise,"[13] which pointed out that the number of Americans who are not affiliated with any religion rose from 15% in 2007 to 20% in 2012—a one-third increase in only five years. Perhaps even more significant, these "Nones" were disproportionately young; one-third of adults under thirty were unaffiliated with any religion. Young adults today, the report says, are far more likely to be unaffiliated than previous generations were at similar times in their lives. Yet these "Nones" of all ages are nevertheless interested in spiritual matters: 68 percent say they believe in God; 53 percent said they often think about the meaning and purpose of life; 30 percent have had a religious or mystical experience; 28 percent believe that it is very important to belong to a community with shared values and beliefs. Most of them, however, say they are not searching for a church, and although many believe that churches have a positive effect on society, many also believe that churches are too political and too interested in money and power.

These are important points for any church leader to understand, but they become particularly vital issues for people who are interested in forming communities of faith among younger adults, those who are alienated from the traditional church, and those who have simply never heard the gospel in any meaningful way. The "Fresh Expressions" church attempts to relate to

12. The Rev. Daniel Velez Rivera and Natalia Derritt, interview.
13. http://www.pewforum.org/2012/10/09/nones-on-the-rise/ (accessed January 30, 2015).

unaffiliated people in a way that is entirely unlike the traditional church. A
Fresh Expressions church may do unusual things to make connections with
people, may worship differently, may not have a building, may have different
leadership structures, may gather at other times than the traditional Sunday
morning, and may be supported in a very different way.

The Rev. Katie Nakamura Rengers and the Rev. Kellie Hudlow are
starting one such ministry in Birmingham, Alabama. From the outside, it
will look like a coffeehouse, and in fact that is exactly what it will be. People
in the neighborhood will come in for coffee, but they will also be welcome to
talk to a priest, deacon, or bishop who might be serving coffee or sitting at a
table inviting people to talk. There will be Bible studies and worship services
and opportunities to explore deep questions of faith. The coffeehouse will
sell coffee and pastries, and eventually the plan is that coffeehouse profits
will cover the cost of rent and operations. It is a completely different model
of church, in style, leadership, worship, programming, and financial support.
Rengers and Hudlow believe that this style of creating community is what
the Millennial generation is searching for. They describe the genesis of The
Abbey[14] idea for both of them:

> Rengers (an associate priest at St. Luke's Birmingham who is starting
> this ministry as an offshoot of her St. Luke's position): When I moved
> to Birmingham in a 10,000-member church, I got hired to work with
> younger adults. But then I discovered there really were no younger
> adults there. Maybe ten children of older members still showed up every
> now and then. This group of ten people ages twenty-three to thirty-five
> approached me at one point and said they wanted to do EfM [Education
> for Ministry]. . . . So we started this group and it's been fabulous. What
> I noticed about two months in is that this group of young adults quit
> coming to church altogether. They come to EfM on Wednesday night,
> but they will not come to worship on Sundays, because EfM has become
> their church. That small intimate group is what they find worshipful.[15]
>
> Hudlow: [When I lived in Tuscaloosa], I got this idea to start talk-
> ing about Jesus in a bar. . . . It started out as young adult and college

---

14. http://www.theabbeybham.com
15. Katie Nakamura Rengers and Kellie Hudlow, telephone interview with the author, June
30, 2014.

ministry, but I'm an attorney, and so I started inviting folks from that side of my life to come and we ended up with a combination of churched and unchurched, this interfaith kind of thing meeting in a bar. It became a group called Pub Church, mainly made up of non-Episcopalians. . . . They started wanting to talk about the Lord in a more specifically Christian way. So we added a meeting once a month in a Monday night in this bar doing Compline or Evening Prayer and dropping a one-hour Bible study in the middle of it. I recently moved to Birmingham. Katie had been talking about this for a while and we started getting together and came up with the idea for The Abbey. For me, what I'm interested in are the unchurched that have been broken from the religion they might have been brought up in, and for a lot of them they weren't brought up in a faith at all.[16]

Rengers and Hudlow believe that the Millennial generation in particular needs this approach to church, a more intimate, community-building group that allows them to explore deep questions of faith and life in an interactive way. They hope to build a community that will pray, study, worship, discuss scriptures, and also engage with the neighborhood around them in community service. They use monastic language to describe the community they want to build, the cycle of daily prayer they will engage in, and the rule of life that they may eventually bring into the mix. And in a way, it does follow an ancient monastic model, as Rengers says:

One of the ways I describe it is old-time monks and nuns who used to support themselves by brewing the beer and making the cheese and selling it to people. Probably for a lot of folks that was they only time during their day that they came into contact with the spiritual life. For my part, I'd like that to be what The Abbey does, really be an open door to the church and spiritual people and to whoever is walking by.[17]

They don't necessarily see this kind of church community as the model for all future generations; as Rengers says, "I fully expect that my one-and-a-half-year-old will get to be my age and say 'Oh, those Millennials, all they

---

16. Ibid.
17. Ibid.

want to do is go to the coffee shop,' and church will have to work differently for people her age."[18]

In the Diocese of Los Angeles, the Rev. Jimmy Bartz leads a community called Thad's,[19] which includes about 225 people in a rented facility on any given Sunday, attending a worship service that is very different from most other Episcopal services. They do not offer a regular Episcopal Eucharist every Sunday, but instead concentrate on the ministry of the word. According to Bartz:

> We really stay focused on the narrative of biblical scripture. We spend almost all of our time on Sunday morning looking at that narrative through reading and teaching with a dialogue after the sermon. That is what allows for that distinct faith diversity to be in the room. People can ask questions, and their questions are honored at every level. . . We do Eucharist, but not every week. One of the things I've said from the beginning is that we have it every week but we don't ritualize it every week. I [didn't] want the Thad's community to take the Eucharist for granted, so I said we will offer it when we really can experience communion with each other. . . . So much a part of our context in LA is that we're surrounded by people invested in producing, creating, and directing stories. So that's where we chose to focus our attention. . . . We have several musicians who create the musical content. We look several weeks out. I might say I'm going to be looking at Jesus's temptation in the wilderness and here are some highlights, some phrases I'll be concentrating on. A few days later there's an MP3 in my e-mail box that somebody's written that uses those phrases. That's how we create music. That's how the hymnal got written; it's not innovative, we're just doing things the way they've always been done. We have prayers of the people that are written by a group of people who get together and write prayers for the church. The person who is assigned to lead the prayers of the people has the authority, if they please, to add into the prayers some of the content they've heard from the teaching or the dialogue that day. When the prayers at Thad's are the best, it's when that person who is praying those prayers is listening intently and brings the language of

---

18. Ibid.
19. http://thads.org/who-we-are/

the day into those prayers; then it's really powerful. It's an area where we restrict participation; we have a lot of people in the entertainment industry who can stand up and read something with incredible expertise, but when someone like that leads the prayers, it's incredibly apparent to people that they don't pray. In our internal leadership we say that everybody is in the bus, but not everybody gets to drive. It's an important part of the way we steward our community.

Bartz and his leadership team have chosen to focus their energies in this way, teaching their way through one book of the Bible at a time, because of the spiritual context of the Los Angeles area.

We have a lot of entertainment industry people. . . . It's a chosen constituency we find ourselves in; we have a really uneven faith topography here. We have people who are really well-formed Christians with missional outlooks who left traditional Episcopal churches to come join us in what we do. We have people who have zero experience in church on the other end of the spectrum, who say, "Wow, this is church? We would have come earlier if we had known." For the most part we have people who have never been to church, or maybe had church in their distant backgrounds but grew up and stopped coming to church because they had a negative experience. But they are still drawn to the story, and drawn to the idea that they need a community of people in order to really develop their spiritual practices.

One of the cool things about being in LA is we're a little bit out in front of the culture in America. People have not gone to church here for so long, and have tried to do that American thing of create-your-own-spirituality and have seen failures from it. They see that it's not sustainable for long. Most of the people at Thad's are very spiritual, inquisitive, and desirous of having some sort of community to help them express their spiritual practice, yet their ability to express that community has atrophied because of the spiritual culture. More than 50% of the people who come to Thad's would call themselves a Christian if you asked them, but not as many as 75%. Some would identify as part of another faith, but they come every week, which fascinates me because we talk about Jesus a lot.[20]

---

20. Jimmy Bartz, telephone interview with the author, September 22, 2014.

Thad's is a very good example of letting the context and the intended audience of a church inform how the church gathers and worships. Traditional Episcopalians often find it hard to fathom how Thad's can worship without offering the Eucharist on a regular basis, or following the lectionary. Yet Thad's is offering the Christian story in a way that people in its community can understand, and that offering allows them to form a community of Christian spiritual practice. If we insist that all people who come into an Episcopal church go from zero experience with the Christian faith to full participation in the Eucharist, that insistence that "they" conform to "us" might be a big reason why we find it so difficult to reach people without a significant church background. If we are serious about evangelism, we will allow space in our worship spectrum for nontraditional expressions of the Christian faith like Thad's.

A completely different model of church is happening in Worcester, Massachusetts, where the Rev. Christopher Carlisle and a team of other ordained and lay people lead the Cathedral in the Night.[21] The worship services happen outside, year-round, in a space defined by lights rather than by walls. The worshipers are a mix of homeless street people, mostly veterans, and young adults from surrounding colleges. Carlisle describes the ministry:

> We gather in front of a Congregational church every Sunday at five o'clock in the evening. A lot of folks who live on the street congregate there anyway, which is why we chose it. . . . Our community is location-specific and territorial, so we realized that the Congregational church was a good place. We wrestled with the question, "Surely you could find a warm room or sanctuary in a church to conduct services?" We decided it would completely change the experience from being a wall-less, boundary-less, permeable experience, where people could come and go as they willed, to something that's fixed, and also for many a place of bad memories, which makes them feel as though they're really not quite welcome. . . . We want them to feel comfortable on their turf rather than our own; that seemed to us really important. So the choice was to be outside and to recognize a space as sacred that was part of their experience in a way that a church building wasn't. . . . I thought that it would be very interesting to create a sacred space out of light rather than out of walls. So that's when we started talking about being

---

21. http://www.cathedralinthenight.org

outside, and realized that too many street ministries are a little bit drab. But if anybody needs to have a beautiful space, it's folks who don't have any home. . . . The space is created by sheetrock buckets and pipe, with paper cranes and fluorescent lights around the perimeter of the worship space. It's very beautiful and very simple. We do that fifty-two weeks a year. . . . Then we decided that we didn't want to have just "homeless food"; we wanted a meal that everyone would feel very good eating with an eye to nutritional needs. We got others involved: we asked thirty-five parishes to bring food and a piece of liturgy—a song, a prayer, a poem. We have a bit of a problem because we don't have enough slots for churches that want to get involved. The service is a very brief Rite III service. We end with a grace and go into the part of Eucharist that has more substance than pita bread, and have a hot meal. It's also just fun; you have conversations with folks you'd never have conversations with. . . . We do lot of pastoral care throughout the week.[22]

Carlisle's experience and outlook on the traditional church is different from mine; he believes that the "institutional church" is dying because it is no longer relevant to younger generations, and because it does not match the model of Jesus' original ministry. While this is not my experience, and in fact in my context I have found that younger families often prefer quite traditional worship and structures, I think it is important for us to hear and consider his views and experiences.

I have come to wonder about the future of parochial, institutional Christianity from the changing demographics across the country, and also my experience in Europe. I see what has happened there; people don't go to church in all sorts of contexts: urban, rural, suburban. . . . I think that other things are at work in the culture, and particularly the younger demographic, that doesn't fit with the idea of going to a church building. . . . The Sunday morning liturgy is wooden to them; it doesn't resonate with their dramatically fluid lives. Does that render the church irrelevant? I believe the answer is no, not at all. . . . To the extent that the institution appears to be breaking down, if we are asking what it might look like in the future, the most faithful model is to look at . . . the first century. It's very Jewish, it looks like what Jesus led, with disciples

---

22. Christopher Carlisle, telephone interview with the author, September 11, 2014.

including women and children, a community of people reaching to the margins of the community and ministering to the people they find there. And it seems to me that whenever Jesus got close to the powers that be, he got into trouble. Whenever he got close to buildings, he got into trouble. . . . When he would go out to the margins, he felt free to be prophetic, free to invoke the power and character of God who binds up the wounds of the lonely and the sad. That changes the paradigm of God being at the center of power to God on the margins. It's a complete inversion of the way that Palestinian Judaism was conducted. It continues to be contrary to the way most of institutional Christianity has constituted itself. . . . We often read the gospels as a story of how Jesus left Judaism for Christianity. I don't believe that is the case; I think what he left was institutional religion that takes power for itself in order to survive. For Jesus it seems as though he saw as untenable the relationship between institutional power and the power of God, which gives of itself even unto death.[23]

But Carlisle readily admits that the "institutional" church is a necessary underpinning of his own ministry. He is paid to do his ministry with veterans, college students, and young adults by the Episcopal Diocese of Western Massachusetts, and thirty-five area congregations are crucial supporters of the feeding ministry of the Cathedral in the Night. In a very real way, the very institutional church he thinks is losing relevance enables his ministry on the margins. Very aware of this tension, he continues:

I don't know what the answer to that is, the incredible tension between those two kinds of power. I don't think there will ever be an answer. Our faith, it's ultimately about the power of giving, which is of God, not the power of taking. What keeps the church alive is that we live in this tension between the demand to keep the institution going, to have the resources there to serve the people we need to serve, but not hanging on to those resources in a way that we deny our commitment to the poor. And I really do believe the gospels are all about the poor. We would like to say it's all about other things, yes, but the portal is always the poor. For Jesus it's poverty, whether it's material or spiritual sadness, being sick, knowing your own mortality, having a sense of salvation in the midst of stress and suffering. Those dynamics are really what I read the

23. Ibid.

gospels to be about. . . . We have a big meal afterwards, and in our case the conventional structure of church is crucial, because thirty-five parishes create food every Sunday. We couldn't do it without them. There's a critical balance between institutional stability and resources to help the wandering, ephemeral ministry of the street.[24]

I believe that every church needs to have elements of both the "wandering, ephemeral ministry of the street" and institutional structures that keep it operating. In the case of Cathedral in the Night, the building and infrastructure are minimal, but the ongoing leadership is supported by money from the diocese and others, and surrounding churches join in the ministry. (Similarly, Luke's gospel tells us that even Jesus was supported by the generous stewardship of several women who provided for the disciples' needs.) In the case of more traditional churches, if they are able to move beyond survival needs, they often have ministries that serve those in need in some way. And a traditional church that ministers purposefully will be intentional about forming disciples who take their Christian faith seriously enough that it informs their actions in daily life, and relieves the spiritual poverty that results from a life focused entirely on self, success, power, and money, the great temptations of twenty-first-century American life.

Every church, whether traditional or "Fresh Expressions," in some way needs both the institutional and outward-moving dimensions. The problem with many Episcopal churches is that the outward-moving dimension has been lost in anxiety over survival. One tremendous benefit of Fresh Expressions churches is that they call us back, reminding us of Jesus's "wandering, ephemeral ministry" that, as Carlisle points out, reached the people on the margins with the good news of God's love for them.

Other models of nontraditional church are also happening. There are exciting stories all over the church:

- In Boston, the Rev. Stephanie Spellers started The Crossing, which worships at the Cathedral Church of St. Paul and brings in a diverse, multi-racial group of people who work together to create eucharistic worship.[25]

---

24. Ibid.
25. http://www.thecrossingboston.org

- In Brooklyn, New York, St. Lydia's Dinner Church, led by the Rev. Emily Scott (an ordained ELCA pastor), gathers for dinner and holds its worship around the dinner table. Its website explains, "St. Lydia's is a Dinner Church. We gather every Sunday and Monday night to cook and share a sacred meal. Our congregation is looking for an experience of the Holy that is strong enough to lean on, deep enough to question, and challenging enough to change us."[26] Every person who attends is put to work in the kitchen, or setting the table, and all eat together, share and discuss a story of faith, and take Eucharist together. St. Lydia's website also has an inspiring video describing the concept.[27]

Each of these models of church is completely different from a traditional church, and also different from each of the others. Each is a creative response to its context, and each works to create community by gathering in ways the people in the neighborhood understand and respond to. The common element in these Fresh Expressions churches is that the founders envisioned something that draws from ancient Christian and Episcopal traditions, yet adapts those traditions uniquely to speak in a new way to a particular group of people.

I believe that these unusual, creative, deeply thoughtful and inspiring forms of church will be essential to helping Episcopalians tell the good news of Jesus in a new era. In order to support these nontraditional models of church, bishops and dioceses will need to be willing to empower visionary leaders who have unusual ideas, and may need to give them permission to adapt our liturgical traditions in some ways. They will also need to trust nontraditional leaders who can envision community needs, hopes, and dreams that not everyone can see.

One danger of a Fresh Expressions concept is that it might not outlive its founder; when the initial visionary leader leaves, the community will have to be strong enough to carry on with new leadership. One of the positive aspects of the institutional church is that institutions provide stability and continuity. Fresh Expressions churches will either need to find a way to provide these

26. http://www.stlydias.org/about.php
27. Ibid.

things (as, for instance, The Abbey may do by having a physical location and a sustainable financial model), or simply accept that some churches are called into being for a season only. The season may be shorter than it is for an average traditional church, but without a long-term investment in land and buildings, a nontraditional church can reach many people in deeply transforming ways, helping them come to know Christ and grow in relationship with God.

All three of these styles of church: traditional church plants, ethnic church plants, and Fresh Expressions communities, are important ways of planting churches. All three of them will be vitally important in the coming decades for helping the Episcopal Church join in God's mission of reaching new generations of people who have not yet heard the gospel of Christ. ❧

∿ 5

How Shall We Do It?
Models of Church Planting

Endicott Peabody arrived in 1882 by stagecoach in Tombstone, Arizona, a town where he had never been and where he knew no one. In this dusty frontier town, he was expected to get to know the townsfolk and plant a church—and so he did. This is perhaps the classic method of church planting, but it is far from the only one. There are many different ways to plant churches, each appropriate for different situations. Some methods are more likely to be successful than others, depending on the context. Church-wide, diocesan, and parish leaders, as well as potential church planters, should think through the possibilities and consider what approach will work best for each situation. They might find that opportunities for evangelism abound in places they had never expected to find them.

The Parachute Drop (or Diocesan Plant)

"Parachute Drop" is the term for Endicott Peabody's model of church plant (though in his nineteenth-century case, perhaps we would more appropriately call it a "Stagecoach Drop"). In the Parachute Drop, a planter is identified and metaphorically dropped alone behind the lines into uncharted territory and left to make his or her way. In the Episcopal context, we could also think of this model as the Diocesan Plant. Generally, it is the diocese that identifies the planter, the territory, and the financial resources to make it happen.

Many nondenominational churches are planted according to the Parachute Drop method, and the planters do everything on their own, including raising all the money for the church as well as their own support (often by working bi-vocationally). In the Episcopal system, it is rare to find an absolutely pure Parachute Drop, since the diocese usually chooses the planter and provides at least some financial and organizational support. This is a very good thing; church planting is difficult and stressful enough without the planter having to worry about where the family's next meal is coming from, or where to find time to plant the church after working a full schedule at the other job, or whether anyone is praying for the church to accomplish God's mission.

Other than the financial piece, however, many Episcopal churches do follow the Parachute Drop method. The Rev. Lang Lowrey started St. Benedict's in Atlanta as a Parachute Drop plant in 2006. With nothing but a territory identified by drawing a circle on the map, and some financial support from his bishop, Lowrey made contacts in the area and launched worship with three hundred people in attendance the first Sunday. The Rev. Canon Frank Logue also started a Parachute Drop church, King of Peace in Kingsland, Georgia, by similarly making contacts and starting programs in a town that the Diocese of Georgia had identified as a growth area. Interestingly, since planting their churches, both Lowrey and Logue have moved on to other calls, yet the churches they planted remain and thrive. The continuing vitality of these plants reflects the fact that the Parachute Drop church plant is the classic model, and carries assumptions that the church will reach stability and continuity by building institutions that will last.

My own Church of the Nativity was a Parachute Drop as well. The identified territory was a suburb in the Phoenix/Scottsdale area with some new subdivisions and the promise of future development; the closest established Episcopal church was twelve miles away. With the help of a group of about two dozen people from churches in the Phoenix area who wanted to see an Episcopal church in our neighborhood, we formed a launch team, met other people in the area and invited them to join, and planted Church of the Nativity.

The Parachute Drop is the classic method of church planting. It is also extremely challenging. The reason is this: no matter how fertile the ground, a church plant will not thrive if the plowing, planting, fertilizing, weeding, and harvesting all remain in the hands of one person. Planting a church is a team project. A lone-ranger planter who tries to make all the connections and invitations personally, and never forms a team, will likely fail. A church planter's first job is to form contacts with people who will connect with each other, commit to God's mission through this church, and form a team. This is what Jesus did, after all—he connected with a team of twelve disciples first, then multiplied that team to seventy, and then sent the seventy out to the countryside to connect with others and spread the good news of God's kingdom. The group became a movement because Jesus knew how to form a team and multiply his connections.

Diocesan leaders and planters who want to plant a Parachute Drop church will have to understand that creating and building a team is the first task, and that this task takes time. A Parachute Drop church that tries to launch worship too soon, without a team of enthusiastic and committed supporters, is likely to fail. Frank Logue tells the story of attending the first worship service of one such plant:

> The church planter was doing everything: the readings, singing, preaching, and acting as lay Eucharistic minister. Everything was just the church planter. As it imploded, I wasn't surprised—because [the planter] had missed a step before it ever got started. [The planter] was relying on personal abilities alone and wasn't developing and nurturing a group. . . . If there's an event and the church is committed to it then you've got to make sure it occurs. But you don't need to be in charge of everything, you have to make sure it happens. It's about finding people with the right gifts. . . . Another thing people do is they start with a liturgy, and they don't yet have a church. I think it's like a shell game if you don't have other things going before you start, like a Sunday school. My target for King of Peace was that I wanted four things going on at least monthly before we started our first service. So [we had] a youth group, children's activities, a Bible study, and a women's group before [we ever had] anything on Sunday. So there's a community you're inviting them to, not just a liturgy.[1]

---

1. Frank Logue, telephone interview with the author, July 2, 2014.

Parachute Drop church plants are appropriate where there is a significant area of population growth without a nearby Episcopal church. Diocesan
leaders who want to start such a church should be prepared to:

- Pay the planter's salary for a significant period of time before the
  church plant offers its first public worship service, while the planter
  builds the launch team;
- Actually insist that the planter build a critical mass of people before
  launching public worship (more on this subject in chapter 10);
- Staunchly back the church plant against other Episcopal churches
  that would prefer to claim the identified territory as their own (even
  if they have not made significant inroads with the area population);
- Support the church plant with prayer, encouragement, and some
  financial operating expenses (more on finances and stewardship in
  chapter 13);
- Provide a coach and some training for the church planter and lay
  leadership. The coach should have planted one or more successful
  mainline churches (not necessarily Episcopal ones), and should have
  experience coaching the type of church you expect to plant;
- Possibly, pay for the church's initial worship space (usually rented)
  and/or purchase land for a permanent location. (The diocese does not
  always do these things; see chapter 12.)

A Congregation Within an Established Church

The Parachute Drop is only one possible church-planting method. In the
New Congregation model, an established parish starts a second congregation
that will reach a completely different set of people than its current congregation, but will worship in the same location. This model may be used for a
parish that wants to start a Fresh Expressions worship service. It is also commonly used when an established parish is located in an area that has seen a
demographic group move into its neighborhood that is significantly different
from the people who already attend the church. For instance, an established
majority-Anglo congregation might discover that its neighborhood includes
significant numbers of Latinos, and start a new congregation that worships
in Spanish. The new congregation may be considered an integral part of
the ministry of the congregation that is already worshiping there, like the

Spanish-speaking La Trinidad congregation at Trinity Cathedral, Phoenix. The English and Spanish congregations there worship separately, but are all included in Trinity Cathedral's governing and leadership structures.

Alternatively, the new congregation may worship at the established church's location, but have separate leadership. The priest in such a congregation is brought in, either by the parish or by the diocese, specifically to start that ministry. Iglesia Santa Maria in Phoenix worships at St. Mary's Episcopal Church, but is considered a separate mission congregation under the oversight of the diocese. Similarly, the Rev. Daniel Velez Rivera started a Latino congregation at Grace Church in Salem, Massachusetts. Three years later, when the diocesan internship program under which he was hired at Grace Church ended, he was called as the new co-rector of St. Peter's / San Pedro in the same city, and the Latino congregation moved with him to the new location. This move highlights the character of that Latino congregation as separate from the parish where it began its ministry.

The New Congregation model has some distinct advantages. First, the new ministry does not require an expensive physical plant; it uses a building that is already in place. Second, this model provides a way to utilize older church buildings, perhaps with declining, aging populations, that need to find new ways to reach out to their changing neighborhoods. By bringing in new leaders who intentionally focus on a different population, the reach of the older congregation is extended in exciting new ways. The neighborhood church finds new life in its old neighborhood.

Of course, this model comes with challenges, too. It might be difficult for the established congregation to see the new worshipers as part of their own church's ministries rather than interlopers who are invading their space. Arranging time schedules and space utilization between the congregations may be challenging. And of course, the biggest challenge for the Episcopal Church is to find enough leaders who are qualified to do this work—bilingual, bicultural, entrepreneurial leaders.

A Mother-Daughter Plant

In a Mother-Daughter plant, an established parish discovers that a number of its members live in a geographically distinct, growing area, and commissions that group to go out from the mother church and plant a new church in that area. In some situations, the lay people who help start the daughter church make that commitment for only a short period of time (two or three years), but often they continue with the new church permanently. The mother church provides some financial, personnel, and management support for a few years. Sometimes, the new church is intended to have a very different worship style and target membership than the mother church, but more often, its genetic heritage shows, and it resembles its parent closely. Eventually, the new plant is expected to become an independent parish.

This model has some important advantages over a Parachute Drop. First, the new plant starts with a ready-made launch team of enthusiastic members, recruited from the mother church with its blessing, who help it build ministries and achieve critical mass. A Parachute Drop planter may take one to two years to make enough contacts in the community to start building a team, but in the Mother-Daughter model, the planter starts with a team in place. Community contacts and inviting the public are still essential, but the initial critical mass from the mother church gives the plant an opportunity to launch large and grow much larger. And although the mother church may experience a drop in attendance and membership after the daughter church launches, often this drop is only temporary. As the daughter church grows by reaching new people in the new neighborhood, the mother church also fills its empty space with new people in its own neighborhood. When done well, the Mother-Daughter church plant can end up benefiting the mother as well as the daughter, and Episcopal Church membership in the combined area multiplies greatly. And very importantly, the negative reaction that neighboring Episcopal churches sometimes have to a Parachute Drop plant does not exist when the nearest, most closely affected neighbor to a new church is its supportive parent. Diocesan leaders will likely find a Mother-Daughter plant to be much easier to sell to surrounding parishes when it has strong support from the nearest church.

Commonly, when a mother parish decides to sponsor a daughter church, it will bring a planter priest on board as an associate at the mother church for one or two years. The planter has permission to use that time to build relationships with church members and recruit them to the planting team, and also will live in the daughter church's area and make community contacts there. This is an ideal situation for the planter, not only because it gives her or him the opportunity to build a team of committed Christians and train them in ministry and evangelism, but also because the planter can spend that time learning from a mother church that is clearly visionary and evangelistic.

The Rev. Clay Lein planted St. Philip's, Frisco (Diocese of Dallas), the most successful recent church plant in the Episcopal Church by attendance, using this model. He was the associate rector at Christ Church Plano, the largest parish in the Episcopal Church at the time, when the diocese approached him about planting a daughter church in the nearby town of Frisco. He and Christ Church both agreed to the plan, and he spent his remaining time on the Christ Church staff, building a core launch team for the new church. Ultimately, he was able to bring about 100 to 150 people from Christ Church to St. Philip's, and added many new contacts from the community in order to launch worship on Easter 2001 with 250 people in attendance.[2] The church grew from there, and reported average Sunday attendance of 712 people in 2012. Inspired by that experience of being supported by another church, St. Philip's has since sponsored two other daughter parishes in the Diocese of Dallas: St. Andrew's McKinney and St. Paul's Prosper.

Lein talks about the experience of being the rector of a mother church that sponsored two daughter churches:

> We [at St. Philip's] actually were getting ready to do our capital campaign, and we asked the diocese if they would please plant a church in McKinney. . . . They came back and said we've never had a church ask us to plant right in their back yard, but we will, and we [St. Philip's] told them, "We will be a place for that person [the planter] to begin. We are not much, we don't have a building, we are in the middle of a capital campaign, but right on!" We were involved in that process in several ways. For one, we were part of the assessment for that church planter. Jim Griffith [Lein's coach in planting St. Philip's] taught us that assessment was a key to success, maybe 90%. A good beginning depends on getting the right person that God is calling to that place. So we were part of the assessment and we provided a place to begin. Mike [Michie, the founding priest of St. Andrew's McKinney] moved

---

2. Soon after the launch, the Diocese of Dallas decided that it would prefer to oversee the new plant directly rather than let it remain as a daughter church to Christ Church. This move proved to be prescient, as Christ Church Plano subsequently left the Episcopal Church over sexuality issues, while St. Philip's Frisco remains as an Episcopal congregation.

here to McKinney, his family was welcomed here, he was on the staff, he preached as much as me, he did pastoral care as much as me, he taught in our Alpha course. We gave him free rein; we said you can have anybody. Start developing relationships, and those relationships will go with you. He was only with us for about six months, and we learned that that was really too short a time to Mother-Daughter, so he took only a few people with him.

We sponsored St. Paul's Prosper and we were a little bit more mature. We had a coach for Michael [Gilton] and a coach for me as a mother church. We had him here for a year. . . . As we got closer, we had a baby shower [for the new church]. We personally challenged people in the congregation to go. I wrote letters to people in that area. We passed out pledge cards. We said a mother is "all in," so every one of us has to be "all in" on this daughter. That means we are either giving, going, or praying. We challenged everybody to do this in a very visible way. Then we had a blessing, a commissioning (with Michael present), and his people went out following a cross that they had brought. I think that was a better model. He took more people and he took stronger leaders. He was blessed in that way. That's how we've helped in that process.[3]

But wasn't it hard for the mother church to decide to give up members and pledges to nearby churches that might be competition in the future, I asked? How did St. Philip's leaders help the congregation to understand the vision of spreading God's kingdom through planting new churches? Lein responded:

For us it was a challenge to step up to, and we were very bold and artic-ulate about it. There were people who would say, "Hey, that doesn't make sense," and we always would say, "This is God's sense, we have to trust him. He will restore everything he takes away. Sure, our ASA may take a hit, we will lose families, they may take their pledges with them, some may be big pledges, but within a year we will have replaced it and we will have the joy of seeing a new child born." It was not hard for me because it had always been what I knew God was calling us to do. I had to always challenge people, "This is a faith-growing experience. This

---

3. Clay Lein, telephone interview with the author, July 1, 2014.

is where faith grows. It's not sitting in a Sunday school class only. It's going to happen, (gulp) can we do that hard thing?" And saying "Yes, we can."[4]

I believe that the Mother-Daughter church-planting model has great potential for growing the Episcopal Church and helping Christ reach many new people through us. The challenge will be to help rectors of large churches see that vision: that growing God's kingdom may sometimes involve short-term sacrifices in attendance and pledges, followed by God's grace in replacing what was lost. We have many large, program- and resource-size congregations that fill their current space comfortably, but have little room to grow. These established congregations are in what Stephen Compton calls the "Equilibrium" stage of the life cycle discussed earlier; they have had generally flat attendance, with small fluctuations, for a number of years. Such a congregation can re-start growth and evangelism in its area by starting a new congregation. The visionary gifts of the mother will often result in growth in both the mother and daughter churches, as both respond eagerly to God's call.

The Multi-Site Church

One strategy with real promise for success, which has not yet been tried extensively in the Episcopal Church, is the Multi-Site model. If it is difficult to get large resource- and program-size churches to envision birthing new daughter churches, for fear they will lose attendance and pledges, the Multi-Site model is one way to address that concern. In this model, similar to a Mother-Daughter plant, a group goes out from an established church to minister in a new location. However, the intention is that the two churches will remain one church with common governance, finance, and administrative structures. The mother church will simply begin to offer worship at two locations, instead of one.

Bishop Andy Doyle of the Diocese of Texas has a vision to plant fifteen new worshiping congregations in the next five years, and fifty-one new congregations in the next fifteen years—a challenging goal, indeed. Why do they want to plant new churches? Mary MacGregor, the Canon for Evangelism and Congregational Development, explains that the vision for the diocese

---

4. Ibid.

is evangelism, sharing the good news. Every established parish is encouraged to grow, but the diocese will also adopt church planting as one of its primary growth strategies. There will be some diocesan plants (such as Parachute Drops), but Texas will go slowly on these—perhaps planting one every three years—because of the difficulty in finding gifted planters and the expense involved (Texas puts significant resources into providing worship facilities for its church plants). The diocese would also like to do some Mother-Daughter plants, but finds that it is sometimes hard to convince established churches to take this leap of faith. Therefore, the most important strategy Texas is adopting is the Multi-Site or Second Campus strategy. MacGregor explains, "Second Campus is a big push because we have a number of resource-size churches, and there's no reason in the world why they can't have a second campus. They can afford it, they can do it, they just need to capture a vision and have the leadership that says they can do it. So we're pushing that with our larger churches."[5] She describes several initiatives that are already underway:

> We currently have one church, Grace Georgetown, which has an active Second Campus. They have had it for three or four years and are absolutely exploding. They're going to have to move, they have leased space, they have about eighty-five people on Sunday, they are maxing out the space. We have another church that is partnering with us. We are purchasing the land and they will pay for the building, probably ten miles south of their current location. They are very strategic about it and it's going to be a success. They already have an in-house associate who is going to be the priest-in-charge at the Second Campus. Those Second Campuses really look like an extension of the mother: they have one vestry, common ministries and programs, and Sunday worship is similar. It's just a whole new location that will accommodate a whole new group in a new geographical area. . . . [In] another [situation], we had a church that left due to sexuality issues, the rector and people left, so instead of selling that property. . . this church came to us and said we have a vision. If you'll give us that property we'll help refurbish it and we have a vision. That church is scheduled to open in 2015.[6]

5. Mary MacGregor, telephone interview with the author, June 27, 2014.
6. Ibid.

The Multi-Site model offers great growth opportunity for an established church that is filling its current worship space, or that sees a way to reach new people in a distinct area nearby. The sponsoring church would need to have the available financial resources to do a second worshiping site, and would need to have leadership it trusts to take charge of the second location and pastor the people there.

As MacGregor describes it, that leadership can be an associate priest who is already serving on the mother church's staff. But Clay Lein (St. Philip's Frisco), has a broader vision for the potential of Multi-Site congregations (and wrote his doctor of ministry thesis on the subject). As he sees it, there are two major obstacles in the Episcopal Church to planting churches. One is the scarcity of financial resources. He points out, "In this diocese (Dallas) we have been successful in planting one church every three years, which is not at all sufficient to keep up with population growth or the natural life processes of growth and decline in a diocese."[7] But the most important obstacle, he says, is the difficulty of finding gifted, entrepreneurial clergy leaders; he laments that "the challenge of finding people who have entrepreneurial, persevering, faith, innovation, communication, preaching gifts, with a collar on them, in our tradition is almost impossible."[8]

Lein continues:

Part of why I'm concerned about this is that I believe that . . . we don't have enough church-planting clergy in the Episcopal Church. Seminaries and Commission on Ministry processes wean out entrepreneurial types because those people rock boats. [We need to] admit that we have a problem that we are powerless to solve and start re-visioning the way we raise up leaders. That's one of the things that Multi-Site structures hold some promise in for me, because I'm thinking Multi-Site may be our best hope. . . . The biggest difference [between Multi-Site and other models of church planting] is that to plant a new church, you need a collar. I don't see any way around that in our tradition. . . . But what if I could find a way to start a new community of faith that did not require a collar, but allowed lay people to lead who start businesses left and right, who are teachers in schools and colleges, who have

7. Lein, interview.
8. Ibid.

communication gifts, who are right in the trenches with real life? What
if I could find a way to mobilize some lay leaders to lay-pastor a community of faith? Sure, I need a priest to do sacraments, but I can find
retired priests who want an altar. I could imagine doing three campuses
at St. Philip's alone. All of those little struggling shoots have their tap-
root connected to a larger church and have access to the staff, and our
staff actually sees every one of those campuses as an integral part of their
responsibility.[9]

An exciting vision, indeed. Is it too much for Episcopalians to accept
lay entrepreneurial leadership of sites under the oversight of a large parish?
Even in the less revolutionary Texas model, with clergy leadership of the new
site, are we able to let go of our idea that a church is equal to a physical location, and re-vision a church as a congregation of people in common mission?
Lein points out that the ancient Celtic monastic model envisioned regional
ministries; can we envision regional ministries in the twenty-first-century
Episcopal Church?

Church Planting: Something for Everyone

In church planting, there is something for everyone. The typical church
plant is the Parachute Drop or Diocesan Plant, which is appropriate for new,
growing areas that can support a new church. But this is not the only way to
plant churches, or even perhaps the most important strategy. We have many
opportunities to plant churches.

In the Episcopal Church, we have many small parishes with large buildings that are struggling to survive because their offerings are no longer relevant to their neighborhoods. A small congregation in this situation should
consider starting a second congregation that *is* relevant to the neighborhood
(often an ethnic church plant) or the diocese should consider closing the current congregation and using the building for a new congregation. If a church
is dwindling because it is not reaching the people around it, then it may be a
valuable asset that should be used in a more mission-oriented way.

We also have many large, program- and resource-size congregations
that fill their current space comfortably, but have little room to grow. Such

9. Ibid.

congregations can re-start their growth by starting a new congregation, either a Mother-Daughter plant or a Second Campus. Or, if an established church sees that despite its vitality, it is not reaching many young adults, it can start a Multi-Site Fresh Expressions ministry for young adults. These are exciting initiatives for growth that can become major strategic investments for the future, and vital ways of answering Jesus's call to go into the world and make disciples.   ❧

PART TWO

Factors that Contribute to Success in Church Planting

There is no cookbook recipe that will automatically lead a church plant to success. Every church plant is different, because each is in a different context. An ethnic church will be planted differently than a traditional church or a Fresh Expressions community. There is a great deal of literature from the evangelical world about how to plant a traditional-model church, but much less is available about planting nontraditional worshiping communities. The chapters that follow use advice from church planting books and from the experience of Episcopal church planters and other leaders to give some general ideas of success factors. This advice is most generally applicable to traditional plants, but I believe that all different types of new churches can glean some wisdom from these experiences.

6

Church Planters: Servants Through Whom You Came to Believe

What then is Apollos? What is Paul? Servants through whom you came to believe, as the Lord assigned to each. I planted, Apollos watered, but God gave the growth. 1 Corinthians 3:5–6

What was it that drove Paul from city to city, starting one church after another, transforming the known world and planting seeds that continue to bear fruit in our lives today? He yearned to tell the world-changing, life-transforming good news of Christ. He was willing to talk to anyone, anywhere, about Jesus. He had absolute faith that even in the darkest hour, Christ was present, and that Christ would empower his ministry. He had a vision of what he believed Christ was doing in the world. He persevered, running the race that was set before him, never wavering from what he believed his course to be. He was a gifted communicator, adapting his speaking and writing to the cultures and beliefs of each audience. He had the gift of gathering people around him and awakening in them a hunger to know more. He knew how to build those people up as leaders and pastors in their own right. He was not afraid of conflict, but engaged lovingly with those who disagreed with him. He was willing to let the Holy Spirit lead him into situations he would not have planned for himself. He knew his own abilities, but he never lost sight of the fact that it was not

Paul who was working miracles, but Christ who was working miracles through him. He prayed.

Those of us who are present-day church planters in the Episcopal Church cannot claim to have anything like Paul's stature, nor his courage, nor his effect on the world. We do not risk our lives to do the things we do. We do not preach to a world that has never heard of Jesus before. Yet twenty-first century planters would do well to pay attention to Paul, the greatest church planter in history, because even today, starting new congregations of faith requires many of the same gifts.

A Burning Desire to Share the Good News

Paul changed the world because his life had been radically and irrevocably transformed by Jesus Christ. To the very core of his being, he was driven to share what he had found with others. He was absolutely convinced that Jesus was at work in the world, overcoming death and sin and bringing a new creation into being, and that every person needed to hear that good news and be part of that divine work. That was the good news he shared, and that is the good news we share. Christ has commanded us to take that good news into all nations, to Jerusalem, Judea and Samaria, and to the ends of the earth. For most of us, there is no need to look to the ends of the earth—those who have not heard this good news in a relevant way, whose lives are spiritually empty, who yearn for a more meaningful life, are right here in our own neighborhoods. It is our call as followers of Christ to share that good news.

The Rev. Canon Frank Logue, who planted King of Peace, Kingsland, Georgia, names the one core motivation that he believes is absolutely essential for church planters to have:

> If evangelism isn't a core part of who you are, and you're not interested in some deeper way in talking about Jesus and finding people who have been deeply unchurched but are interested in asking these deeper questions, then you're probably not going to be successful. We're not talking about finding people who are already church broke and convincing them to come to yours instead of another one. We're talking about finding people who are not in church and bringing them into the church, so that's who you're looking for. If that's not something worth getting up for every morning, you're not going to really be very successful. . . . There might be things that could make you a very effective rector but

[not] a church planter, so we're looking for something other than that, something additional.

When we're looking for an effective rector, you've got to attend to all the basics, you can't miss them. You don't have to preach home runs every week, but you have to get base hits every time you go to bat, [you have to] connect with the people, connect with their lives, you've got to be able to teach and lead. But for church planting you need this other thing. You need this: "I have a passion for spending my time talking to people who don't have this whole framework, who have all these questions." They come from all sorts and conditions but you have to have a passion for that because that's the thing.[1]

I believe that every priest, and every Christian, has a certain group of people that tug at her or his heart in particular. For me, the group of people who make my heart ache are people in the same state of life I was when I came back to the church after many years away: young families, people immersed in professional, business, or work life, people whose lives are almost unbearably busy but who still feel a deep spiritual emptiness. Nativity's neighborhood is full of people in this situation, and my passion is to share the life-changing gospel of Christ with them. I want them to hear the voice of God, to be moved by the breath of the Holy Spirit, to be inspired by the example of Jesus as it touches their lives. These are lives I know and understand, because I have been there, too. Other church leaders have a passion to share the gospel with different groups, which is as it should be. Very few of us can be like Paul—we cannot be all things to all people—but each of us can reach some people and tell them the good news of Christ.

A Gift for Communicating

A church planter must be an excellent preacher. There really is no avoiding this fact. People attend church for many reasons, and preaching is only one of them. But in a church that meets in a school, an office building, or a movie theater, a sense of beauty and transcendence might be hard to come by. The community may be lively and welcoming, but people who are new to the church will want to hear engaging sermons that can be applied to their everyday lives.

---

1. Logue, interview.

A gift for communication must go beyond mere preaching, however. It certainly should encompass teaching, too—the planter should be able to help Christians deepen their faith through study of Christian scriptures and tradition. But more than this, a church planter needs to be a person who can cast a vision and convince other people to follow in helping to create it. The planter must be able to describe what God is doing in his or her community in such a compelling way that people want to join in God's mission. This communications gift should be evident in groups, in one-on-one conversation, and in writing. A diocesan leader who is wondering whether a person should be called to plant a new church should look very carefully at the way the person speaks and writes. Does she describe the vision in such a way that the bishop is tempted to join the new church? Does he open the eyes of his listeners to a new way of looking at God's work in his community? This person might be a naturally gifted church planter.

An Affinity for the Community

Closely related to having a heart for evangelism and an ability to communicate is the issue of "affinity." The planter, in most situations, needs a close affinity with the community the new church is trying to reach. There are some people who have the gift of cross-cultural evangelism, but far more common is the gift of deep understanding and love for people who are part of a very familiar world. My description of the people in Nativity's neighborhood above, for instance, mentions that they have a great deal in common with me. Affinity with the people one is called to serve is important not only because those people will be attracted to a planter like them. It is because the planter is able to communicate in stories and images that connect with the people's lives and touch their minds and hearts. Tom Brackett, the Officer for Church Planting and Redevelopment for the Episcopal Church, says:

> The core things are a compelling expression of the gospel that is appropriate to the context we're called to serve. . . . We have several planters right now who are very gifted, but they don't love the people they're called to serve. It's not their culture and context.
>
> [There is] nothing more compelling than stories that illustrate what we say. We believe stories are the best containers for truth, but they gotta be local stories. As the saying goes, it's hard to sing the blues

from the back seat of a brand new Volvo. If your stories aren't accessible to the culture you're called to serve, then you need to change or move on. To me the questions are, "Do you love the stories of the people you're called to serve? Do you love the story by which you're conveying these truths of God's presence among us and how we fit into God's story? . . . . Can you sustain a story that is you as much as them, given the culture?" [2]

Paul famously found ways to connect with local cultures. When speaking to Jewish Christians like himself, he reached deeply into the well of ancestral Jewish stories to explain Jesus Christ's mission and ministry. When speaking to Greeks in the Areopagus (Acts 17:22), he found a way to appeal to their own tradition in order to proclaim that what they worshiped as unknown—the yearning they felt for something they could not name—was in fact the God who sent Jesus Christ and raised him from the dead. Like Paul, we who plant churches need to be able to connect to the deep beliefs and cultures of the people we are called to serve.

Faith

I sometimes think that if I had known before I became a church planter all the challenges that it would involve, I might not have accepted the call. But in a way, I did know. I knew that we were going to try to build a congregation starting with zero, and that we had three years to do it before my diocesan money ran out. I knew that this nonexistent church had no land, no building, and no steady income, yet would need a place to worship. I knew that we did not have staff, volunteers, or any means to make the ministries happen that I felt were absolutely crucial (children, youth, music, administration). And yet somehow I didn't worry about those things. It seems crazy now, but going in, I was absolutely confident that Christ was calling me to do this, and Christ would be there with me, making miracles happen. And the miracles did happen—the people, money, facilities, staff, and volunteers all came exactly when they were needed. I still can't describe exactly where that certainty came from. Is there a special kind of insanity that leads church

---

2. Brackett, interview.

planters to assume that things will work out somehow, unlikely though it
seems? Or is it just faith?

Lang Lowrey, the founder of St. Benedict's, Smyrna, Georgia, thinks it
is faith:

> I think faith is the most important criterion. The idea that God won't
> abandon you. This is scary, you're out there by yourself; the vicar has a
> lot of pressure. More fail than succeed—this is not a time when churches
> are proliferating. You need to have faith that this is important, it has
> real value, and that God won't abandon you.[3]

Clay Lein, the founding priest of St. Philip's Frisco, expresses it like this:

> I think the first [thing a church planter needs] is faith, and I don't mean
> right doctrine necessarily. There are lots of people that have right doc-
> trine that are not spending every minute of every day trusting [that]
> God will be faithful to us and helping us in this new work. It's the faith
> that says everyone says this is impossible, but God says it is possible,
> and I will trust him. It's the kind of faith that Job had, saying, "Even if
> you slay me, I will still trust you." So even if this church plant is going
> to end badly, and my reputation will be stained permanently, I'm still
> going to trust you in it. That's a sort of desperate trust you need in
> church planting.[4]

Where does this kind of desperate trust come from? Certainly it comes
from prayer, and from discernment of God's presence in the call to plant a
church. It comes also from experience that confirms that trust: from watching the most improbable doors open, and the most unlikely opportunities
unfold. In the first few years of Nativity's existence, I became accustomed to
miracles. The right people would show up to lead the right ministries. The
problem of a place to worship would be solved in ways I would never have
expected (several times!). Money would be provided in exactly the amounts
needed. The Holy Spirit would show up and compensate for my weaknesses.

Ten years ago, before I planted this church, I took an assessment instru-
ment provided by the Episcopal Church to see whether I was gifted as a

---

3. Lowrey, interview.
4. Lein, interview.

church planter. That assessment is no longer available, but I am not sure that it tests for the most important criteria anyway. I am not sure any assessment can test for a burning desire to share the gospel, or an ability to share in the stories of a local culture, or the sureness of faith. Certainty may be foolhardiness, or it may be confidence in God's call. Ultimately, I believe it comes down to discernment of God's call. If God is in the movement, then God's work will happen, even if the church plant does not ultimately survive.

The Ability to Live with Uncertainty and Risk

Though a church planter has faith, there are going to be many times when it is not clear how the next dilemma is going to be solved. He may discover next week that the school where the church has been worshiping has decided they don't want a church there any more. She may realize that it will be years before this church ever reaches the kind of stability she enjoyed in her last call in an established church. He may not have a job in a year's time, because the church may no longer exist. (I have been in all of these situations.)

A church planter has to be able to live with, and even thrive on, uncertainty and risk. Church planting is all about making things up as you go along. There are no parish traditions to fall back on. There are no tried-and-true ways of doing things. There is no altar guild director who has been in charge for twenty years and knows how everything works. Everything is invented by trial and error. Many traditions will change as the church grows. There will never be anything comfortable or cozy about leading a church plant. A true planter is the one who knows that once the church grows to the point where things are comfortable and cozy, it will probably be time to move on to the next call.

Diocesan leadership can help with the uncertainty inherent in church planting in one area: ensuring that the planter at least has a decent salary, benefits, and basic operating expenses for a clear period of time, agreed in advance. Nervousness over where the family's next meal is coming from does not contribute to creativity in starting a church.

Many people involved in church planting will tell you that we have a problem calling, preparing, and ordaining risk-taking, entrepreneurial leaders in our church. Bishops and dioceses should be looking for people who have a history of starting things or growing things from small to large, who are restless in the face of stability, who are always looking for something just a bit more challenging. Unfortunately, our Commissions on Ministry often weed such people out of the process. One leader who wished to go into church planting told me that her Commission on Ministry ordered her to undergo spiritual and psychological counseling to determine why she was not willing to be a "normal" priest in an established parish. Her spiritual director just laughed and answered, "That's their problem, not yours." It is indeed our problem. We need experienced, entrepreneurial leaders who are willing to think in new and creative ways.

Such leaders may make Commissions on Ministry uncomfortable, because most COM members come from established churches and envision that such an entrepreneur would turn things upside down there (and they are probably right). Seminaries are led by academics, few of whom have ever been involved in planting a church, and may not even see it as an important task. New priests generally serve their first few years, either in small churches where they become priest-in-charge with very little mentoring, or in large churches that have been in existence for many years. Lowrey suggests a different model of preparing church-planting leaders:

> We are not calling [the] types of people [we need]. We are calling much
> different people. Risk-taking is not engendered in our church, and this
> is a risk-taking enterprise. [It should start] with the profile of the kind
> of people we need in the priesthood, then nurture [them] with place-
> ments that expose them rapidly to church planting. I [would take] a
> person who meets the criteria, put them in a church plant, pay them to
> spend a year there. The church planter will teach them. Invest in get-
> ting the right profile person. Don't train them in the traditional way in
> a status quo church, put them in a church plant. The plant won't have
> them for long, they will go start another one. Train them, use them,
> teach them.[5]

Leadership and Management Skills

It is vitally important for a church planter to have a history of leadership, and also to have the underlying management skills necessary to make their leadership effective. People experienced with church planting, both planters

5. Lowrey, interview.

and diocesan executives, wax eloquent on this subject—not only on the importance of calling people with very strong leadership skills, but, as Lang Lowrey points out above, the difficulty our system has in approving innovative, experienced, skilled, entrepreneurial leaders for ordination. He goes on:

> Also [you] need to be good at something before you do this. It's not the type of job for someone just out of seminary who has a new idea. You need entrepreneurial skills, math skills. Maybe the person is not a sales person, but they need entrepreneurial skills to create things from nothing and organize them. [They should have a] proven previous career. I would not have succeeded as a young man right out of college. They need faith, stick-to-it-ness, vision, moxie. It takes someone with a previous career who was successful in it and chose this vocation.[6]

I would second the idea that we should be looking for experienced leaders to plant churches. This does not necessarily mean elderly leaders—young people can be experienced leaders too. We need to look for people who are burning to lead and to innovate, and whose life history shows that they have the leadership skills to do it, and the management skills to sustain it.

Vision, Innovation, and Entrepreneurship

A church planter should be able to see the church that does not yet exist, as if it were already a tangible reality. She should be able to look at a community and discern where God is working within it, and understand how a new church can participate in God's vision for that community. And the planter should be able to envision the steps that would get the church from point A (where it is now) to point B (where God wants it to be). That is a creative process; it involves innovation. A church planter should be exhilarated by innovation, creating something from nothing.

Lein describes his background:

> In my business career I worked for Intel and was a manager for product innovation. That was part of what I liked to do from the beginning—I like new things, new products, new processes. Even in seminary, I convinced the diocese to restart a neighborhood inner-city church in field education. I had trouble just doing what the system said to do, and from

---

6. Ibid.

the beginning I was wired to start new things. I knew I wanted to be doing new stuff.

I think that entrepreneurial innovation . . . is a necessary quality. You're not getting a coloring book with all of the pictures traced out, you're getting a blank piece of paper, and in fact you're not even getting a blank piece of paper, you're being told by someone in charge, go paint a beautiful portrait, you're on your own. Church planting can be really outside the lines and sometimes not even on the paper, so I think innovating is important.[7]

In assessing a prospective planter, leaders should look for a history of innovation. Can this person point to experiences of creating, growing, and leading? Is he an entrepreneur, someone who can not only envision something new, but also follow it through to completion? Ideally, the planter should have proven herself in a successful previous career that used a wide variety of skills: business skills, organizational skills, and leadership skills.

The Ability to Gather and Empower a Team

A church planter in the Episcopal system is usually a priest. But in every church, and in a new church in particular, the priest has to be acutely aware that lay ministry is a vital underpinning of the congregation. The very first, and most important, task of a church planter is to gather a group of people who will commit to the church and work together to make it a reality. Each person's gifts are essential and it is the whole group together who will bring the church to birth. The planter is only as good as the team of people she or he can inspire to make this church a life's work. So a gift of drawing people together and making them want to work together for a common goal is essential. A planter should have leadership experience that shows that he or she has the gift of gathering a team. (This is such an important subject that chapter 8 is devoted to the topic of gathering and empowering leaders.)

Willingness to Work Through Conflict

Paul was famously unafraid to say exactly what he thought in any situation, but he always said it with love, doing his best to remain in loving relationship

---

7. Lein, interview.

with the person with whom he disagreed. This ability, which Rabbi Edwin Friedman called self-differentiation, is a mandate for any church leader. Church planters especially should understand that conflict will arise, and it might be acutely painful to experience it in a church you have helped midwife to birth; it may actually feel like being rejected by one's own child. But it is natural for any church in its formation stages to experience conflict, once the initial excitement has worn off. A planter needs to understand this, anticipate it, and be prepared to face conflict when it arises and work through it in a mature way, including being able to apologize and admit when he is wrong. Conflict, after all, when handled well, can be a way for a community to exercise discernment and find creative solutions to new problems.

Ego and Humility

Paul was zealously confident of his mission, his beliefs, and his leadership abilities. He had a notoriously healthy ego! At the same time, he had a deep humility. He knew that he could not accomplish the things he did on his own power: Christ's was the power that allowed him to do great things. "I have been crucified with Christ," he said, "and it is no longer I who live, but it is Christ who lives in me" (Galatians 2:19–20). Paul's mission was not his own, but Christ's.

Lein offers a very interesting insight on ego and humility.

Perseverance is essential. You have got to be able to persevere and continue to press forward. You have to have a little bit of egotism that goes with that perseverance. People push back and say we shouldn't do that. You kind of have to have a sense that you've gotten clarity, and you are going to persevere in that. It may appear bullheaded even to people, but when you're doing something that's new, that didn't exist before, your perseverance will be tested.

I think prayer covers all of it too, that's part of the faith; it's the conversation with God that says, "Help me Lord," because this is scary. I think [another quality the planter needs] is humility. I guess that's what balances out the egotism that says, "I think God is calling me to plant this church." The humility says, "Yeah, but I don't think I can do it on my own." Some people call that insane; trusting God.[8]

---

8. Lein, interview.

The qualities Lein is describing—a curious mixture of ego and humility—seem to have a lot in common with what business writer Jim Collins calls "Level 5 Leadership." In *Good to Great: Why Some Companies Make the Leap . . . And Others Don't*,[9] Collins and his team researched companies that became great (measured by stock performance) and sustained that greatness for at least fifteen years. He found that all of the companies that made the leap had a "Level 5 Leader." Oddly, a Level 5 Leader is not a celebrity superstar—in fact, Collins found that having a celebrity superstar leader was negatively correlated with performance. Instead, a Level 5 Leader "blends extreme personal humility with intense professional will. . . they were self-effacing individuals who displayed the fierce resolve to do whatever needed to be done to make the company great."[10] They were not personally famous; their ambition was for the company, not for themselves, and they often gave credit to others for their success. They made sure that the companies were organized so that they would last long beyond their own tenure: they provided for successors and helped their employees become strong performers.

Level 5 Leadership seems a tailor-made concept for Christian leaders. If we are truly followers of Christ, we know our own faults. As the Psalmist says, "For I know my transgressions, and my sin is ever before me."[11] Personal humility is a characteristic of the committed Christian. Yet church planting is hard work, and "intense professional will" (in Collins's words) is necessary in order to accomplish all that needs to be done—reaching out to make connections in the community, creating ministry systems, managing a non-profit organization, inspiring others.

It is tempting to think of the church planter as the kind of celebrity superstar who draws the crowds and ensures that everything in the church is centered on the pastor. And indeed, a church planter must have some of these qualities, or people would not become part of a fledgling, uncertain, under-resourced church. The church planter must be someone that other people want to be around, and are willing to follow. And the planter must be a person who can speak compellingly about God's vision for humans in

---

9. Jim Collins, *Good to Great: Why Some Companies Make the Leap. . . And Others Don't* (New York: HarperBusiness, 2001).
10. Ibid., 21.
11. Psalm 51:3, Book of Common Prayer, p. 656.

the community. But I think it is vital, if a new church is going to outlive its founder, that the founder take care to create systems that do *not* depend on herself. Churches must be planted with the long-term goal in mind. The church planter will be with the church for a season only. If everything depends on the founding pastor, it may very well all fall apart when the pastor leaves. A wise planter will create strong systems of lay leadership and will make a priority, not of building a cult of personal adulation, but of building a church that can someday survive without him. After all, that's what Jesus did. In his extreme humility, he gave himself for the sake of others—but not before creating a community of disciples, training them in evangelism, ensuring that they practiced doing the work on their own (Luke 10:1–24), and leaving them behind to carry on the work without him.

Prayer

A church planter should pray regularly, and depend on prayer to sustain her. There will be exhilarating success, and crushing failures. The planter will need to depend on a strong relationship with God to help navigate these ups and downs. A church planter should also seek the prayers of a group of intercessors that will commit, not only to praying for the church and its leaders every day, but also to giving prayer support for special requests the planter might send. Jim Griffith, Methodist church planter and founder of the Griffith Coaching Network, suggests that the prayer team should not include members of the church; it should be a group of interested people who make this their long-distance ministry.[12] The reason for enlisting folks for this ministry who are not members of the new congregation is that the planter may need to share serious concerns about church conflicts and personalities with the prayer team. If the prayer team is to be effective, the members must be kept informed about the everyday truths that the planter faces, and this kind of honesty is very difficult to achieve with folks who are too close to the situation. Of course it makes perfect sense also to ask the congregation's regular prayer team to pray regularly for the mission of the church and its leaders.

---

12. Suggestion made at Church Planting Bootcamp offered in the Diocese of Arizona, September 15–17, 2014.

Family Support

If the planter has a spouse, that spouse should be completely on board. That doesn't mean that the planter's spouse must be an equal partner in ministry. The classic church planting model of years past has a priest whose spouse is equally committed to the plant and contributes significant ministry to the new church. In this era of two-vocation households, I believe that such a model is increasingly impractical. My husband has his own career, and I don't expect him to share in mine. But he is completely supportive, and has patiently listened to all my anxieties, frustrations, hopes, and dreams for the church for eight years now. He worships at Nativity and participates in a few ministries. But he is not unpaid Nativity staff, as the old-fashioned model would expect. Don't get me wrong—if the planter's spouse is willing to act as an equal partner in the ministry, that's terrific. But it shouldn't be required. What is absolutely necessary, if the planter is married, is a stable and supportive marriage, with a spouse who understands the kind of tremendous effort that church planting requires. The spouse must be willing to do the one important ministry that no other church member will do: listen understandingly and offer unqualified love and support.

Selection, Training, and Assessment

Perhaps it is true that church planters are born, not made. The Rev. Canon Carmen Guerrero says:

> I don't consider myself a church planter. However, I know I have started churches and I have brought dying churches to life. . . . As the saying goes, "I can do no other." Like Paul, I share the gospel, educate about the gospel, teach self-sufficiency, help people discover their gifts and be willing to let them utilize them, prepare people for my leaving. I don't see myself as a church planter, but I start churches. Some people take courses, but in Spanish we say, "*si no te mace*," if it isn't born in you and through you, you don't have it.[13]

I believe that across the church, in dioceses, seminaries, and church-wide, we need to be taking special care to raise up and train the kind of leaders who

---

13. Guerrero, interview.

will be required to lead the church into a new era. Not all of these leaders will be ordained, and it will be very important to offer leadership training to lay people with leadership potential. It will also be vital to raise up ordained leaders who can lead the work of church planting.

Mary MacGregor offers a summary of the profile of the ideal church planter:

> [Successful church planters] seem to be clergy who have a high degree of enthusiasm for the mission of the church, a real spirit of joy about what the church has to offer. . . They're not afraid to go out into the community, they're not afraid to introduce themselves, they're not afraid to grow something out of nothing. I think [they should be] entrepreneurial, having a history of growing something, particularly a ministry that evolved perhaps from nothing to something that was successful with a number of people involved. We always look at people's experience [and ask], "What have they grown, where have they demonstrated leadership?" We want leaders, we don't just want people who can manage or who can shape liturgy well, we want people who have relational skills, can build relationships, can empower people, are discerning about people's gifts for ministry, and are not so controlling that they can empower others to work as a team. It doesn't mean that they don't have a lot of power themselves in a church plant, but they have got to build a team, so they have got to have those kinds of people skills. So [they should be] fearless, faithful, mature, [they should have] a degree of emotional intelligence, they know when it's important to be a non-anxious presence, they can self-differentiate, [they are] relational, empowering, and [they are] not lone rangers or silos.[14]

Eight years ago, when I was thinking of becoming a church planter, the Episcopal Church's Office of Congregational Development offered a church planter assessment that had been developed by the Gallup organization for six mainline denominations. (Undependable as a screening tool according to Tom Brackett, this assessment is no longer available.) Today, the best way to screen and select church planters is to look for those people who have a

---

14. MacGregor, interview.

burning sense of calling to minister in a particular community, who have a history of leadership and growing things, and who have the ability to gather a team of enthusiastic leaders around them.

Diocesan leaders who want to plant churches should seek out training and coaching for their planters. While there are a few experienced Episcopal planters who could lead training and coaching sessions, there are many experienced trainers available outside the Episcopal world; we should take advantage of their expertise and invite them to help in our ministry of proclaiming the good news. It is true that some non-Episcopal church planting experts take stances that are anathema to us in ministry (e.g., excluding women from leadership), but there are some from mainline contexts who have done spectacular church planting work themselves, and who are called to coach and assist others. Some non-Episcopal church planters have planted very large and successful churches, and they have very valuable insight and experience to offer. I have attended training offered by non-Episcopal, mainline church planting consultants (such as United Methodists Jim and Kim Griffith), aimed at people planting churches according to a traditional model. This training is very practical in orientation, offering a step-by-step approach. The Episcopal Church could take advantage of such expertise, not only to train planters, but also to bring planters together in training sessions and help them form supportive relationships with each other.

Tom Brackett also offers training for all categories of church planters. He describes that training as follows:

> The training I offer is an Episcopalianized version of Church Multiplication Center Boot Camp. I added my experience with coaching church planters and added stories and vignettes; real life examples of what I've learned from bishops about how to make it in Episcopal Church culture. It starts with a point of compassion. There are a lot of people that we might say should be planting but they have no reason, because they have not yet themselves come in contact with the kind of experience of belovedness that would make it worth it. I don't think what's plaguing us is a lack of strategy or rational thinking; we have a lot of people in leadership who don't come from a place of belovedness. They haven't had a compelling expression of good news that they can talk about.

I start with [asking people] in five hundred words, to give us a glimpse of your version of good news that you sense is a compelling enough expression that you can engage the context you're called to serve. A good number are there in spite of the way they've been brought in. They do have a compelling expression but haven't been asked before. If it feels like we're getting too far from our sense of belovedness, we need to start over. I want to help you realize that you are qualified to reach a certain audience, and help you get clear about that.

We talk about the basics of how to talk about what sustains their hope. It's a cousin conversation to evangelism: How do you sustain hopefulness? How might we share good news?

We talk about who are your neighbors, what does it mean to be a neighbor? We look at demographics, community organizing, what are the needs here, what is God doing, how do we identify ourselves, what does it mean to be neighbors to these people, how Jesus talks about the neighbor in Jewish law. It's a way of inviting people to rethink what is sacred, how to be archeologists of hope.

We talk about how to gather a core team, and the six primary conversations the core team needs to have.

We ask what is the invitation, the genuine invitation to join? Many Episcopalians have never been invited, nor have had the experience, or the gift of genuine invitation. We talk about how we will deal with dissent. We talk about how do we invite and create multiple streams of invitation.

We also offer a two-day training on the intermediate level, then monthly telephone video conferences.[15]

I think that both approaches—the step-by-step approach offered by some church planting consultants and the training currently offered by the Episcopal Church—may be valuable and may complement each other well. I have also attended training offered by the conservative evangelical world, which I found disempowering (for a female leader, in particular) and very difficult to translate into our context. I think most Episcopal church planters should approach such training with care.

---

15. Brackett, interview.

Servants Through Whom You Came to Believe

All kinds of people make good church planters. Certain characteristics are essential, however: leadership skills, willingness to get out into the community and meet and recruit people, ability to take a risk, faith that God is in this unusual and taxing ministry, a compelling ability to share a vision and inspire others to follow, combined with personal humility and willingness to empower others. But the most important qualification today, just as it was in Paul's time, is a driving passion to tell the good news of Christ.   ❧

~ 7

Faith and Vision:
Mission Discernment
in the New Church Plant

For I am convinced that neither death, nor life, nor angels, nor rulers, nor things present, nor things to come, nor powers, nor height, nor depth, nor anything else in all creation, will be able to separate us from the love of God in Christ Jesus our Lord. Romans 8:38–39

Paul was the most influential church planter in history, yet he went through very difficult times—much more difficult than most of us will ever experience. After all, not many North American church planters are thrown in prison, shipwrecked, given thirty-nine lashes, or driven out of town for their work. We do take some risks, though. Our work may be lonely; the community around us may simply ignore us; the church we are pouring our heart and soul into may not flourish. What kind of faith does it take to plant a church, and how do we know what kind of church God is calling us to plant?

A church planter is a person who has confidence in a vision of the church, because it arose through a relationship with God based on prayer. Beyond this, a church planter is someone who can lead a group of people to take prayerful, informed risks for the sake of the gospel. The initial years of planting a church will be uncertain and unstable, and the church will have to risk failing, in confidence that God is calling them to action. Frank Logue describes taking a risk at his church plant, King of Peace:

> Starting a preschool, we had less than $5,000 in the bank and we were starting a $250,000-a-year business. It wasn't foolhardy; we had income, we had a plan, and the church was going to be able to cover some things initially so there would be no cost for the building or the power. We had it all figured it out. But we were overstaffed for the students from day one: the student-teacher ratio was nearly one-to-one on day one. I [had] a school board that [was] one hundred percent behind that, and when we had a meeting to decide if we were going to pull the trigger, I had people saying to me, "Frank, I thought you said that if we were going to do something and God wasn't in it, we were going to fall flat on our faces. This is that thing, Frank, remember when you talked about that? This is that." When people talk in these ways to [Commissions on Ministry] and bishops, they get scared. It sounds unsafe, and it is unsafe, and we need more of it.[1]

Logue's story is one example of taking a large risk, in confidence that God would be in it. But the confidence that King of Peace had was more than a dream. It was based on concrete, in-depth knowledge of its community and the needs of the families in it. In order to discern God's vision for the church, Logue went from door to door and asked people what a church could do for the neighborhood. The answer he heard over and over was that families in the community needed a safe, reliable preschool. King of Peace's willingness to take a risk on a startup preschool was based on its research and knowledge of its community. You will hear more of Frank's story of starting the church in chapter 9.

Church plants go about researching their communities and discerning God's vision for the church in different ways. In chapter 4 you heard about Katie Nakamura Rengers's and Kellie Hudlow's vision for their non-traditional new community called The Abbey. Their design was founded on their experience of how young adults best experienced Christ in community. They saw Millennial generation members dropping away from traditional churches despite being interested and engaged in growing in

---

1. Logue, interview.

discipleship through small group experiences; they saw people without any church background who were willing to engage questions of faith and participate in Christian prayer in groups that were open to wondering and experimentation. They observed the need for a "third space" that would bring people together in community and give them a place to gather. Based on these observations, they designed a Christian coffeehouse that would allow people to gather for Bible study, discussion, prayer, worship, counseling, and fellowship.

Similarly, Christopher Carlisle based his vision of Cathedral in the Night on his years of experience in campus ministry. He saw young adults who were less and less interested in going to a traditional church, yet were passionate about helping the homeless. In his outdoor cathedral of worshiping together and feeding those without homes, he was able to bring these two passions together. He describes how the vision took shape:

When I left the university campus . . . I thought about Cathedral in the Night. I had done some street ministry; that was one of the things I did that seemed to most resonate with my students. When I taught the homelessness course there was a great response. We got a sizeable grant from the Episcopal Church to get us launched, then we started it. . . . [It was] a two-pronged thing, or a three- or four-pronged thing. One was street ministry, responding to the gospel wind, and we also wanted to appeal to students and young adults. . . . We have folks who just come, either homed or homeless, from all sorts of different age groups and circumstances. Our hope, which was fulfilled, was that we would be an inclusive community to which people with and without homes would be welcome. At a conscious level we were thinking how to reach the student demographic. Then what came out of my experience of the past was the resonance I saw between students and homeless ministry. Then when Bishop Fisher [Diocese of Western Massachusetts] said he wanted to do something about homeless veterans, especially female veterans, that became a focus. I'm just starting that part now. That's how ministry lives, by evolution. You can predict certain things, but then you have other needs and opportunities; other people get involved.[2]

2. Carlisle, interview.

Some traditional planters, like Carlisle, go about discerning God's vision for the church in a very informal way. Clay Lein, the founding priest of St. Philip's Frisco, describes his process:

> I don't ever remember a systematic process to create a strategic vision. I went to church planters' boot camp and they talked about Post-it Notes and putting them up on the board, getting a flow and all this stuff. I'm more intuitive; it sort of emerged. As I spoke with people inviting them into this, it sort of emerged. I'm an extrovert, which means I know what I'm thinking when I tell somebody, and the strategic vision came out of that. I begin to flesh out a straw man, a general sense of where and what is important. Then I bounce that off people and I begin to hear God speaking in community. Really, by the time the launch team formed it had been this intuitive prayerful dance, that as people resonated with it, I knew that was God. It was like Michelangelo who said, "I carve away the stone that's not the sculpture." Our mission statement is "Growing faith that impacts the world for Christ." We didn't have that until we were a year into it, and when that emerged it was like, "Yeah, that's us, that's it."[3]

St. Philip's Frisco is the most successful recent church plant in the Episcopal Church, measured by attendance, so Lein's method of discerning God's vision for the church was certainly effective. However, St. Philip's was also a Mother-Daughter plant whose community, worship style, and methods of outreach were very similar to those of its mother church (Christ Church Plano). A majority of the initial launch team came from a common church background and probably understood what to expect from the new church and from the community.

Most church plants in the Episcopal Church are not Mother-Daughter plants, however. In many cases, it is helpful for the church's mission and vision to be discerned a bit more formally. But the reason is not because the planter doesn't know the vision before the discernment process begins. In most cases, the planter has (and should have) a fairly clear vision of where the church is going before a discernment process begins. The vision-discernment process, then, is about bringing a team together, building relationships among the

---

3. Lein, interview.

members of the team, and making sure all members of the team are on board with the vision. The last thing a planter needs is a team full of people who each have a different idea of where the church is going, and unconsciously try to pull the church in many different directions. The advantage of a vision-discernment process is that all members of the team can become clear about what kind of church God is calling them to plant.

At Church of the Nativity, during the months before our launch, we spent a great deal of time discerning our infant church's mission. I wanted to go through a process in order to develop the launch team. I met with the launch team as a full group at least every other week, in order to keep the project of creating a church foremost in their minds and hearts. The launch team meetings were opportunities for people to invite friends and family to become involved in the new church, to create relationships with others that would bring a new community into being, and to pray, study the Bible, and discern their own call to be part of this church. We had prayer time, mission discernment time, and social time at each gathering. At our first meeting, we had fourteen people present; by the last launch team meeting several months later, we had sixty-five people crowded into one house. The process of discerning our mission created excitement and ownership in the people God was calling to join our team.

The other, more important, reason I spent a great deal of time with our launch team developing our church's mission is that I wanted to have an opportunity to pray and study the Bible with the group in order to discern God's mission, rather than to follow our own disparate ideas of what a church should be. I also wanted to have a mission statement and a list of values or purposes that we could always refer back to. We have used the resulting mission and purpose statement in multiple ways since our launch. Everything we do as a church needs to fit within our stated set of values, or we don't do it. The mission and purpose statement serves as a guide by which we organize our ministries, our budget, and our vestry meetings.

The rest of this chapter will describe some ways that Nativity and other churches have discerned their mission. While there is not one right way to do it, and while any process should be adapted for people who decide to undertake it, this discussion will provide some basics in thinking through and discerning God's mission for the church.

The Hedgehog Concept

In *Good to Great*,[4] Jim Collins explains that great companies know their business in a very focused and specific way. From interviews with these companies, Collins determined that each has what he calls a Hedgehog Concept. A fox, says Collins, is very clever and knows how to do many things moderately well. A hedgehog, however, knows only one thing, how to roll up in a ball. But he knows this one thing thoroughly, so thoroughly that he is the best in the world at it. For a great company, the Hedgehog Concept is the answer to these three questions:

- What are you deeply passionate about?
- What can you be the best in the world at?
- What drives your economic engine?

The place where these three questions intersect, says Collins, is a company's Hedgehog Concept. If it concentrates on its Hedgehog Concept, a company will move swiftly from good to great.

I think every church needs a Hedgehog Concept. But the questions we should be asking are different. Here are the questions that churches need to ask:

- Who are we? What do we, specifically, have to offer the world?
- Who are our neighbors? What are they like, and what do they need from a church?
- Who is God? What is God's mission for the church, and for our congregation?

I believe that the intersection of the answers to these three questions forms a church's Hedgehog Concept: the one thing it should do, and do very well, to thrive.

Our launch team spent weeks working on our Hedgehog Concept. Of course other churches may not want to do such a formal vision-discernment process. But I do think each church planter and team should have a good idea of the answers to these questions.

---

4. Collins, *Good to Great*, 90–97

Figure 7: The Church's Hedgehog Concept

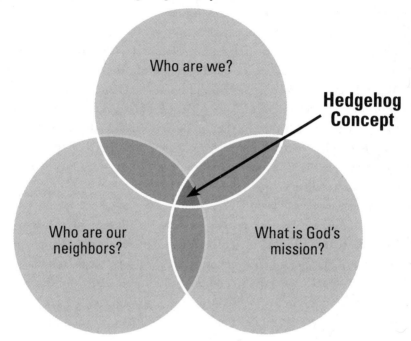

Who Are We?

Why is God calling your church to start a church in your community, right now? I know there are many unchurched people there who need to hear the good news of Christ's love, who need to grow in discipleship, who need to worship and serve and learn to love. I know there is much work for Christians to do in your neighborhood. But why your church? What do you have to offer that is special?

Not far from Nativity is a satellite campus of a Phoenix area super-megachurch that is aiming to have a hundred thousand people worshiping at ten campuses by the year 2020. They worship according to the familiar megachurch formula: several praise songs with a hard rock beat, followed by a communion that most Episcopalians wouldn't recognize (tiny crackers and grape juice cups, passed down the rows in little trays), followed by a forty-minute sermon projected on the three large screens (since the preacher is at the main campus) giving useful life lessons, accompanied by a handout outline of the sermon on which church-goers take careful notes. This church packs in the crowds on Sundays. What does Nativity have to offer in the face of such overwhelmig numerical success?

This is a question that all Episcopal churches should be asking themselves. What about our sacramental, thoughtful, Anglican tradition gives us something special to offer to our communities? Though the worship services at the megachurch in our area are crowded, I believe there are many people like me who are left cold by their approach. I honor that church for what they accomplish, but I think that there are many kinds of churches in the world because there are many kinds of people. What does our tradition have to offer that is distinctive?

Your answer will be different from mine, not just because we value different things, but because we live in different communities. It is true, for instance, that our Anglican approach to scriptures is thoughtful, and some of our sermons go into far more depth in history, theology, and life application than some other sermons you might hear elsewhere. But those virtures are more valuable in my well-educated suburb than they would be in, say, a church for homeless people. The question your launch team needs to ask is what, specifically, do we have to offer to our community that is distinctive?

One key factor in this discussion is worship style. Worship is often the front door to our church communities; growth in discipleship and service frequently follows attendance at worship. Our Anglican style of worship is generally familiar to Episcopalians, Roman Catholics, and Lutherans, but not as easily accessible to people who truly have no church background. How will you worship in a way that touches the hearts of people who are not just transplanted Episcopalians, but who are truly without a church community? How will you help people to understand the significance of the things you are doing in worship?

A very important consideration is musical style. Ten or fifteen years ago, Episcopalians often assumed that new church plants would worship in the "contemporary" style our megachurch neighbor uses. At Nativity, however, we looked at ourselves—the people gathered in the room—at the Anglican tradition, and at the opportunities in our neighborhood, and we made a different decision. Ultimately, we decided that what we have uniquely to offer our community is a traditional style of music, and formal liturgical worship. We are located in a city with a large university whose classical music program allowed us to hire an extremely talented music director, trained on the organ and devoted to Episcopal liturgical tradition. We had a number of talented classical singers on our launch team, making it possible for us to offer excellent traditional music from the beginning. Everything pointed to our call to worship in a traditional Episcopal way, with traditional music, vestments, and formal liturgy; our community responded well.

St. Benedict's in Smyrna, started in 2007, also worships in a traditional style, which its founder, Lang Lowrey, sees as a sign of hope for the Episcopal Church. Our traditional worship still has the potential to touch many people. St. Philip's in Frisco worships with a combination of traditional and contemporary styles, which is appropriate for its community. The key in thinking about worship is to select a style that speaks to people in the community, while holding on to Anglican essentials. Carmen Guerrero says that "music that is relevant to the people" is absolutely vital for a Latino congregation. "They are working all day with the radio on, playing Latino music," she says. "Then they come to the church and they hear the organ? That doesn't make any sense to them. They need to hear music that is relevant to their lives."[5] Iglesia Santa Maria hires a mariachi band (easily available in the Phoenix area) to play at its worship services every week. The Crossing in Boston offers a style of music Stephanie Spellers called "groove-based chant," which celebrated the intersection of culture and tradition in her community.

I believe that every new church should go through a similar analysis of its gifts and talents, and how the distinctive offerings of the Episcopal tradition can be made relevant to its community. Some launch teams will bring different gifts, and will be touched by worship in different ways. Some cities will have many talented guitarists and drummers, but not many classically trained pianists or organists. Some communities will have an overabundance of traditional worship offerings, with nothing offered for those who yearn for contemporary worship. Some new congregations will not be able to afford professional musicians (though I strongly recommend making every effort to have as high-quality music as you possibly can; this is is something I believe most churches need to find a way to provide before launching worship) . We will not all arrive at the same answer, and we should not. What we should do

5. Guerrero, interview.

very carefully is discern our own gifts and discover what God has given us to offer our communities.

Who Are Our Neighbors?

Every church needs to be intimately familiar with its neighborhood. The planter and launch team should live in the community and should be acculturated; you must understand the people in the community, their hopes, dreams, and worries. The team should go out into the community and ask questions. Frank Logue went door to door and asked people what they thought their community needed. Stephanie Spellers intervewed people she met in the neighborhood and asked them about their dreams. Lang Lowrey hung out in coffee shops and talked to people about their personal, pastoral needs. Daniel Velez Rivera joined the boards of community organizations and got involved in advocacy groups. At Nativity, we made appointments and interviewed community leaders, like school principals and business owners, about the problems they see and the opportunities the neighborhood presents. We also went door to door and talked to whoever would answer.

We also did significant work on our launch team analyzing demographic data. At the time we used Percept data via the Episcopal Church's website; similar demographic studies are now available from MissionInsite.[6] We looked at economic status, education levels, age groupings, religious backgrounds, and what people named as their joys and concerns. We created profiles of people we thought might be typical Nativity members. We talked about people we knew in the neighborhood who didn't have a church, and what we thought might be important to them. We asked team members to go home and pray for people they thought might need a church, and then invite those folks to join us. Some of the people who received those initial invitations are now beloved longtime members of our church.

Who is God? Or, What is God's Mission for the Church?

Aubrey Malphurs quotes the business guru Peter Drucker about the church's mission: "What matters is not the leader's charisma. What matters is the leader's mission. Therefore, the first job of the leader is to think through

---

6. http://missioninsite.com

and define the mission of the institution."[7] The leader of a church plant is, in one sense, the lay or ordained planter who has been appointed to lead the project. In a more important sense, the leader is Jesus. What does Jesus want for your church? What is God's mission in your community? We discern the answer to this question through prayer and scripture study. Although not all church planters go through a formal mission discernment process, Malphurs recommends it. He describes a discernment process that asks three critical questions:

1. Where are we? Core values
2. Where do we want to go? Mission and vision
3. How will we get there? Strategy[8]

The core values drive the new church's ministry: they spell out the bottom line, they affect behavior, they move people to action. Malphurs defines a church's core values as its "constant, passionate, biblical core beliefs that drive its ministry."[9] He points to Acts 2:41–47 as a helpful beginning in determining the core values that drive the universal church:

> So those who welcomed his message were baptized, and that day about three thousand persons were added. They devoted themselves to the apostles' teaching and fellowship, to the breaking of bread and the prayers. Awe came upon everyone, because many wonders and signs were being done by the apostles. All who believed were together and had all things in common; they would sell their possessions and goods and distribute the proceeds to all, as any had need. Day by day, as they spent much time together in the temple, they broke bread at home and ate their food with glad and generous hearts, praising God and having the goodwill of all the people. And

---

7. Peter Drucker, quoted in Malphurs, Aubrey, *The Nuts and Bolts of Church Planting: A Guide for Starting Any Kind of Church* (Grand Rapids, MI: Baker Books, 2011), 81. Malphurs's book is very useful for a church planter, but please know that it is written from a theologically conservative perspective and, for instance, has a very distinct idea of the proper roles of men and women in the church. If you can overlook this flaw, the book is helpful.
8. Malphurs, 64.
9. Ibid., 66–67.

*day by day the Lord added to their number those who were being
saved.* Acts 2:41–47

From this description, Malphurs discerns that the five essential core values
of the church are evangelism, instruction, fellowship, worship, and service
(or, in traditional New Testament Greek terms, *kerygma, didache, koinonia,
leitourgia, and diakonia*). A church, he says, often emphasizes one of these
values above the rest, whether that emphasis is stated or unstated. That
emphasis will drive the church's ministries, and while it is natural for different churches to have different emphases, every church should include these
five core values.

Some churches, however, effectively ignore some values in favor of others.
Malphurs says he frequently sees churches that concentrate on worship, fellowship, and instruction, but ignore the outward dimensions of the church's
ministries: evangelism and service. Many Episcopal churches certainly fall
into this trap, staying inwardly focused at the expense of engagement in their
communities. An inward focused church will have a very hard time growing,
because it will emphasize serving its own members above welcoming and
serving others. It is also easy to find churches that concentrate on evangelism but fail at the task of service—usually not Episcopal churches, however.
More frequently in the Episcopal Church, one finds churches that excel at
service but neglect evangelism. Yet Jesus gave us the Great Commission to
"make disciples of all nations," and Episcopal churches must proclaim the
good news in words as well as in deeds. I believe that it is vitally important for new churches to emphasize the core value of evangelism—not to
the exclusion of the other values, but as an absolutely essential reason for the
church's existence.

I also believe that it is possible for a church to have additional values
besides the foundational ones Malphurs lists. These values may be stated or
unstated. An Episcopal church might value a particular style of liturgy, for
instance, or a certain outlook on social issues, or a distinctive way of reading
the scriptures. All these values are valid and important, but they should not
override the core biblical values of the church. We don't bring churches into
being in order to worship in a particular style, for instance. We bring them
into being to answer God's call, and we need to be open to hearing that call in
a way that speaks to the hearts of those in our communities.

Malphurs makes an interesting distinction between a "hot start" and a "cold start."[10] A "hot start," he says, is a church that begins with a group of people who are interested in starting a church. A Mother-Daughter plant would fall into this category. In a hot start, the planter works with the group to discover the group's core values, which become foundational to the church. There is a risk that these essential values will simply be personal preferences, unless the planter works carefully with the group to draw out the core biblical values. The advantage of working with a local group to discover their values is that if that group is immersed in the community, they will understand the hearts and minds of the people in that community and will have an intuitive grasp of how to reach them.

A "cold start," on the other hand, is one in which the planter arrives in a new place and starts a launch team from scratch. In a cold start, the values of the planter often become the values of the church. The danger in this approach is that the planter may not understand the local community and may simply try to create his or her own "dream church," and then not understand why those in the neighborhood seem unresponsive. The best approach, in my opinion, is for the planter to be immersed in the community for a period of time, and to use that time to build a team of local people who understand their neighbors. The values of the church will then be communally discerned between the planter and team, with the planter guiding the group in making sure those values are directed by God's biblical vision for the church.

Malphurs goes on to describe what a church's mission, vision, and strategy are. The mission, he says, focuses on the new ministry's function or what it is supposed to be doing.[11] The biblical basis for the mission is found in the Great Commission of Matthew 28:19–20. Based on the values the group has discerned and the biblical mission that Jesus gave the disciples, the church creates a mission statement that is clear, focused, and brief. While the mission statement is brief, the vision of the church is a longer description of where the church is going; a picture of what it hopes to be. The strategy, then, becomes the specific plan for how the church will achieve the things that are described in its mission and vision, following its core values. Again,

10. Ibid., 74.
11. Ibid., 83.

while I don't believe this group mission discernment process is always necessary, and many Episcopal planters don't go through it in a formal way, for my
launch team it was a very helpful way of forming a team that understood and
worked for the same mission.

Mary MacGregor describes the very different pre-launch visioning processes of two successful church plants in the Diocese of Texas:

> St. Aidan's in Houston was a diocesan plant. What inspired me was
> Justin [Lindstrom]'s approach. I went to church planters' boot camp
> with Jim Griffith back in 2000 as a coach for church planters. I learned
> some things and was assigned as a coach to one of our planters. One of
> the things I learned at boot camp was the critical nature for articulat-
> ing vision, mission, and core values as an initial activity for planting a
> church. You have to know the kind of church you want to plant specifi-
> cally. Justin is that kind of guy: he had an extremely clear vision and
> core values, and every single decision that launch team made was based
> clearly on those things, with very little going off the map. They were so
> focused. To watch that congregation develop was amazing and stun-
> ning. It was one of the best starts I've ever witnessed. To know what you
> want, to be faithful, to be strong, to be confident, to clearly define these
> core values, and Justin was all those things. And to watch him work
> with his launch team and his initial Bishop's Committee: every decision
> they made was based on their core values and mission and vision. They
> would talk about it all the time.
>
> Miles [Brandon's] story [at St. Julian of Norwich in northwest
> Austin] was terrific. He started out building relationships with people.
> He had gone and recruited people from churches: he asked neighboring
> churches to recommend a couple of people who might be interested. He
> took them to lunch to share the vision. Once he had the initial group,
> they didn't even talk about church. They built relationships. They spent
> the whole time talking about each others' life stories, faith stories, to
> see if this group would gel. He was so wise to start out that way, and
> St. Julian's of Norwich is an immensely successful plant, born on Miles'
> incredible gifts and his intuitive leadership ability. . . .
>
> [That church is] very healthy, grounded in who they are, what
> they're about, who their [typical member] looks like. You can talk about
> Rick Warren's stuff pro and con, but sometimes it's good to articulate

what's the profile of the person who you think is most likely to become a member of that church. He's done a great job of that.[12]

At Nativity, we followed a two-pronged approach to discerning our mission. First, we worked on the first two questions of the Hedgehog Concept: Who are we? and Who are our neighbors? Then, in order to answer the most important question: Who is God and what is God's Mission? we studied the Great Commandment and the Great Commission.

The Great Commandment:

> *[Jesus said,] " 'You shall love the Lord your God with all your heart, and with all your soul, and with all your mind.' This is the greatest and first commandment. And a second is like it: 'You shall love your neighbor as yourself.' On these two commandments hang all the law and the prophets."* Matthew 22:37–40

The Great Commission:

> *And Jesus came and said to them, "All authority in heaven and on earth has been given to me. Go therefore and make disciples of all nations, baptizing them in the name of the Father and of the Son and of the Holy Spirit, and teaching them to obey everything that I have commanded you. And remember, I am with you always, to the end of the age."* Matthew 28:18–20

From the Great Commandment, we discerned that God was calling us to love God (worship) and love our neighbors (service and fellowship). From the Great Commission, we discerned that God was calling us to make disciples and baptize (evangelize), and to teach about Jesus' commandments (teach). Interestingly, using this approach, we came up with the exact same list of core values for the church: evangelism, worship, teaching, fellowship, service, just as Malphurs did using Acts 2:41–47, even though we were using completely different scriptures. It seems that the scriptures are fairly consistent in describing what God wants the church to accomplish.

Nativity's launch team considered carefully how to encapsulate these purposes of the church into a mission statement that was short and memorable,

12. MacGregor, interview.

and decided that all of these purposes could be summarized as ways of transforming people's lives with Christ's love. Out of this discernment process, we created the following mission and purpose statement:

> OUR MISSION is to transform lives by helping the people experience the love of God in Jesus Christ.
>
> WE WILL ACCOMPLISH THIS MISSION BY ACCOMPLISHING THESE PURPOSES:
>
> - We will reach out to our community with the good news of Jesus Christ through active invitation and servant EVANGELISM, contributing to the planting of new churches when the opportunity arises;
> - We will WORSHIP together in a way that connects with people's lives and gives them a sense of spiritual connection with God;
> - We will bring people into deeper FELLOWSHIP with each other through active hospitality, newcomer welcoming and orientation, and pastoral care;
> - We will TEACH the Christian and Episcopal traditions and scriptures to children, youth and adults through enriching education programs;
> - We will REACH OUT IN SERVICE to our community and beyond.

This mission and purpose statement is more than a boilerplate for us at Nativity. It is the guide to how we organize our common life together. Our ministries are organized into these five categories plus a sixth (administration and stewardship), with two vestry members assigned as liaisons to each area. Our budget is also organized into these six areas, so that we can analyze whether our actual priorities, the things we are willing to put money into, match what we say our church should be doing. At each vestry meeting, we begin by sharing stories of how we have seen lives transformed in the past month (how we are accomplishing our mission), and then proceed through all the ministry categories in order, to discuss opportunities, challenges, developments, and decisions in each area. When a big decision comes before the group, we look at our mission and purpose statement to see whether this new initiative is consonant with what we have said our priorities will be. This focus is possible because our launch team, years ago, established these priorities as the DNA of our congregation.

There is no one right way to discern the mission for a new congregation. Sometimes the mission will simply emerge. But if you are a planter working to build a launch team that will be of one mind and hold a common understanding of what your church is planning to accomplish, some serious work on discerning God's mission may help this happen. You should ask the core questions: Who are we? Who are our neighbors? And what is God's mission for the church? Working through these questions will bring you together as a ministry team that knows each other, feels like a community, and is ready to take action to accomplish great things for Christ.   ❧

⌁ 8

Gathering and Empowering
a Team of Leaders

For just as the body is one and has many members, and all the members of the body, though many, are one body, so it is with Christ. For in the one Spirit we were all baptized into one body— Jews or Greeks, slaves or free—and we were all made to drink of one Spirit. Indeed, the body does not consist of one member but of many. Now you are the body of Christ and individually members of it. 1 Corinthians 12:12–14, 27

Paul was the most remarkable church planter in history, but he did not plant churches alone. He prayed and asked for Christ's strength to guide him. He took ministry partners on his journeys. He also set to work immediately, wherever he went, gathering, training, and empowering a team of leaders. As he watched these teams work together, he realized that together they could accomplish wonders; the whole was truly greater than the sum of the parts. Gathered together, they were not simply an organization, they were an organism, with each part knowing its own function and also dependent on every other part. Together, the team became the Body of Christ.

One of the most fascinating aspects of Paul's work was that in every city, he trained and empowered leaders who would guide the flock long after he was gone. He was humble enough to understand that no team should be dependent on a single, heroic leader. If he gathered a group of people who were attracted to his charismatic personality but who fell apart when he left, he would have achieved nothing. He knew that the leader who initially creates the team is responsible to train leaders so that the team will be greater than the founder alone, long outlasting the founder. As Paul moved from place to place, he looked for people with leadership potential, like Priscilla and Aquila, with gifts of teaching, and Lydia, with the gift of hospitality. When he moved on to his next call, he left behind trained and experienced leaders to guide the flock. Paul knew his own role in the Body of Christ—the planter—but he also knew that the head of the church was Christ, not any human leader.

Tom Brackett talks about the importance of team building as one of the core competencies of a church planter:

> When I first came into my position . . . I was charged with doing the back testing of the Gallup skills inventory that six denominations paid to have Gallup create [a test that assesses people's giftedness for church planting; see chapter 6]. What we realized was [that it did a good job of predicting good planters] but not dependably, because we had eleven church planters in the Episcopal Church who already had a great track record, who scored really low on their inventory despite all their best work. So I was sent out into the field to interview them. Of the eleven, seven were women; they scored really low but were doing remarkable work. I found [that] of those seven, five of them were doing amazing work because they didn't necessarily contain within themselves all the skills needed, but they had the capacity to gather a team around them whose aggregate strengths made up the profile for a really great church planter, the skills constellation. When I asked [about it] . . . several of them laughed and said, "I never imagined myself as a church planter, this is just what the Spirit led me to do, and early on I realized that I didn't have all the skills." I realized that the old heroic model of church planter is probably not as relevant to our context as a lot of our traditional church planting models would have us believe. One of the primary characteristics [of a good planter] is actually the capacity to gather around herself/himself a team that together has the strengths required to call together a genuine community.[1]

---

1. Brackett, interview.

I believe that it is vitally important for the church planter to have certain competences: a passion for evangelism, leadership skills, management skills, the ability to raise money, the ability to preach and teach and cast a vision in a way that people can understand it and want to make it their own. The special skills that I believe a church planter needs are outlined in chapter 6. But I also believe beyond a shadow of a doubt that the planter must make it a top priority to recruit others to join in the team and do important ministry work. I am a former CPA and am perfectly capable of doing our church's finance work, but that is not my primary role in the Body of Christ. I am also a former director of Christian education and can teach children (and sometimes do), but again that is not my primary role. If I did these things for our church, I would not only be over-extending myself and leaving no time to do the leadership tasks that actually are my primary roles (and exercising inappropriate control, in the case of the finances), but I would also be robbing others of the joy and satisfaction of serving God by doing the things they are gifted at and called to do. One of the most important aspects of any person's growth in discipleship is learning to exercise ministry in whatever way God calls her. Priests should be in the business of empowering ministry in others in any situation: equipping the saints for work of ministry. Empowering others to create a team that will truly grow into a Body is absolutely imperative in the church plant.

Nelson Searcy, who started the Journey Church in New York City, a non-denominational church that now has over a thousand members, says, "Learning to ask people to join you is an absolute prerequisite to effectively building a team and launching your church. . . . You must learn how to seek out the people God intends for you to work with." Those people will become the launch team of your church. He offers the following definition of a launch team: "A team of committed individuals who will assist you in preparing for and executing an effective launch. This is a team of people currently living in the area where your new church will meet—a team that you will build from scratch. The launch team is in existence only through the first weekly service."[2]

---

2. Nelson Searcy and Kerrick Thomas, *Launch: Starting a New Church from Scratch* (Ventura, CA: Regal, 2006), 141–2.

Finding Initial Team Members

One person with many individual relationships is not a church. I have seen planters with excellent one-on-one evangelistic skills who could never manage to bring all the people they were in relationship with, into relationship with each other. If the planter tries to create a church on the model of a bicycle wheel, where all spokes lead into one center point, and all things depend on that center point, that church will have a very hard time growing and thriving. The church is not a wheel—it is a network. Or, as Paul puts it, the church is a Body. All the parts are in relationship with, and dependent on, all the other parts. The planter must start by gathering a group of people, helping them create relationships with each other and interacting with each other, not just the planter.

There is another reason to create a team. On the first Sunday your new church worships together publicly, you don't want to be preaching and presiding to an empty room. A couple of decades ago, people could start Episcopal churches by simply putting a notice in the paper announcing that a church was beginning, and Episcopalians would show up. The Episcopal brand name is not that strong these days. People who might be interested in attending a new church will lose interest quickly if there are only a few people in the room when they arrive. Your church needs to feel vital and active. Jesus is alive—our churches should be, too. You need a team of enthusiastic leaders to welcome folks and help them feel that they have entered into something special and life changing.

How to find the initial team? The answer varies depending on the model of church you are planting. In a Mother-Daughter church, for instance, the initial team is usually gathered from the congregation of the mother church. The advantages of having a team from a mother church, or several churches, are many. The team members are usually committed Christians who understand the power of lay ministry and know that their gifts and talents will be vitally needed. Their presence substantially reduces the amount of time it takes to build critical mass to launch worship. They have made the decision to move from an established church to a new church that is as yet only an idea in someone's mind, specifically because they are entrepreneurs who are excited by the prospect of creating something out of nothing. Such entrepreneurial skills will be invaluable time and again. These folks also are generally hoping to grow closer to God as they experience the joy of watching a new church flourish, so they are open to prayer and spiritual growth. Indeed, many launch team members find that being part of the birth of a new church is a life-transforming experience.

Carmen Guerrero has started several Latino congregations in the Phoenix area, and she uses leaders from one congregation to start the next. To start her current congregation, Iglesia Santa Maria, she identified six leaders from other area congregations and asked them to attend a Spanish-language Cursillo.[3] As part of attending Cursillo, she asked them to commit to a future ministry and empowered each to see themselves as leaders. Those six leaders then helped form an initial ministry team at the new church. Some have stayed with the new church, and some have returned to their original congregations. This approach recognizes that a priest simply cannot start a congregation by herself. Committed, empowered, trained lay leaders must participate. Without a team, a church planter who attempts to start worship alone, or with a few participants who are consumers rather than leaders, will be very lonely for a long time, and building critical mass to launch worship will be a difficult challenge.

Starting with a team of other Episcopalians does have some disadvantages, however. Brackett says, "New church plant[ing] in this time, a time that is increasingly post-Christian and post denominational . . . asks of us some different disciplines than you're going to engage in an established church." Traditional Episcopalians may prefer to transfer the traditions of the established church. They will likely see things through traditional Episcopal eyes and will expect the new church to be similar in many ways to the other churches they have experienced. The new church will almost certainly bear a strong resemblance to the mother church. If you are attempting to plant a church that is quite different from any other church, folks from an established Episcopal church may not "get it" and may try to change

---

3. Cursillo includes a three-day weekend that begins on Thursday evening and concludes on Sunday. The weekend includes fifteen talks, five meditations, and a Eucharist every day. The Cursillo weekend is not a retreat, but an opportunity to meet clergy and laity seeking to strengthen one's faith. It provides an environment to experience the reality of the gift of God's love through shared prayer, individual meditation, worship, study, fellowship, laughter, tears, and unconditional love. http://www.nationalepiscopalcursillo.org

the vision to make the church more like what they have known before. They may not understand the importance of true evangelism, because most Episcopal churches do not emphasize or teach it. Danger arises if they left the mother church because of discontent or conflict; they may bring that conflict with them. Be wary of people who complain about their former church or former pastor.

If the initial team is not to come from another church, how should they be gathered? Chapter 9, regarding ways to connect with people in the community, names numerous creative ways that planters in the Episcopal Church have gone about finding the people God is sending. There are advantages to gathering an initial team of people who have never been Episcopalians, who have recently made a decision to follow Jesus, or who have been away from church for a long time but who are drawn to your vision of a new way of creating a community of faith. Recent converts may be more eager to tell others about what they have found, and much more willing to go outside the Episcopal "box" and construct a new kind of church that looks completely different from any other. They will be less anchored to Episcopal ways of doing things. (You will never hear them say, "But we've always done it this way!") But as newer Christians, they also may be (appropriately) less committed to ministry and leadership, needing first to receive—Christian education, ministry, fellowship, the benefits of church community—before they can give back.

The launch team should pray together, vision together, form a Christian community together, and discuss and strategize the best way to reach others together. These folks will get to know each other well, and will learn to function as a team, building on each other's strengths. Interestingly, Searcy, in *Launch,*[4] cautions against spending too much time building close relationships among the launch team. His concern is that the team members might develop too tight-knit a community and be reluctant to let others in. I don't know whether this is truly a problem for many Episcopalians, but Searcy is correct at least in this: the priority for the launch team is to be outward-focused, concentrating on reaching new people in the community, rather than inward-focused, simply building relationships with each other. The launch team's task is to create the skeleton of a church that will touch the

---

4. 142–43.

lives of many people who need to know the love of Christ. The planter's task is to lead them and continue to help them focus on the people God wants your church to touch.

In any case, the planter should make it a priority to grow a team for ministry. The initial group of committed folks will create, in concert with the planter, the formative vision and values for the church. This launch team will also comprise the ministry teams that must be in place before launching Sunday worship.

Identify Gifts and Call People into Ministry

The story goes that someone once asked legendary Oklahoma football coach Bud Wilkerson to describe the game of football. He replied that football is a game that involves eighty thousand fans who desperately need exercise sitting in a stadium, watching twenty-two players on the field who desperately need rest.[5]

Church, unlike football, is not a spectator sport. Every Christian, lay or ordained, should have both feet planted firmly on the field. The Book of Common Prayer tells us that the ministers of the Episcopal Church are lay persons, bishops, priests, and deacons.[6] Lay persons are listed first for a reason. Our baptism is the sacrament that calls us into ministry—every baptized person. In our baptism, the Holy Spirit gives each of us gifts that empower us for the ministry we are called to. The role of the pastor is to equip: to provide the worship experience, the scriptural background, and the training and opportunities so that people can answer God's call.

Paul lists a number of spiritual gifts in his letters, but I believe there are many gifts beyond those Paul listed. I have never seen woodworking in a list of spiritual gifts, but woodworking was a talent that one person developed over a long period of time and then dedicated to building beautiful things for Church of the Nativity. Any of our talents—bookkeeping, care of children, cooking, woodworking—can be used for the glory of God.

An absolutely vital skill for the planter is the ability to discern people's gifts and call them into ministry. This does not mean identifying all the slots there are to fill, and diverting people into those slots. It means starting with

---

5. Quoted in Malphurs, *The Nuts and Bolts of Church Planting,* 152.
6. The Book of Common Prayer, 855.

the people God has sent, assuming that God has provided everything that is needed, and finding out how God has gifted these people, and what God is calling each one to do. Each person God sends is a precious gift to all the others. For the planter, calling people into ministry is a privilege, because it allows them to be transformed as they feel the power of the Spirit working through them. We can watch miracles happen as God works through ordinary people whose baptismal call to ministry has been awakened and empowered.

One of the miracles that happen time and again at Nativity, continuing to reassure me that God is in this enterprise, is that God always sends us the people we need exactly when we need them. The first four members of Nativity were Mark and Jennie Dobbins and Alastair and Mary Longley-Cook. The remarkable dedication and gifts of these four people have proved absolutely essential to the birth and growth of Nativity. Other people soon followed. Nativity's early launch team meetings included people with amazing gifts of welcoming and hospitality, an expert woodworker, an experienced bookkeeper, two gifted Sunday school teachers, a couple who were excited about leading youth ministry, a man whose organizational skills directed our setup and takedown crews, people who were absolutely dedicated to serving those in need in our community, people with leadership skills, a nursery worker, talented singers, public relations professionals, and many more. I connected with some of these people personally and invited them to join us in our great enterprise. Others came because people already in the group invited their friends.

To a great extent, we learned what our church was called to accomplish by looking at the people God sent to us. I would have assumed that youth ministry could wait for a year or two, but for the couple who were eager to share their gifts with teenagers, and taught us that ministry with young people would be a cornerstone of our church. Because of them, we were able to launch worship with an active youth group that was already seven teenagers strong. I would have thought a regular folding table would work for an altar, but the expert woodworker demonstrated that our new church had the gift of creating and worshiping in aesthetic beauty no matter how uninspiring our setting, a gift we have carried into all our worship locations.

How formal does the discernment of spiritual gifts need to be? Many church planters seem to fly by the seat of their pants, and simply have the gift of interviewing people, listening to them, discovering their heart's desire, and calling them into ministry in that area. This is the way we operated at Nativity, partly because we were so busy with other things during the buildup to the launch process that we did not have time for formal spiritual gifts discernment. Other planters have more time in the pre-launch period. One possible development activity during this period could be to do formal spiritual gifts education and discernment as part of the visioning process. For launch team members who have not previously been involved in ministry, spiritual gifts education may help them come to understand that every Christian is called to ministry, and that God has gifted them with unique talents to be shared with the Body of Christ. Such a formal process could help the team members get to know each other, as well as introduce them to the concepts of spiritual gifts and God's calling to each Christian. Whether spiritual gifts discernment is done through a formal process or through a more intuitive interview method, the goal is to look at people's gift sets and understand what they are telling the group about what God is calling the church to do.

Calling people into ministry should remain a priority long after the church has launched worship. I believe that active and engaged lay leaders are the cornerstones of ministry in the twenty-first-century church. Building a launch team and calling people into ministry may be a seat-of-the-pants, intuitive process in the church plant. This is fine in a small, fast-moving, task-driven group like a launch team. But the church (by God's grace!) will not remain small for long. A church planter should give serious thought to how newcomers will be assimilated and called into ministry after the church is launched. This is one of the most important systems a church will need to create, and will be discussed in chapter 10.

Bring Them on Board with the Vision

In chapter 7, we talked about discerning God's vision for your church. This is a project that the launch team may undertake together, with strong leadership from the planter, who has probably done significant research and church leadership practice before beginning this plant. The members of the launch team will likely be people who live in your target area and who are similar to your target demographic. They will have good insight into the mission field and how to reach it. It is possible, however, that some of them will have a different vision for the church than the one God is leading you toward. Perhaps their vision will be that the new church will be just like their favorite old church, or exactly opposite to their least favorite old church. Perhaps their vision is that they will have a lot of power in the new church. Guard against letting the launch team direct the vision, especially with personal agendas. There are times when the church you are creating just won't be right for some of the folks that would like to be part of it. You, as the planter, might need to deliver that message, suggesting that they find a different church that is more suited to their needs. The planter needs to be open to hear the thoughts of others, but not so open that others can manipulate the church in unrecognizable ways. The launch team that starts the church should understand the church's vision and be enthusiastic about it.

Get Them To Commit

Churches in America are full of consumers: people who choose among a smorgasbord of worship options according to their music, preaching, and youth activities. Consumer Christians expect to be fed, and they will attend the church with the menu that suits them the best.

People who join a launch team must realize that they are not there to be consumer Christians. It will be a long time, after all, before your new church becomes what they dream of. In the meantime, the people you need on the launch team should be those who are ready to feed others, not those who are looking to be fed. Consumer Christians will take up an inordinate amount of the planter's time, requesting new menu options, and will not provide what you need from your launch team. Therefore, it is vital that you make sure that your launch team members are ready to commit, and know what is expected of them.

Nativity's launch team had about sixty-five members by the time we started public worship. These sixty-five folks were excited about their ministries and were unshakably committed to the church. They staffed the ministries of the church and they gave generously of their time and money. Their commitment made our launch possible. I believed that it was essential to make sure in advance that the launch team members had thought carefully about their commitment to the church. I did not want people to join us just because they thought we might be better than the church down the street; I wanted them to be convinced that God was calling them to a ministry unlike any they had experienced before, one that would demand their best.

Therefore, I asked everyone who wanted to be a part of the launch team to sign a covenant. I gave them the covenant on paper and asked them to take it home, pray about it, discuss it with their families, and then return with a signed copy if they were able to commit. If not, they probably belonged elsewhere. The covenant asked them to:

- **Pray** daily for the church, its ministries, its leaders, and the people in the community God wanted us to reach;
- **Attend** every launch team meeting and every event and public worship service of the new church, unless they were ill or out of town;
- **Invite** at least one person to every event and public worship service of the new church during our pre-launch season;
- **Participate** in at least one ministry of the church (and the covenant asked each member of the family to name what those ministries would be);
- **Give** generously and sacrificially to support the ministries of the church (and the covenant asked the family to list the dollar amount of their stewardship commitment for the first year).

Almost everyone who had attended launch team meetings before I introduced the covenant went on to sign the covenant. Only four people took it home, thought about it, and then let me know kindly that they could not make the commitment. I believe that that was the right decision for those four people, and I was glad to know about it up front.

Of the others, all signed enthusiastically. Our new church was immediately staffed with volunteer ministers who made our church hum. These folks worked hard for the spread of God's kingdom through the church. They not only showed up for everything, they made special efforts to invite others, even when it was outside their comfort zones, so we had many new people from the community try out our church. They gave generously, and from the beginning, we have always had enough money to do the things God called us to do. And always, I have known that their prayers have sustained everything we have done. I believe that for these launch team members, seeing our church grow and flourish was a true experience of God's life-transforming grace and presence.

Create Structures that Will Outlast You

One of the most important disciplines for the church planter, I believe, is to come to a deep, spiritual, personal understanding that this church is not the planter's baby. It is God's baby. God entrusts the church for a time to a particular leader, or set of leaders, to nourish and support as it grows. A healthy leader is vital to the church's flourishing. But good health in a leader, like good health in a parent, means recognizing that the child will someday need to grow up and stand independently of its founder. A church with a charismatic founder on whom everything depends will fall apart when the founder departs, and every founder will inevitably, eventually depart. If you are working to create something that will last, it means working to create something that will outlast you. This is why the planter needs to learn to exercise the spiritual discipline of encouraging others to take leadership. Like Paul, the planter will eventually be called elsewhere by God. It is imperative to leave strong, trained, empowered leaders to carry the church into the next era, with God's help.

9

Evangelistic Outreach to the Community

So they took [Paul] and brought him to the Areopagus and asked him, "May we know what this new teaching is that you are presenting? It sounds rather strange to us, so we would like to know what it means." Now all the Athenians and the foreigners living there would spend their time in nothing but telling or hearing something new.

Then Paul stood in front of the Areopagus and said, "Athenians, I see how extremely religious you are in every way. For as I went through the city and looked carefully at the objects of your worship, I found among them an altar with the inscription, 'To an unknown god.' What therefore you worship as unknown, this I proclaim to you. The God who made the world and everything in it, he who is Lord of heaven and earth, does not live in shrines made by human hands..."

When they heard of the resurrection of the dead, some scoffed; but others said, "We will hear you again about this." At that point Paul left them. But some of them joined him and became believers, including Dionysius the Areopagite and a woman named Damaris, and others with them. Acts 17:19–24, 32–34

We plant new churches to reach new people and tell them the good news of Christ. That's evangelism, and it is the main, if not the only, reason to do the challenging work of planting new churches. Evangelism is sometimes a scary word to mainline Christians, who hear the word and picture fire-breathing television preachers. But at its heart, evangelism recognizes that Jesus came to proclaim good news. God is active in this world, from the miracles, death, and resurrection of Jesus, to the creative work of the Father, to the ongoing work of the Holy Spirit in making God's kingdom an active and present reality in the lives of those who put their faith in Christ. As Jesus' followers, it is our God-given task to invite others to share in that kingdom, here and now. Jesus said so, in Matthew 28:19–20: "Go therefore and make disciples of all nations, baptizing them in the name of the Father and of the Son and of the Holy Spirit, and teaching them to obey everything that I have commanded you."

How do we reach new people in our community? Paul sought out public places where he could speak to people about the good news of Christ. Often, he spoke in synagogues, recognizing that people there would likely understand the language and stories that formed the foundation of his faith, and might be open to learning about a new spiritual path. Synagogues offered him an entrée to people who were part of his target audience. Sometimes, he sought out other public places, including the Areopagus in Athens, where he gathered a curious crowd. Though he was not as successful with this less targeted approach, he did connect with a few people this way, by researching their own culture and their own spiritual understandings, and speaking in a way that resonated with their experiences. The church planter's job is to seek out the Areopagus of his community, the places where people are likely to gather, and speak to people about Christ.

Of course, in twenty-first-century America, standing on a street corner, or in a public park, or in a marketplace, preaching as Paul did, won't get you very far. Most people will simply give you a wide berth, or call the police. So how do you make connections with people so they can hear the good news we have to tell? How do you invite them into a community that will embody Christ's love?

Marketing Strategies

We can talk about connecting with people in terms of both marketing and evangelism. These are different, but interconnected, activities. Marketing lets your target audience know that your church is there, in a way that makes them want to experience it for themselves. Evangelism communicates the fact that following Christ changes lives, in a way that awakens a desire to follow him. Both are vital.

At its most basic, marketing conveys basic information about the church. Nativity's greatest early marketing success happened when we went to a sign company and had them create ten bright yellow, solid wood, sandwich board signs that had basic information about the church (not much information, just enough for them to find us) printed in bright red letters that were large enough for people to read as they drove by on the main road at fifty miles per hour. At least half of our new attendees in the first year found us through those ugly, heavy, low-tech signs.

On the other hand, many church planting books advocate the use of direct mail as the most cost effective way of reaching huge numbers of people. Nativity tried several direct mail campaigns, with attractive print and photos on large, custom-designed postcards, and finally gave it up as too expensive and completely ineffective. I am not sure that anyone has ever found us through something we sent them, unsolicited, in the mail. As far as I can tell, those beautiful print pieces went directly into the trash. After all, that's what happens to direct mail advertisements in my house.

For many audiences, the most important marketing tool you will have is your website. One of your goals should be to find a launch team member who can build a basic, attractive website that will describe your church in a way that appeals to the people you are trying to reach. Include lots of photographs of people (not buildings) looking happy and engaged. Use realistic photos of people that someone might expect to meet if they attend your church. Make it easy to find information like where and when you meet, what activities there are for children, and who the leaders are. In addition, I believe it is important to include information about the style of service (many people will be flummoxed by the liturgy otherwise), what it means to be an Episcopalian, and what it means to be a Christian. Please feel free to visit Nativity's website at http://www.NativityScottsdale.org for examples of these pages on our website. (You may use our verbiage, but please do contact us for permission first.) I also recommend reading Rebecca Wilson and Jim Naughton's book, *Speaking Faithfully: Communications as Evangelism in a Noisy World,*[1] for many helpful suggestions on creating a lively website.

Very few church planting books mention creating a social media strategy (perhaps because they're not quite up to date yet), but depending on your target audience, such a strategy may be anywhere from helpful to absolutely essential. If your church is in a suburban community, the social media strategy might be slightly important to a certain subset of the neighborhood; if your target includes young adults, you may want social media to be the keystone of your outreach efforts. In any case, I believe this area of marketing and connecting with people will continue to grow in importance, and you should not ignore it. If you as the planter are not particularly interested in social media, find a launch team member who is willing to make this his or her primary ministry. Again, Wilson and Naughton's book provides many helpful suggestions.

George Martin, who founded an Episcopal church near Minneapolis in the mid-1980s, reached many people through phone calls and door-to-door evangelism, an experience he writes about in his book, *Door-to-Door Ministry: The Easy Way to Make Friends for Your Church.*[2] Rick Warren also famously used door-to-door visits when founding Saddleback Church in California. I tried going door to door when founding Nativity, and found very few people at home; I reached an actual human being at perhaps five percent of the doors I knocked on, and not many of those were interested in engaging in conversation, though they were friendly enough. I think that the success of this method depends greatly on the culture of your neighborhood. If your neighborhood allows for door-to-door ministry, Martin's book gives many helpful examples and pointers.

On the other hand, I did have success with the more contemporary technique of working in a coffee shop. A person in a clerical collar (especially a

---

1. Rebecca Wilson and Jim Naughton, *Speaking Faithfully: Communications as Evangelism in a Noisy World* (New York: Morehouse Publishing, 2012).
2. George Martin, *Door-to-Door Ministry: The Easy Way to Make Friends for Your Church* (Rosemount, MN: George H. Martin, 2012).

woman) working in a coffee shop seems to be an unusual enough phenom-
enon to inspire others to talk—sometimes out of curiosity, sometimes out of
true, deep spiritual need. Of course if you are going to work in a coffee shop,
it is important to have something that sets you apart as a person available
for conversation: just a collar and Bible, perhaps, or even a sign that invites
people to talk. And certainly it is important to have business cards on hand
for an informal invitation to be part of the church community.

Another vital approach is to join community organizations, such as the
Chamber of Commerce, the ministerial association, groups addressing poverty and racial issues, and others, depending on the most important issues
facing your neighborhood. These groups will help you become more aware
of the problems and issues of your community, as well as allow you to make
contacts with community leaders.

Jim Griffith, an experienced United Methodist church planter and con-
sultant, recommends becoming a "chaplain" for community organizations,
schools, restaurants, fire departments, funeral homes, nursing homes, and
so on. A chaplain would be available for community events, for counseling
employees in need, and for pastoral emergencies for people who don't have a
pastoral caregiver of their own.

What is vital is to make personal connections with people who might be
hungry for God's presence. Perhaps the coffee shop or the community non-
profit organization is the twenty-first-century equivalent of the Areopagus.
They are the public spaces where we speak and listen to each other.

Community Service and Events

Another way to connect with people is through community service and
meet-and-greet events. Nelson Searcy recommends both of these strategies in
Launch.[3] In a community service event, the church's leadership team (however many people are part of it at this point) identifies a community need
and sends a team out to meet it. The main objective is to actually perform
the service. But the people doing the service do it in the name of the church,
and are happy to tell others about the reason for their service. It is important
that these projects, if they are to result in invitations to the church, occur in
the church's neighborhood. In Nativity's neighborhood, building a Habitat

---

3. Searcy and Thomas, *Launch: Starting a New Church from Scratch,* 176–7.

for Humanity house or running a soup kitchen would not apply. But we have done community service events such as handing out free water bottles at a school carnival (with information about the church, of course, and free prayers to anyone who wants them), or offering free gift wrapping at a mall at Christmastime.

Special events might include get-togethers that allow people to "dip their toe in the water" of the church and find out if they seem to fit. Social events are good examples: barbecues or picnics that are invitation possibilities for neighborhood folks. Religious holidays provide an opportunity: St. Francis' Day could be the occasion for a pet blessing in the parking lot of a local pet store (with the store's permission, of course) or in a park where many pet owners walk their dogs. One good principle to follow is to always have a follow-up invitation. If you expect many people to show up for a particular offering, be ready to give them an invitation to the next event. On Easter, invite them to come back the following Sunday for a special day of service. On Christmas, invite them to come back the first Sunday in January for a special children's event. At the pet blessing, invite them to the November adult education series on sex and the Bible (or whatever intriguing topic you have dreamed up). People are much more likely to join the church if they have attended two or more events in a row, and have gotten to know a few members by name.

The pre-launch process for church planting will often include sample worship services. Say a church plans to launch in September, in time for the start of a new school year. The launch team might offer four sample worship events, open to the community, in May, June, July, and August. These sample worship events give those who attend a picture of what they can expect from the new church, and they offer the planter and launch team an opportunity to get contact information from people who might be interested so they can send them information later. The planter can then follow up personally with all who attend, with special attention to those who seem particularly interested and might be interested in participating as part of the launch team. These folks should receive an invitation to coffee, lunch, or a newcomers' event with the planter or launch team members. Each of the sample worship events might include an invitation to all who attend to come to a social or education event before the next public worship service. These worship "sampler" services also allow the launch team to refine its procedures and work out all the kinks before the launch of regular Sunday worship services.

Personal Evangelism

The best invitation is a personal invitation. Word of mouth is the most effective form of evangelism. The launch team, from the very beginning, should understand that inviting people into the church's fellowship is not just the job of the paid staff. It is the ministry of every Christian. That means that the launch team should be equipped to do the job. They should have whatever paper is helpful to hand out to their friends and acquaintances (church business cards, brochures, invitations) and they should also have the knowledge of the church's vision to share with others. The planter can do nothing but make community contacts for sixty hours a week, and still not make as many contacts as thirty team members making one contact each every week. People telling their friends about something that is bringing hope, excitement, and transformation to their lives is a great way to spread the news of your new church. Asking people to bring their friends to special events where they can socialize, get to know other church members, and learn about the church is even better. Multiplying the church's invitational evangelism by enlisting the skills and contacts of the launch team is crucial.

Of course, none of these techniques of connecting with people in the community matter very much if they do not result in an invitation to grow in relationship with or knowledge of Christ. The whole point of starting the new church is to evangelize—tell the good news of Christ—and help people grow in discipleship. Always be ready to account for "the hope that is in you," says the apostle in 1 Peter 3:15. The planter and launch team members should be able to say not just why this church is a nice church, but how it brings people closer to God, and why that is important to them. Who is the God that they are inviting people to meet in this new church fellowship? Some people will find it very difficult to do anything more than mention that they are part of a new church that is exciting. Some will be eager to talk about the difference Christ makes in their lives.

At Nativity, we have offered different kinds of training for our lay people in evangelism, with varying degrees of success. The *Unbinding the Gospel* series by Martha Grace Reese[4] has been especially helpful. We studied this book during a Lenten series, and the homework and exercises it provided

---

4. Martha Grace Reese, *Unbinding the Gospel: Real Life Evangelism* (St. Louis, MO: Chalice Press, 2008).

offered a number of thought-provoking ways for lay people to engage their acquaintances in deep, meaningful, non-threatening, spiritual conversations.

Stories of Engaging the Community

The ideas above are just some ways that you can engage the community and invite people to be part of your new church. But Episcopal church planters have done this work in many creative ways. I will let some of them tell their own stories.

Lang Lowrey, the founding priest of St. Benedict's, Smyrna, Georgia, tells how he began reaching out to the community before St. Benedict's launched worship:

> I used both the pastoral and program approaches, two prongs simulta-
> neously. The pastoral approach is not supposed to be the way to plant
> a church. I was an ambulance chaser for Christ. If someone's mother
> was in the hospital, I would ask, "Do you mind if I visit and say a
> prayer?" and if they said yes, I visited. In the drugstore or coffee shop
> every morning I would start conversations. Everyone has a pastoral
> concern; everyone needs God. I was doing weddings, going to nursing
> homes; the whole day was virtually all pastoral outreach to the com-
> munity. It took six months. People would ask where my church is. I
> would say, "I'm doing God's work, hoping God will send me people.
> Let me know if you know someone." I would leave them my cards.
> It was amazing. People started calling, e-mailing, giving me names.
> Soon I had fifty people, including ten from the mother church. They
> didn't want to leave St. Anne's but they wanted to help. We started
> small group meetings, talking about what kind of church we wanted.
> The key was hospitality—food, wine, cheese, coffee, cake—whatever
> it was, I needed hospitality. [When] I finally had people I did a ques-
> tionnaire [and created a] newcomers committee. They agreed that they
> would go out to look at every Episcopal church and competing church
> in the area and come back in a month with all the information to cre-
> ate a detailed plan. We spent weeks developing the best newcomers'
> procedure. We appointed greeters and ushers, we provided training,
> we held monthly newcomers' events at my house for wine and cheese
> or afternoon tea. We would have twenty to twenty-five people at these

monthly events, and follow up to get them into a small group. It just kept growing.[5]

Guerrero talks about her methods for starting several Latino congregations in the Phoenix area:

We told people about the church by word of mouth. People from an older church would help start new ones. We put out thousands of fliers in the neighborhood. The people came to join us out of patience and persistence and a belief in what can be. At Santa Maria we worshiped for weeks with only the launch team there. I said be patient, give it time, it will happen. Finally one lady came, then the next week she brought her daughter, then the next week her husband, then she brought her whole extended family. Latino culture is family-oriented; if you get one, you get the whole family. I also did "shoot from the hip" stuff. When I started worship at St. Mark's, one lady came with lots of children. I told her she was just in time because I was starting catechism next week, so then I had to hurry to create the catechism class. Soon we had ninety people.[6]

Frank Logue talks about how he started King of Peace, Kingsland, Georgia:

I started out with the demographics, reading them, seeing about the community. I took the maps for a ten-mile radius and asked, where do I need to knock on doors in order to make my door-knocking demographically significant. . . . I knocked on one hundred doors and said, "I'm here to start a new Episcopal church. I don't want you to come to the church, I just want to know what can a church do for this community." The words people told me were children, teens, community, spirituality. . . . There was a need for a full day preschool because both parents were working.

At the same time I had been separately doing things to get the word out about this new church. Victoria and I had worked in newspapers and knew how they worked. I did not want to arrive at a newspaper with a press release that said we are starting a new church because I

---

5. Lang Lowrey, telephone interview with the author, July 8, 2014.
6. Guerrero, interview.

know what that article looks like. It runs on the religion page and it reaches people who have churches. . . . So instead I got on the schedule for the Kingsland City Council and told them about knocking on doors. I talked to the council to ask them the same questions, what would you like to see a church do? I did this in part because I wanted to hear what they had to say, and in part because I knew newspapers. I got a news story out of it instead of a religion story. Basically what you do is you go make news, you don't tell them you're a new church. Because of the article that resulted from that I started getting phone calls, and I started making lunch and dinner dates to go meet people in a restaurant and talk to them.

We were aiming toward a Christian education offering [before we launched worship services]. At the local rec center I rented a room and did "Questioning Your Faith," a thirteen-week series talking about things like: Why does a good God allow a world of suffering? What about science and religion? and Can other religions be true? That gave us something else to advertise and something else to invite them to.

So as I began to get the sense that this was a group that I could work with, we began to get together for other meetings. We talked about what I'd learned about launching a church over time. We talked about the sorts of roles we need and how we're going to need to do them. It seemed clear as we were heading toward Advent that year that we could probably begin doing trial worship services just to work the kinks out as we were worshiping in that space. We did four of those and then launched Christmas Eve.

Clearly we had the team that would give us what we needed. So I think the two things have to come together—you have to identify a need in the area, but you also have to have the gifts to meet that need. And there are some things the church never really needs to do, and there are some things that are yours, and the crossover is the need in the community, combined with your group having the gifts to meet that need.[7]

Clay Lein, who founded St. Philip's Frisco in the Diocese of Dallas, tells the story of gathering his initial group of people:

---

7. Logue, interview.

Once I knew I was going to be doing this, I just started tracking contacts. I had a big Excel spreadsheet. I started putting in it any conversation that anyone had with me. . . . We put a couple of ads in the Frisco paper saying we're doing a new thing. What we found was that a lot of the word of mouth got out, and I started having lunches and coffees and dinners at my house or other people's houses. I just basically threw myself into creating relationships with as many people as I could, telling them what we were trying to do, casting a vision of a place that was focused on growing faith that impacted the world for Christ. I tried to be as winsome and relational and gracious and attractive as I possibly could. And people came; they wanted to see what was going on.

We had a preview service on . . . Ash Wednesday [because] we knew that people needed to have some incarnational example of what we actually meant. It wasn't that different from the mother church—a blend of contemporary and traditional, but Rite II biblical preaching that was grace-filled and focused on real life, with personal examples from my life. . . . That service had about 150 people at it. We got a great picture with everyone looking at the camera with ash crosses on their forehead. That got the buzz going. We spent the rest of Lent having a Wednesday night worship and Bible study time at [a non-denominational] church here in Frisco. They lent us some upper rooms and they provided a nursery. They said, "We were a church plant just two years ago, so we'll help you." So we met there every Wednesday night and we started doing the things that were going to be our values. We were teaching children; we had some people from our mother church who were doing a children's Alpha [course]. I taught through the Gospel of Mark. I had a friend who played keyboard, and we sang traditional and contemporary worship hymns. Then we had fellowship time; we had coffee and talked about what this was going to be like.

I also met with focused teams. I had a children's ministry team I met with in my home every week. We were putting things in place for a launch: a worship team, a music team. We spent the season of Lent preparing and communicating with everyone we could, and inviting people who were going to be on the core team to communicate with everyone they could to come for that first Easter service. We had it and it was a wonderful thing, with 250 people at that service. The . . . service was in jeans and boots in a school cafeteria. We had a children's sermon, lots of people, and we said this is what we were going to do.

We were very intentional about word of mouth [advertising]. One of the things we really understood was that buzz matters. We wanted momentum, and we knew people were talking about this experience they'd had of a God who is relevant. That really was probably one of the most effective ways of reaching our community, because I can only do so much. While meeting in the school I think we grew to about four hundred. I knew that if we're going to grow we needed a lot more people telling people about what's going on. We did a lot of preaching focused on felt needs, but it was always out of the scriptures, always applying it to life, and if there's one thing people really gave us feed-back on, it was that the preaching really changed the way they looked at their lives.

We did "come and see" months where . . . the focus was on one thing that people were dealing with: stress at work, kids, relationships, finances, or whatever it was. We would give them postcards and we would invite people to invite people, for a month, not just a day, because [if it was just a day], if they missed it they would miss it. So everything was oriented toward that, and we had greeters and ushers that were focused on new people. We created a machine that was focused on wel-coming people and connecting them to the body and encouraging them to be changed. We had burgundy registers that we would pass down during announcement time and we would ask everyone to sign in. We had calls that would be made that day by me or by the other clergy associate. We had letters that got sent out and follow-up calls, so it was a multi-tiered system of following the leads that God gave us. Our web-site [brought] probably more than 50% of our visitors. We had a lot of info and pictures on the website so people would know what they were getting into. We had test drive CDs with pictures, sermons, music, and lots of those kinds of things.[8]

Natalia Derritt, who is a Latina lay leader working with Daniel Velez Rivera to start a Latino congregation at St. Gabriel's, Leesburg, Virginia, talks about how she got involved with the project:

---

8. Lein, interview.

I worked in this community for several years. I used to work for a
non-profit organization that provided different kinds of support for
families, single mothers, couples, sometimes in very difficult situations—economical, psychological, physical. I worked for that organization for around three years and also as an interpreter for the school
system in Loudoun County. I noticed that besides [physical and mental
needs], this community needs a place, a spiritual place, where they can
connect with themselves, connect with a spiritual guide, continue being
strong and survive in whatever difficult situation. I met Daniel because
we have a small school and church in St. James', the mother church
of St. Gabriel's, with a reading program for the community. Middle-
and low-income people come and bring their children to prepare those
children for kindergarten. That was how I met Padre Daniel and we
started talking and working together.[9]

Daniel Velez Rivera continues:

The sextons at St. James' are Spanish speakers and we became very
good friends. . . . One of them said, "My father died in Mexico and I
can't go to the funeral," and I said, "You need to have a funeral here, so
we'll do a memorial service in honor of your father and we'll do a full
funeral for your benefit, for you and your brothers and their families
who live here." Natalia is their friend so she went to the funeral, and
there were fifty or so people there. The other sexton's parents were here
visiting from Mexico and it was their fiftieth wedding anniversary and
they asked, "Can you do the blessing of the renewal of the vows?" I
said sure, and fifty people came. That's the soul of the church planter.
It's not an opportunity, it's the gift that we can give to the community,
so why not?[10]

Velez Rivera also shares how he started the Latino congregation at Grace
Church, Salem, Massachusetts:

My best friend, Ema Rosero-Nordalm, is from Colombia, and has been
a friend of mine for twenty-four years. . . . When I went to [Grace
Church] Salem, I said to Ema, "I need a female partner." It's important

9. Velez Rivera and Derritt, interview.
10. Ibid.

to have both genders in order to reach out appropriately to the community. Ema and I literally took to the streets together.

Rosero-Nordalm, a deacon who is now the Missioner for Latino-Hispanic Ministries in the Diocese of Massachusetts, began working with women in the community, gathering them and responding to their needs. She created two programs. Abuelas, Madres y Más (Grandmothers, Mothers, and More) was a program that helped grandmothers and other caregivers learn how to raise children in American culture. At the same time, the grandmothers and older caregivers helped younger mothers who were familiar with American culture learn how to care for their children. The second program grew out of the first and was called Ruth and Naomi, a program to help older Latina women mentor younger ones. From these beginnings, the women who gathered started asking for a spiritual component, and began attending worship services.[11]

Velez Rivera continues:

I got on the boards of the homeless shelter and community organizations. . . I became actively involved with labor organizations for unjust job issues. . . I have a social work background and I worked with young kids that have been incarcerated and were being released into the community. I had a program called Moral Reasoning and I met kids and their parents who then started to come to church. We did our first religious service in the Latino community agency where I volunteered to teach citizenship preparation courses. They also took their GED in Spanish.

Here [at St. Gabriel's], my first Spanish service was on Good Friday. We had outdoor Stations of the Cross on the land that was given to us. Natalia called me on Monday and said the community wants to know what you're doing for Holy Week in Spanish, [so we created that service]. About thirty or so people came, and they came to the Easter sunrise service.[12]

It should be clear from these inspiring stories that the ways of interacting with the community and inviting people to be part of the adventure that

---

11. Ema Rosero-Nordalm, telephone interview with the author, December 9, 2014.
12. Velez Rivera and Derritt, interview.

is your new church vary widely. The best techniques will depend on the people in the community. What are their hopes and dreams? What keeps them awake at night? In what ways are they empty and searching, hoping, for more? How might they best come to feel and understand the presence of God in their lives? What does God want to say to them, and how is God already working with them and inviting your church to join in? The task of the church planter is to come to a deep and nuanced understanding of the people in the neighborhood, and to connect to them in ways that touch their hearts, souls, and minds. ❧

~ 10

An Energetic Launch

When the day of Pentecost had come, they were all together in one place. And suddenly from heaven there came a sound like the rush of a violent wind, and it filled the entire house where they were sitting. Divided tongues, as of fire, appeared among them, and a tongue rested on each of them. All of them were filled with the Holy Spirit and began to speak in other languages, as the Spirit gave them ability. . . . So those who welcomed his message were baptized, and that day about three thousand persons were added. They devoted themselves to the apostles' teaching and fellowship, to the breaking of bread and the prayers. Acts 2:1–4, 41–42

The Day of Pentecost lit the fire of the greatest church launch in history. The apostles had no idea what was about to happen to them, but they prepared themselves by gathering in a community of faith, praying, and waiting for the action of the Holy Spirit. Like the apostles on Pentecost, people today can sometimes be surprised and amazed by the Spirit. We prepare ourselves by prayer and by immersing ourselves in the words of God and in the power of Christ's resurrection. And the goal is for the Spirit to light a fire that will launch God's new church into orbit.

For most modern-day churches, laying the groundwork of an energetic launch takes careful preparation. Church planters meet and speak with people wherever they can, inviting them to experience Christ through the new community they are planting. Making these individual contacts and invitations is the first step of creating a church. The second step is to gather a team of people who will eagerly join in the adventure of planting the church. The third step is to reach out to the public to make sure as many people know about the new church as possible. The fourth step, then, is to invite the (hopefully energized and enthusiastic) public to join in worship at a consistent place and time, where they will devote themselves to the apostles' teaching and fellowship, to the breaking of bread, and to the prayers.

How this fourth step happens is partly a function of the church's vision. If the church intends to remain a house church permanently, then the fourth phase—opening up worship to friends as well as family—might look very similar to the first, second, and third phases, except a bit larger, and the invitation process might happen gradually over time. If the church intends to be a nontraditional Christian community in a coffeehouse, like The Abbey in Birmingham, the official launch might look like the grand opening of a business, with different classes and worship offerings added from time to time as appropriate. Or, a street ministry like Cathedral in the Night in Worcester, Massachusetts might open small and grow by word of mouth.

For most new church plants, however, the beginning of public worship is a major strategic move, which needs to be thought through carefully and planned to take place at a good time of year, a time when all the essential pieces are in place. Church planters need to do significant work to build ministry infrastructure, leadership, enthusiasm, and public awareness before launching public worship. Jim Griffith and Bill Easum write that launching public worship too soon is one of the most common reasons they see church plants fail. "In our experience, many planters and their teams misunderstand the purpose of the public launch," they write. "They wrongly assume that the goal of the launch is to 'get started.' It's not. The goal of the launch is to get into orbit where the new church can begin to develop with minimal amounts of effort to stay aloft."[1] Therefore, the church must launch powerfully and energetically.

---

1. Jim Griffith and Bill Easum, *Ten Most Common Mistakes Made by New Church Starts* (St. Louis, MO: Chalice Press, 2008), 36.

A premature launch, say Griffith and Easum, is like a premature baby. Such a church has to fight to grow, and may never increase beyond its size at birth. A church that launches public worship with just a few people will probably still have just a few people several years later—if it lasts that long. One problem with premature launch is that once regular Sunday worship has begun, preparing for Sunday becomes a huge focus of the planter and launch team, and they spend time on preparing worship, offering pastoral care, and administering a church rather than reaching out to the community.

Griffith and Easum compare the pre-launch development period to the gestational period of pregnancy, an absolutely vital time to build strength for a healthy life. They recommend that during this time, the launch team hold periodic "preview" or "taste and see" events that allow the public to sample what the church has to offer, moving to an "exhibition season" with weekly celebrations that allow the team to refine their ministries and prepare for the public launch.[2] The official launch, then, happens after the exhibition season has allowed the team to gather momentum and perfect its approach. In order to grow, a church needs to launch with critical mass, enough people to staff the needed ministries and to give new attendees the feeling that the church is an exciting place to belong. How many people it takes to form a "critical mass" depends on the vision of the church and the community in which it is located. Frank Logue describes the development period and launch of King of Peace, Kingsland:

> We launched on Christmas Eve 2000, and we had forty-two people, which was about our target. We wanted to hit the average-size church in our community, and that was about it. A large church in that community was over one hundred. This is a town of 8,500 people with 25,000 in a ten-mile radius and 105 churches already in existence, with an Episcopal church at the end of that radius in each direction. So it wasn't a natural place to start a church, but the reason the bishop wanted to plant another was that he saw the town's population more than double in a decade in which the two Episcopal churches went down in attendance. It was a more blue-collar place, some college was

---

2. Ibid., 39–41. I highly recommend reading Griffith and Easum's short, readable, and very useful book.

typical but college graduates and advanced degrees was not typical. We were a church for sailors, not officers.[3]

King of Peace launched, meeting its goal of forty-two people in attendance based on the population of its community and the typical church there. Church of the Nativity launched in fall 2006, after an exhibition season that grew our attendance from 65 people (the launch team) to 106 (attendance at launch). St. Benedict's in the Smyrna area of Atlanta aimed for a much larger launch, according to Lang Lowrey:

> The bishop saw that groups that started with less than fifty or one hundred socialized small; they never grew or became self-supporting, [so the bishop insisted that we have two hundred people before we launched]. We had people sign a petition with 150 to 175 signatures, and we hung there for a month or two. I knew it was almost ten months in now [since I began building the launch team], and I had a sense of tempo. If we didn't start worship soon, we would start losing some critical mass. In the tenth month, we rented out a community amphitheater, invited the bishop, all surrounding priests, my family and friends, and all 175 names. We created a mailer; we called and followed through, inviting people to a community day. We invited everyone to come hear from the bishop some good news about St. Benedict's. . . . I gave a presentation and told everyone that if they were willing to listen to God's call, we would worship starting February 1, 2007. . . . At our February 1 launch, we had about three hundred people that day. I was panicked about how many people would show up. It was so emotional, overwhelming, when I walked in the room and there were three hundred people. After that I worried a hundred of them were my friends and the others wouldn't come back, but we held over two hundred every week afterwards.[4]

Clay Lein was prepared to be patient and build his launch team, heeding advice not to launch too soon. But he discovered that he needed to launch earlier than he had expected.

> I had been released by Christ Church Plano [the mother church of St. Philip's] in June 2001. I knew that I would be on staff there through

---

3. Logue, interview.
4. Lowrey, interview.

the end of the year, then released on January 1 to go do this new work. I had a church planting coach who had had a lot of experience planting. He had helped plant Willow Creek, had done some coaching with Saddleback, so he was really good at coaching planters. [The coach was Jim Griffith.] At first . . . my coach was real clear, you gotta go slow to launch, you gotta have enough core team, you can't rush to a Sunday morning service. Most church planters are too fast with that and end up with this small group that's meeting once a Sunday, and suddenly that becomes the focus of the planter's life. You can't do that, he was really clear. I thought okay, I've got time, maybe in August, eight months later, it might work. In one of our coaching sessions, I'm telling him about how many leaders we have and how many people are saying we want to be part of it, when he [Griffiths] challenged me to launch earlier than we had thought. So it was kind of a change and it was a recognition as he said, "Clay, you've got all these people. In some sense you are transplanting, planting a shoot, you're not just planting a seed hoping it grows, you're actually transplanting [from the mother church]. Having them be nomads for eight months is going to drain off some of that momentum that you would actually need to continue that growth." So he really pushed me to start thinking more about an Easter launch, March 31 that year. . . . We had 250 people at that service.[5]

In contrast, Guerrero discusses launching her Latino congregation with only the team members present, and letting her lively church grow one family at a time.

We grew by word of mouth. We got people from older Latino churches to help start new ones. We put out thousands of fliers in the neighborhood. The team came to worship and waited for others to start coming. You have to have patience and persistence and belief in what can be.[6]

The number of people that you need to launch will vary by community and culture; the point is to work very carefully toward the goal of being able to launch with the critical mass of people, and lay ministries, that will help

5. Lein, interview.
6. Guerrero, interview.

the church become a growing, thriving community, and with the necessary systems in place.

What systems should you have in place before launching? New churches should avoid trying to have everything in place before launch, I believe. You may have ministers to staff a children's program but not a youth program; you may have an education program but no community service ministries yet. Don't try to achieve the final vision on the first week. "Failure of the new church to act its age and size" is one of the top ten mistakes made by new church plants, according to Easum and Griffith.[7] Small churches need to act small, but strategic. Searcy and Thomas provide a list of the systems they believe need to be in place in *Launch*.[8] Some of their thoughts don't carry over to the Episcopal system (for instance, an Episcopal church plant does not have to create a corporate/legal structure, because the sponsoring diocese or parish will direct that decision). But most of their suggestions are very helpful. Adapting their list for the Episcopal context, here are the systems I think you need to have in place before you launch:

- Sunday service and all related lay ministries
- a plan for evangelism and marketing
- a website
- a newcomer assimilation system
- a recordkeeping system
- an accounting system, bank account, and clear financial structures
- a leadership system
- an approach to Christian formation (this is so important that it gets its own chapter, chapter 11)
- a facility in which to worship (discussed separately in chapter 12)

Sunday Service and Lay Ministries

Each church should determine what the "front door" of the church will be according to its mission and vision. How will most people find you and become engaged with your ministries? For Fresh Expressions churches, the front door might be the coffeehouse, the Wednesday evening pub theology

7. Griffith and Easum, 93.
8. Searcy and Thomas, 183.

discussion, or the home group that you invite friends to join. The front door might be a service ministry to the neighborhood, or a person who is involved in the community. For most churches, however, the front door of the church will be the weekly worship service, usually (though not always) on Sunday mornings. Worship will be the event that brings church members together in one place to glorify God. Worship will be how people discover whether what you are offering speaks to their lives and helps them build a relationship with Christ. Worship will give you the opportunity to offer hospitality, get to know people, and invite them to join in your other discipleship offerings.

Preparing for Sunday worship takes a great deal of careful planning. You need to decide about worship style, according to the church mission and decisions you have discerned. What style of music does the church eventually desire to have, and how can you start worship in a way that will lead the church naturally to that vision? Nativity's vision included traditional music, but we did not have access to an organ or piano. Instead, we bought a high-quality electronic keyboard that we could move in and out of the school each week, and played traditional music on it with a talented musical director and a volunteer choir. Your church's eventual vision will dictate worship style decisions like whether to use bulletins, prayer books, or projectors and screens, or whether to worship in the evening by candlelight, singing ancient chants. Wherever you intend to lead the congregation, you should begin with some approximation of that style, or a later change will be disruptive. If Nativity had begun worship with guitars and drums and attempted to change later to traditional organ music, we would have lost the people who were attracted to the original style. Instead, we started with traditional music played on an electronic keyboard in classical style. Find a way to provide a high-quality worship experience in the style you want to make permanent, to the extent your resources allow.

If you are worshiping in a space that is used for other purposes during the week, you will have to figure out how to do setup and takedown without this becoming the exclusive job of the clergy and family. At Nativity, we had a finely tuned setup and takedown system. One of our launch team members, Fred Brown, was in charge, and he directed a group of volunteers who each had assigned roles. Two people were in charge of setting up the sound system and taping down cords so no one would trip over them. Several people put together our portable altar and credence table, so that the altar guild could come behind them and set up the linens and the altar. A group was in charge of helping set up chairs. Teachers set up the Sunday school classroom and the nursery. The choir brought in the keyboard, plugged it in, and began practicing. The hospitality ministers set up their tables in the back of the school cafeteria, and the greeters set up a newcomer welcome table. I was available for consultation and advice, but the able lay ministers each took care of their own areas. The same people stayed behind to take everything down after each service. Since the school where we worshiped had no storage available, most of our altar setup was stored in the back of an old Ford Explorer that someone owned and never used, and drove to and from the church each week. This whole process took significant time and volunteer energy. But it was a terrific team-building and enthusiasm-generating undertaking each week. Beginning an hour before the service, you could see the Body of Christ in action, preparing to worship God. Figuring out your physical setup—what items you will need, where you will store them, and who will set them up—needs to happen, under the leadership of lay ministers, long before your church launches.

Plan to set up similar systems for every ministry you need for Sunday. Appoint lay leaders to recruit, train, and assign lay ministers in each area. Consider how you are going to provide the order of worship: with prayer books and hymnals (very heavy and bulky, and difficult to store and set up), full bulletins, projector and screen, or some other method, and put people in charge of preparing these items. Plan how you will greet newcomers (more on this in a moment) and provide hospitality. Know when and where your Christian formation classes (see chapter 11) will be. Appointing lay leaders in each area is a terrific way to involve the team and increase their sense of ownership and commitment to the church.

Remember, don't rush to Sunday worship too soon. Once you have launched a regular Sunday worship offering, it will become the primary focus of the clergy leader's week: writing sermons, preparing bulletins, selecting and rehearsing music, making sure lay ministries are scheduled, following up on newcomers, providing pastoral care to those who feel they have a real "church" now, supervising staff and volunteers, preparing for Christian formation offerings, and so forth. The launch team also will tend to breathe a sigh of relief once you have launched, knowing that they have worked together as a team to achieve something important. It is natural for the group to experience an emotional letdown after the high emotions and anticipation of the launch. The challenge will be to keep the energy high enough to continue reaching new people and expanding the church's ministries once the team has achieved its first milestone.

A Plan for Evangelism and Marketing

While it is natural for the team to breathe a sigh of relief once you have launched, the launch is only the beginning. Most of the evangelism work that the church will do over its lifetime will happen after the launch. The last thing you want to happen is for the church to turn inward once worship has started, but this is a real risk. Begin your regular worship services with a plan in place for evangelism: How will you reach people in your community who don't have a church and help them develop a relationship with Christ? How will you get out into the community to meet new people and touch them with the love of God? How will you teach and demonstrate who Christ is and why that is important to us today? What if people are touched by the church's ministries and want to take a life-transforming step? What action should they take if they want to know more about Christ? Should they contact the pastor, attend a class, prepare for baptism?

Have a plan for marketing, too. How will you continue to get the news out to your neighborhood that a new church is worshiping there? Make sure that your launch team understands the church's basic identity: What is distinctive about it? What sets it apart from the other things people could be doing on Sunday mornings? Consider plans for marketing at special times: Christmas, Easter, the beginning of the school year, the blessing of animals, the opening of a new subdivision or apartment complex nearby. Find out if there are free advertising venues in your area. Do something newsworthy and issue a press release to your local newspaper. Staff booths at community festivals, with free prayers or free water bottles, and tell people about your new church. Give church business cards with the time and place of your services to every member of your church and ask them to pass the cards out to friends and acquaintances who don't have a church, with personal invitations to attend. Personal invitation is the best kind of marketing; train your people to simply invite others to "come and see" (John 1:39) at Sunday worship or special introductory events.

Jim Griffith and Bill Easum say that one of the most common mistakes that church plants make is to cease evangelism after the launch. Somehow, people assume that once worship services begin, no other method of telling the good news is necessary. We no longer live in a "build it and they will come" culture, Griffith and Easum say. We now live in an "invite" culture, where people are far more likely to come if a personal friend invites them.[9] Make personal invitation part of the DNA of your church, so that evangelism continues to be part of your core identity.

Chapter 9 includes many suggestions for reaching out to the public, and stories of how others have done it. Don't forget that evangelism and marketing ministries need to continue—as a priority, with a plan—long after your church launches public worship.

A Website

It should go without saying that you need a website, and your website will probably form your most effective marketing strategy. Most people will research your church on its website before setting foot in a worship service. You can build an attractive and inexpensive website using platforms like WordPress. Make sure your website truly describes who you are, according to the identity and vision you have created. Include lively looking photographs of people (real people who are part of your church, not stock photos of models) and make sure that basic information about when and where you worship is easily found on the home page. Include some information about who you are, what kind of programs you provide for children, who your staff is, what you believe, and what people can expect to experience at your worship services. You don't need fancy upgraded features (flash, video, podcasts) right away. Many helpful suggestions about websites can be found in Rebecca Wilson and Jim Naughton's book *Speaking Faithfully: Communications as Evangelism in a Noisy World* (New York: Morehouse, 2012). Building your website is another great job for a lay ministry leader.[10] Note that the Episcopal Church offers affordable ways of putting together simple websites.[11]

---

9. Griffith and Easum, *Ten Most Common Mistakes*, 50.

10. You are welcome to explore Nativity's website, www.NativityScottsdale.org, for ideas, and to copy some of our general content, if you write and ask permission.

11. See information about church websites available through the Episcopal Church at http://www.episcopalchurch.org/page/affordable-websites-congregations-and-diocese.

A Newcomer Assimilation System

You've been hoping and dreaming and praying for the new folks that are going to be part of the adventure you are starting. What are you going to do with them when they show up? How will you greet them, how will you welcome them, how will you connect them to others, what will you give them so they can understand who and what this church is? Most importantly, how will you follow up with them and assimilate them into the church? The greeting and welcoming system you create now will become a cornerstone of your growth for years to come. Find a person on your launch team who has the gift of hospitality and welcoming, along with significant leadership skills, and make that person the leader of your welcoming team. Plan how to recognize newcomers when they arrive. How will you make it easy for first-time attenders to understand what is going on and how to find important areas like the restrooms, children's area, and even the front door to the worship area if you are worshiping in a nontraditional space like a school? (At the school where Nativity first worshiped, people had to find their way to a side entrance to the school and then walk down a long hallway to the cafeteria where we worshiped. We placed numerous sandwich board signs outside so people could find the church entrance and the Sunday school classrooms, which were in a portable building, and we stationed our newcomer greeting team in the hallway so we could personally conduct newcomers to the cafeteria for worship.) Decide how you are going to get contact information from newcomers, and whose job it will be to follow up with them. Will you send them a letter, invite them to lunch, ask them to attend newcomer classes, provide newcomer events, or have a team of lay leaders to follow up? Who will receive their names, contact information, and begin to pray for them?

Newcomer welcoming involves more than simply smiling and helping people find their way through the Sunday morning event, important as that is. It is equally vital to help people get to know others to feel like they belong. Griffith and Easum recommend having not only a greeter team, but also a connector team.[12] Greeters are stationary, they stay in one place; connectors walk around. They introduce people to others who are like themselves; they conduct people to Sunday school classrooms and worship areas; they look

---

12. Ibid., 56.

for people they have met and greet them happily when they show up again. I recommend *not* combining these functions with the ushers' duties; ushers have their own function and it is difficult for them to spare time for more than a friendly "hello" when people arrive.

Newcomer assimilation involves more than simply getting folks to show up consistently. It also means getting them involved in the ministries and activities of the church that are right for them. I recall long ago attending a church for the first time, and going to coffee hour. Five or six choir members immediately surrounded my husband and me, and enthusiastically badgered my husband about joining the choir, because they needed male voices. My husband was not the least bit interested in joining the choir, but I would have joined if they had asked me. They weren't interested in my voice, however, or in whether I felt left out because they were only paying attention to my husband. They were responding to their own needs, not ours. Newcomer assimilation does *not* mean badgering first-time attendees to fill the church's needs. It means finding out what is important to the people God sends your way, and inviting them to go deeper in those areas. Often, for first-time attenders, they simply need to get to know the church and its members a bit before understanding where they are called to minister. You should plan to offer some low-commitment, entry-level ways people can be involved, perhaps something as simple as bringing snacks for hospitality or attending the adult education classes you offer after the service.

Much newcomer assimilation happens by way of personal conversation, with an interviewer who truly listens to the new person and tries to understand his heart or her needs. It is best if the pastor does not try to take on this role personally for long. A church that depends on the pastor to make all the personal connections and get to know each member on a deep and personal level will plateau at 125 members, say Griffith and Easum.[13] This happens because no one person can hold many more relationships than that in his or her head. If all centers on the pastor, the church will remain small. (Griffith and Easum caution that this problem is especially common in churches with a "sacramental" tradition.[14]) Make newcomer assimilation and deep personal

---

13. Ibid., 66.
14. Ibid., 62.

connection the mission of a gracious, personable, and hospitable newcomer team.

Lang Lowrey tells his success story of newcomer welcoming and assimilation:

> [We got people] into a newcomers' committee. We met and agreed they would go out to look at every Episcopal church and competing church in the area, and come back in a month with all the information to create a detailed plan. They came back with every piece of information the other churches passed out. We spent weeks developing the best new-comers procedure. We appointed greeters and ushers. We had training. We had monthly newcomers' events at my house: wine and cheese or afternoon tea. We said everybody is a newcomer; if you consider your-self a newcomer you are. We would have twenty to twenty-five people at these monthly events. We would follow up and get them into a small group. The groups had leaders and we would send them the names. It just kept growing. That Christmas, ten months [after our launch], we had 550 people at our Christmas Eve service.[15]

A Record-Keeping System

Don't spend too much time or money developing a record-keeping system before your launch; this is the time for evangelism, not administration. But do keep track of attendance, baptisms, and children in Sunday school. You can buy and use the Episcopal church registers as official documents, but I would supplement these with a simple Excel spreadsheet tracking num-bers over the course of the year. Doing this allows you to analyze trends, see where your high and low attendance times are, and watch your growth (or non-growth) over time. These are vital statistics to know for leadership and evaluation.

Also have a simple way of tracking member and newcomer contact data. A Word or Excel document will work at first. Eventually you will want to upgrade to a more complete and flexible software package, but this is not necessary at first, and would probably take too much administrative time. A basic way of keeping people's information is sufficient.

---

15. Lowrey, interview.

Accounting and Financial Systems

Don't wait until you receive your first offering to figure out what to do with it. Have your accounting system in place well before you launch. If you have worked carefully with your launch team on stewardship issues, you will have money in the bank anyway. You need a treasurer and accountability systems well before beginning to worship.

In the Episcopal system, you will likely receive at least some guidelines from your diocese or sponsoring parish. Assuming you are not incorporated, you will need another legal entity (diocese or parish) to open a bank account for you using their tax identification number. Do not under any circumstances use someone's personal accounts to hold church money, or transfer money back and forth from personal to church accounts. Your church finances need to be above ground and above reproach from the beginning. Appoint a treasurer to keep books and make reports, using a simple bookkeeping software package. Make sure your treasurer knows something about non-profit accounting; if she is a competent accountant but doesn't know non-profit accounting, ask someone from your diocese to help train her. Appoint a finance committee to provide oversight to the treasurer, create budgets, and make sure spending stays in line. Spread financial authority so that not all power is in the hands of one person. (This is a basic rule of internal controls, created to avoid the possibility or appearance of fraud; it protects not only the church, but the persons doing the financial work). Have two unrelated persons count the Sunday offerings and sign off, including providing a deposit slip and a calculator tape showing the receipts, and have another unrelated person check the count and create the deposit. Make deposits as soon as possible after money is received. Put someone who does not write the checks in charge of balancing the checking account and making sure the cash balance is in accord with the amount recorded on the books.

Consider how to handle payroll, if you have employees. Your diocese will have policies about how to do payroll, and may handle it for you. If not, find a reputable payroll service to do it and to make sure all tax filings are kept current. The last thing you want to do is get in trouble with the IRS! Make sure also that you have a simple way of sending out year-end tax statements to your donors.

Ask your diocese or sponsoring parish what kind of financial oversight and accountability they expect, and provide the reports they need.

A Leadership Development System

Every church needs strong lay leadership. A church plant, if it is going to grow, will need to work on developing new leaders from the beginning. Griffith and Easum caution strongly against formalizing leadership structures too soon, however, which they say is one of the ten most common mistakes of new church plants:

> Formalizing the leadership and organization of the church too soon is dangerous. Whether it's bowing to pressure by zealous supervisors, current "unofficial" leaders, personal insecurities, or personal experience with a previous "church," the net effect is the same—a major sea change in the life of the church, and, more importantly, redirecting youthful energies away from mission to management. Either way, formalizing leadership too soon *always* hinders the growth of a plant. The organization of the plant needs time to find its indigenous roots in the mission field. Future leaders need time to prove themselves on the battlefield.[16]

I can verify from my own experience that when Nativity formed a Bishop's Committee and official structures quite soon after our launch (at the request of our diocese), doing so diverted an enormous amount of our energy away from evangelism toward creating and following bylaws and procedures and holding administrative meetings.

However, you do need leadership structures. As I mentioned above, a treasurer and finance committee is imperative from the beginning. Early on, Nativity also had a Ministry Council that met to take counsel for the good of the church and to brainstorm new ideas. This group generated great enthusiasm and commitment for the church's ministries.

The most important aspect of leadership development in a new plant is not to provide oversight, but to identify new potential leaders and empower and equip them to grow. You do not want your initial launch team to retain the iron grip of control over all ministries, you want them to be identifying

---

16. Ibid., 102.

and training their successors. That way, your ministry leaders won't burn out, and most importantly, new people will grow in their relationship with Christ as they watch Christ do powerful ministries through them. Bringing someone into leadership is the best way of generating commitment and enthusiasm for your church.

To develop leaders, the planter should focus on staff and lay leaders, meeting with staff weekly or semi-weekly, discussing leadership books together, sharing stories of what is going well and not so well, and encouraging each other in their ministries. The planter should meet with ministry leaders to train them on what leadership means, including recruiting and empowering others, and training successors. For ministry volunteers, it helps to have a job description for every ministry, along with on-the-job training and clear assignments. Clarity and purposefulness helps your members grow spiritually through the ministry work they do through your church.

An Approach to Formation of Christian Disciples

Christian formation is so important a subject that it gets its own chapter. It is to this subject that we will turn in chapter 11.

A Worship Facility

Where will you gather to worship, teach, pray, and send people out into the world to do God's mission? The answer can be simple and obvious, or complex and expensive. We will discuss this question more in chapter 12.

The Most Important Ingredient: Prayer

The day of a new church's launch is exciting, nerve-wracking, stressful, exhilarating, and joyful. It happens after months or even years of planning, gathering a community, raising up leadership, discerning God's mission, and plain hard work. The most important thing that the planter and launch team can do to ensure the kind of launch that will get the church into orbit is to pray. Pray for God to send people, resources, and miracles. Pray for God to give you strength, courage, and excitement for the days ahead. Pray for God to bless the new church that is coming to birth.   ❧

~ 11

Forming Christian Disciples

And Jesus came and said to them, "All authority in heaven and on earth has been given to me. Go therefore and make disciples of all nations, baptizing them in the name of the Father and of the Son and of the Holy Spirit, and teaching them to obey everything that I have commanded you. And remember, I am with you always, to the end of the age." Matthew 28:18–20

I appeal to you therefore, brothers and sisters, by the mercies of God, to present your bodies as a living sacrifice, holy and acceptable to God, which is your spiritual worship. Do not be conformed to this world, but be transformed by the renewing of your minds, so that you may discern what is the will of God—what is good and acceptable and perfect. For by the grace given to me I say to everyone among you not to think of yourself more highly than you ought to think, but to think with sober judgment, each according to the measure of faith that God has assigned. For as in one body we have many members, and not all the members have the same function, so we, who are many, are one body in Christ, and individually we are members one of another. We have gifts that differ according to the grace given to us: prophecy, in proportion to faith; ministry, in ministering; the teacher, in teaching; the exhorter, in exhortation; the giver, in generosity; the leader, in diligence; the compassionate, in cheerfulness. Romans 12:1–8

In Jesus' last words to his friends in the Gospel of Matthew, he commands them to go and make disciples. Disciples are people who have been converted to a new life in Christ, but they are more than that. As Paul said, they are people who have been transformed by the renewing of their minds. As they have immersed themselves in the gospel, worshiping and learning about Christ, they have begun to discern God's will, and they have been transformed from the inside out. As transformed people, they begin to discern and exercise their spiritual gifts according to the grace God has given them. They serve others, teach others, pray for others; they advocate for justice and work for a better world. They learn to walk in love, as Christ loved us and gave himself for us. Discipleship is a lifelong journey of transformation.

From Paul's standpoint, then, making disciples is a process that begins with evangelism, proclaiming the good news. It continues with Christian formation, which transforms people through the renewing of their minds. It comes to fruition as those disciples begin to minister to others in the church and in the world, using the grace given by God in their spiritual gifts.

As Christian leaders, we know that simply filling a worship service with enthusiastic participants is not enough if those worshipers are not becoming Christian disciples in their daily lives. How, then, do we form disciples in our newly planted churches? This should be a central, vital question for any church planting team, because it gets to the heart of the mission of the church, according to the Great Commission Jesus has given us. How we address the question of Christian formation will depend on each church's vision. Forming Christian disciples will look different in young adult congregations than it will in Latino congregations or suburban congregations. As with any aspect of church planting, your approach to Christian formation should be strategically tailored to your community and your population.

Be careful not to take on too much too soon, however. A church plant cannot excel in every area from the start; each church needs to carefully discern where God is calling it to concentrate in the beginning. As Frank Logue says, "I think that God gives you [the ability] to identify a need in the area, but you also have to have the gifts to meet that need; the two things have to come together. And there are some things the church never really needs to do, and there are some things that are yours, and the crossover is the need in the community together with whether you have the gifts to meet it."[1] A strategic focus on what God calls the church to do here and now is essential for a new church. Every church is called to make disciples, but not every church has to do it the same way. Some practices will be strategic imperatives for a church from the beginning, and some will develop over time. Each church must learn how to focus on the programs that are most important in the beginning; no church can spring into being fully formed, the way Athena sprang fully-grown from the head of Zeus. That was something that happened only in Greek mythology—even Jesus was born as a small child!

Therefore, every church needs to think carefully about how it will develop mature Christian disciples, but not every church will be able to accomplish every project from the very beginning. A church needs time to grow into full strength. As mentioned previously, Jim Griffith and Bill Easum name "failure of the church to act its age and size" as one of the ten most common mistakes made by church planters. They counsel that the new church must "decide on the essential ministries for your particular mission field, and delay all others until they are necessary."[2] The decision of what is essential depends on the community and the mission field. The error of trying to do too much at once is certainly one that Nativity has fallen into from time to time; one member of our church early on jokingly called it the "Church of the Activity." We had to learn to slow down and work on doing a few things very well, and not take on more projects until we had the resources and people to do them. Try to avoid burning out the planter, core team, and staff by doing too much at once; select a strategic focus from the beginning and build from there.

Formation of Adult Disciples

Many Episcopalians assume, tacitly or otherwise, that Christian formation is a service that a church provides for children and youth: adults worship and children go to Sunday school. But I strongly believe that the Episcopal

---

1. Logue, interview.
2. Griffith and Easum, *Ten Most Common Mistakes*, 97.

Church needs to grow out of this traditional attitude. Everyone needs to worship, and everyone needs to be formed in the Christian faith. Adults as well as children need Christian formation.

This desire for strong adult formation is not about wishing for well-attended programs. It is truly about wanting to make sure that Christians are constantly being "transformed by the renewing of their minds" in a way that helps them discern and exercise their spiritual gifts. It is about wanting people to have the experience of making deep friendships in the Body of Christ, praying, studying the Bible, caring for one another, and serving our community. Important as it is to learn about the Bible and the Christian faith, adult formation is not simply adult Christian education. Learning, according to Paul, is only one step in a lifetime of formation as a disciple. We are formed as Christian disciples as we learn and then put our learning into practice by ministering to others.

For instance, although strength in adult Christian education was not one of the charisms that Nativity prayed about and heard God leading us toward in the beginning, we have gradually increased and improved our offerings in adult Christian education over time. We have added Sunday, weekday, online, and small-group options, until adult formation has become a significant emphasis of our parish. Our part-time associate priest, whom we were able to add to our staff in our fourth year, leads this ministry, and several lay leaders facilitate small-group options. Participation in our many adult educational offerings is growing as we have devoted increasing attention to this area. Every year, we offer in-depth courses to help ground people in the Anglican approach to scriptures and worship, and these courses double as adult baptism and confirmation preparation. In developing these courses, we have been significantly influenced by The Restoration Project's approach, developed by Christopher Martin.[3] This approach involves offering four basic introductory modules over the course of a year (or several years), in Anglicanism, Bible, Christianity, and Discipleship. This basic education is integrated with encouragement to pray daily and serve others regularly. Our next step will be to develop discipleship groups to help people enter into

---

3. See The Restoration Project's website at http://www.therestorationproject.net and Christopher H. Martin's book, *The Restoration Project: a Benedictine Path to Wisdom, Strength, and Love* (Cincinnati, OH: Forward Movement, 2014).

deeper relationships with each other as they encourage each other in these practices and develop a Benedictine Rule of Life. These discipleship groups will be lay-led, an important step in developing lay persons as spiritual leaders and also ensuring that our discipleship ministries multiply, as they are not limited to clergy leadership.

But remember that as far as Paul is concerned, the "renewing of your minds" is only one step in being transformed. Christian transformation is lived out as disciples begin to exercise their spiritual gifts and serve others. From the beginning, the charism that Nativity has exercised is a talent for calling people into ministry. We are told that what strikes people when they attend worship at Nativity is our joyful welcome and our true interest in getting to know our members well, and inviting them to join us in serving others. We have been known to hand people a broom on their first Sunday and invite them to help clean up after coffee hour—and those people become committed Nativity members and coffee hour ministers. But we don't believe that service happens just inside the church; we are enthusiastic about our ministries in the community, and offer many different ways to serve those in need. The transformation that people experience in worship and education is put into action through our many ministries, including unusually active and generous outreach and social service ministries.

Nontraditional churches operate in different ways, and for some, Christian formation is foundational to their ways of gathering a community. For a nontraditional community like The Abbey in Birmingham, the "front door" to the community will be hospitality in the coffeehouse. The next step for someone who wants to experience the community, however, will be adult formation in the form of discussion groups, Bible studies, and one-on-one opportunities to talk with clergy. These activities will be the primary entrance to faith for The Abbey's young adult audience. Worship will follow as the groups find it appropriate. And as groups are formed into community, they will seek ways to serve their neighborhood by joining with others who are transforming the area. The Abbey's founders see this focus on service to others as a way of providing the kind of genuine authenticity that Millennial adults seek. Deacon Kellie Hudlow says:

> We are . . . talking about service, something that is really a long-term investment. Figuring out a way that we as the community of The Abbey

can plug into a variety of things: community kitchen, service projects. Because of the neighborhood we're going to be positioned in, it will open us up to participating in more long-term projects rather than just showing up on Saturday and painting a house. I think that touches a bit more deeply for folks that just don't want the Saturday morning experience, they want a longer-term relationship with someone that comes with a long-term project.[4]

Leaders in Latino churches talk about the extreme importance of adult Christian education for their congregations. Carmen Guerrero says that Christian formation for all ages is one of the foundational methods she uses to plant churches. For young people, first communion and confirmation classes are culturally expected. For adults, the classes can be truly transformative. "Bible study for everyone is a key, key thing," she says. "It helps them see who they are and how much they are worth in God's eyes. It affects how you behave, when you understand that. So many people just don't know that. I write a lot of teaching booklets. They have to come to class."[5]

Anthony Guillén agrees that adult Christian formation is essential for Latinos:

Often [in the Episcopal Church], adult formation is an inquirer's class in which we talk about the church, not about the gospel, Jesus, praying, or the spiritual journey. I'm as guilty as anyone. I tried in my church, but I spent a lot of time focusing on Sunday worship, not doing other things. One day my Latino congregation leaders came to me. There were fifteen or twenty people in my office, and they said, "You say we have a ministry, we have gifts. We believe it, but you need to teach us." I asked how, and they said, "Some of us would like to be teachers. We don't have the tools. You need to teach us. We want to study scripture, so teach us the Bible, church, leadership." I said okay, and did that for the next five years, developing leaders. They called me to it.

We have a lot of strengths we can build on. I think today if you were to ask most Latinos in our churches about why they're there, most would not tell you because it's a catholic church or because of the liturgy. They would tell you that what they found, what attracted

---

4. Rengers and Hudlow, interview.
5. Guerrero, interview.

them, was preaching that seemed directed to them. Many people have said, "I heard the gospel for very first time when came to the Episcopal Church after going to church all my life." . . . We are a people who are thoughtful; we think things. Latinos find they come and ask questions and people are willing to answer. It's okay to ask, you're not dumb.[6]

Other populations face different challenges. Clay Lein recognized the severe time challenges facing congregations full of busy suburban families, which limit attendance at church programming:

One of the key ways [of doing adult formation] for us was our sermon series. In a sense we recognized early on that we were getting a Sunday morning and more than that was going to be a challenge. So we had specific sermon series where we were opening the scriptures and explaining various things. So we had a sermon series on "how to": how to pray, how to read the Bible, how to share faith, how to have more of the Holy Spirit, how to hear God. We did a sermon series on viewer's choice, where we let the congregation pick their top five questions, for instance evolution. We would do a sermon series on a book of the Bible, and we would focus on Ephesians for over eight weeks while Ephesians was in the lectionary. I wrote a daily devotional on a section of it, and we read through the whole of Ephesians with a commentary kind of devotional each day. Then we would preach on that passage assigned for Sunday, so over the course of the summer we would be getting people to engage with it in a devotional way. So our sermon series were really built around trying to disciple people *in situ* in their worship time. . . . We had a sense that people needed to be involved in ministry, and that's how they were going to grow their faith, so we were always creating ministry opportunities both inside and outside the church. We have been externally focused from day one. Part of that is because if you are focused on helping someone in the community, you will probably meet Jesus in a way that is more real than just in a Sunday school class, so we were always creating service opportunities. We would meet with our core service staff, who were mostly soccer moms who had felt a call to be more active in leading others. We would go through a list of our

6. Guillén, interview.

people (we were always tracking), we called it Shepherds' Heart, who was being connected and involved and who was not. We would have a list of follow-up items to track people and invite them to get involved. All of that was trying to get people connected into the body's life and into the scriptures, and we felt that combination was going to disciple people and help them become Christians.[7]

But, as we discussed above, a church planter cannot do everything. Lang Lowrey expresses the challenge that confronts many church planters who take on the all-consuming job of making contacts in the community and starting a church:

> It was a real challenge for me to be intentional and develop faith. I didn't have time. I was spending all my time trying to identify people, respond pastorally, making ten calls a day, going to homes, hospitals, being the chaplain for a local high school, offering prayer on the sidelines. I was reaching out, doing anything I could. Offering programs was taking so much energy that I realized I would have a difficult job trying to develop lives of faith and spirituality. I went to the bishop and said, "Here's the bottom line—at some point you can't do too many things extremely well. I know you're supportive but I'm going to ask for help. I need a priest or a deacon. I will get people on the hook and reel them in, but I can't also do all the quality work. We need to develop spirituality." Our numbers were growing and he made the faithful decision to give me a young curate. He paid him for a year and let him be the center of that activity. His job was to develop prayer disciplines. . . . He did some of the other programs, started some in-depth teaching and spiritual practices, led some retreats, and online stuff. He also gave [us] the appearance that we were going to be a bigger church, not just a small Episcopal church.[8]

Lowrey's experience illustrates the truth that the church planter cannot do everything. More than that, the planter *should* not do everything. A planter who does not remember to ask God for the people to do the work, and who expects to take care of everything himself or herself, will needlessly

---

7. Lein, interview.
8. Lowrey, interview.

limit the kind of ministry the church can accomplish, because the planter will not be able to do everything well. And a planter who tries to do every ministry personally will be depriving others of the opportunity to exercise the spiritual gifts God has given them. One of the most essential things a planter can do is to call others into ministry.

John Adler, who founded Iona-Hope Episcopal Church in Fort Myers, Florida, writes about how the church created a small-group culture that helps people form relationships, develops church leaders, and accomplishes many areas of ministry without church staff directing those ministries.

> One of the ways we live into our core values is through collaborative leadership practiced through the use of small groups. From the beginning, we set up small groups to manage the usual necessities of a congregation (altar guild, hospitality, office angels), in answer to needs as they arise (adult living facility services, soup kitchen, technology team), and in response to a good idea (book club, memoirs for healing, shawl ministry).
>
> Our policy has always been if you have an idea we will help find a place for that idea to be fulfilled. Whenever someone has an idea for ministry all that is required is that they help identify a leader, complete a brief statement of purpose, and agree to follow the covenant established for small groups. Each vestry member is assigned a small number of groups to stay in touch with and to report on needs and activities at vestry meetings. Group leaders meet monthly with the rector.
>
> All of our groups operate on the same principles. Each small group has a lay pastor, a lay pastor apprentice, and a host as well as a statement of purpose and written agreements between the rector and each of the positions listed above. Each group also has a set of guidelines. Leadership positions are limited to three-year terms to prevent burn out and to make certain there are always positions for newcomers to move into leadership roles.[9]

This small-group culture is a wonderful illustration of how empowering lay people in the congregation to become leaders releases the spiritual gifts of not only those leaders, but of the many people they shepherd. Multiplying leadership in the congregation helps create a culture in which every person

---

9. John Adler, "Small Groups, Big Impact" in *Vestry Papers: Leading Change* (July 2014). http://www.ecfvp.org/vestrypapers/leading-change/small-groups-big-impact/.

can be formed as a Christian, whether they concentrate on Bible study, service within the group, or social justice ministries within the community. As people begin to serve, they grow in faith and knowledge of Christ. As church leaders help people grow, they are answering Jesus' call to go into all nations and make disciples.

Formation of Children and Youth

For some communities, formation of children and youth will be non-essential; for others, it will be crucial. At Nativity, from the beginning, we have known that our mission included a deep focus on children's and youth ministries. Our first hire was a musician to help lead worship, but very soon thereafter we hired a part-time children's ministries director, and we had lively Sunday morning children's and youth programs from the time we launched worship. In fact, our ministries with youth began before launching worship, as young people were full members of our launch team and helped us discern our mission. Our focus on children's and youth ministries has not happened by accident. It was a strategic focus, based on our answers to the questions outlined in chapter 7: Who are we? Who are our neighbors? And what is God calling us to be? We discovered that our launch team included several adults who were passionate about the importance of teaching and forming disciples of children and youth, including me (with my pre-ordination background as a lay Christian education director).

We researched our neighborhood and found large numbers of young people there, and knew that their parents would be looking for ways to raise their children in the faith of Jesus (or, at the very least, hoping to find a church their children enjoyed attending). We prayed and discerned that God was calling us to care specially for the least and smallest of people, specifically in this case, our young people. From the beginning, we knew that we needed to offer the best discipleship programs we could for our youngest members. Our staffing, budgeting, and programming has consistently reflected this priority.

A church that wants to focus strategically on ministries with young people needs to think through a number of issues. Who will lead these ministries? Lowrey narrates his experience with finding a children's ministries director for St. Benedict's:

Another godsend happened: one of the best children's ministers in the city . . . who lived in Smyrna . . . called me and said, "I know you can't pay me, I know you have office space, I can bring my computer, I live with my mom, I have insurance, I don't need attention, but I would like to help you build the church and become the children's director."[10]

This generous offer allowed St. Benedict's to build an excellent children's program from the beginning. At Nativity, we had a similar godsend, when an experienced Sunday school teacher joined our launch team, offered to become our unpaid children's director, and recruited a friend to join her in becoming our first Sunday school teaching team. (We began paying her as a staff person as soon as we had money to do it.) This was one of the miracles we grew accustomed to seeing at Nativity; when there was a need, God anticipated it before we did, and provided the person to fill the need.

I firmly believe that God provides the resources necessary to meet whatever needs a church has. If a resource is not provided, the church should think carefully about whether there is truly a need or simply a wish. Nativity also had a launch team member who dearly loved small children and wished to coordinate our nursery (which was staffed by that member and a paid professional caregiver), and a couple who had taught youth Sunday school and wanted to start a small youth program. The youth program in the beginning consisted of Sunday morning education, plus monthly evening gatherings at the youth leaders' home that included both confirmation classes and social events. We have grown our youth programs from there, and we now have a staff youth director, weekly youth gatherings, and a number of other offerings.

Leadership is, of course, the biggest challenge in developing programs for young people. As a lay Christian education director, I learned never to simply put out a public call for teachers and youth leaders, because of the risk that spiritually and emotionally unhealthy people would be the ones to respond, and I would not be able to accept them into that ministry. Leaders for children and youth should be handpicked and personally invited into the ministry. With vulnerable people like children, it should go without

10. Lowrey, interview.

saying that you must assign your best, healthiest, spiritually strongest leaders. Therefore, anxious as you might be to find someone to lead children, do not accept an offer from someone who makes you uncomfortable, or who seems to be looking for a place to exercise power, or who wants to do this ministry for personal gratification and not as a service to the young people. Yes, our ministries should bring us joy, but they should be exercised out of a deep desire to serve others and help them grow.

In a new church, you will have some handicaps because you will not have much history with the people on the launch team, and will not necessarily be able to determine on short acquaintance whether people are healthy enough to work with children. Get references for people you haven't worked with before who want to minister with young people, to discover a measure of comfort with their emotional functioning, and whether they have a gift of teaching. It is one thing to use untested volunteers as ushers or lay readers; it is quite another to let them loose on your vulnerable young people.

On the other hand, I have found that many healthy people who are invited into teaching ministries are too humble; they think they don't know enough to teach. As a lay Christian education director, I learned to anticipate this response to almost every invitation. My reply was always the same: they were invited because of their Christian commitment, creativity, and care for young people, not because of their extensive knowledge of the Bible. The church will provide a curriculum, and it will teach leaders what they need to know; the best way to learn something, after all, is to teach it. What is important in teachers is not their level of knowledge, but their levels of love and commitment.

In assigning leaders to work with children and youth, we felt it was important from the beginning to ensure the young people's safety. Of course we insisted that all leaders take the "Safeguarding God's Children" training offered by our diocese. We also developed a policy that we would always have two adult leaders present with any child, both to protect the children from a harmful encounter with an adult, and to protect the adults from any accusation of wrongdoing. When ministering with young, vulnerable people, I believe that having such a safety policy is imperative, for the good of all involved.

When choosing a leader for your children's and youth ministries, look for a person who is able to recruit and empower others. The best children's ministry leaders I have worked with have been those who quickly develop friendships with the parents of new children, discern their hopes and dreams for their children, and invite them into ministries they are suited for. A children's or youth leader who insists on doing all the ministry herself or himself will be just like a priest who fails to empower a team of lay leaders. Hoarding ministry means the church will be able to do much less. Empowering ministry results in a true blossoming of offerings, as people bring talents into service that you didn't realize you needed. One of our early Sunday school teachers, for instance, was an accomplished actress and director, who helped us develop a family drama ministry, something that had never occurred to me to start. Several years later, just after that teacher moved away, a new, similarly experienced actor and director joined our church and took over leadership of the drama ministry. Again, God provided exactly what was needed at exactly the right time, and our possibilities for ministry multiplied because the people God sent led the way, rather than my preconceived ideas of what we should offer.

One of the primary questions church leaders who expect significant involvement from families with children and youth need to address is how to involve those young people in worship. Sunday morning scheduling will be a major strategic decision, and your children's and youth programs will need to be considered carefully in your scheduling. As I said before, I believe that both children and adults need to worship, and both children and adults need to be educated. That does not mean they need to worship or be educated in the same way. At Nativity, for instance, we offer Sunday school for all ages, at a time separate from worship. We also offer a children's chapel during the first half of our major worship service, for children ages four through second grade. This is a Liturgy of the Word offered at a child's pace, to help the children understand the gospel and join in the prayers. The children join their parents in church for the Liturgy of the Table. Like many ministries, we were not able to offer children's chapel when we first began, because we did not have the leaders for it; we have added this option as we grew. We arrived at this method after deep consideration of how best to make sure our children can worship. Some churches take different approaches: full inclusion of children in adult worship, on one end of the spectrum, or offering Sunday school during worship and not including children in worship at all, on the other end. There are advantages to each of these approaches, but the church needs to address them strategically. What do we want our children to experience, how do we feel that they can best enter the presence of God, and what leaders do we have available to accomplish these goals?

It will be important early on to think about sacramental preparation with families. As a church planter, you will likely find yourself doing far more baptisms and confirmations than funerals, orders of magnitude more, a wonderful problem to have. You will need to decide what kind of preparation to offer for both adults and children, and how to emphasize these rites as true conduits of the Holy Spirit. Some families will also expect First Communion preparation for their children, especially if the parents are former Roman Catholics. Although I prefer to give communion to children from the time they are baptized, I do follow their parents' preference. I have found it essential to provide First Communion instruction from time to time in a format that doubles as simple Lenten (or other) enrichment for children who already take communion.

As your programs develop, and as new leaders present themselves, you will want to think about adding to your offerings for children and youth. At some point you will want to add special holy day events: Ash Wednesday, First Sunday in Advent, Christmas pageant, Easter children's events. Do not wear yourself out in the beginning by offering all of these things, but add them as people become available to lead them. If you are worshiping in temporary quarters, like a school, which you do not have access to during the week, it will be a big challenge to offer midweek or summer Vacation Bible School programs. You can consider combining with another nearby church to provide these offerings, or you can simply wait for the right time. Building a full children's and youth program happens slowly, beginning with the essentials.

The formation of Christian disciples, whether children, youth, or adults, is one of the most important ministries a church can undertake. Your team should approach these questions carefully and strategically. Most of all, you should pray for God's guidance. Ask God to show you the way to begin with the most essential ministries first, and to provide the people necessary to do the things God calls you to do. In my experience, God always provides.   ❧

12

A Worship Facility

On the sabbath day we [Paul, Timothy, and Luke] went outside the gate by the river, where we supposed there was a place of prayer; and we sat down and spoke to the women who had gathered there. A certain woman named Lydia, a worshiper of God, was listening to us; she was from the city of Thyatira and a dealer in purple cloth. The Lord opened her heart to listen eagerly to what was said by Paul. When she and her household were baptized, she urged us, saying, "If you have judged me to be faithful to the Lord, come and stay at my home." And she prevailed upon us. Acts 16:13–15

Paul gathered people to hear the word of God and to worship, wherever and whenever he could. Sometimes he spoke in public places, like the riverside in Philippi, where he met Lydia. Often, he spoke in local synagogues, continuing weekly until the synagogue leaders asked him to leave (see Acts 19:8–10). He used public gathering facilities when necessary, like the lecture hall of Tyrannus in Ephesus (Acts 19:8–10). When a group of disciples was ready to form a consistent community, they often began meeting in the house of one of the leaders, like Lydia, and when Paul moved on to the next city, he left a cadre of leaders behind to shepherd the church in that house. In Paul's letters, for instance, he sends greetings to and from the church in the house of Prisca and Aquila (Romans 16:3-5 and 1 Corinthians 16:19). By that time, the church in their house had reached some measure of stability and structure, enough that the group of believers was known by the place where they met. We don't hear much about how those house churches fared, though. Did their move to a more permanent, private location insulate them from their surrounding communities, making it more difficult for them to meet others and tell them the good news of Christ? Or did having a regular place to gather offer the stability they needed, both to worship and to reach out to others?

People need a place to gather. Churches are communities of people gathered together to glorify God, and scattered into the neighborhood to serve God in their lives. It is fashionable these days for church leaders to declare that buildings are a thing of the past and that the ideal future church will not have facilities. This is an easy concept to dream of if you have never tried to lead a church without a reasonably dependable facility in which to gather. The simple truth is, whether it is owned, leased, or borrowed, people need a place to gather. Generally, a church needs to worship in a consistent, reliable place—one that has walls, a roof, climate control, and restrooms.

Bishop Kirk Smith of Arizona speaks wistfully of the dream that a church might be able to operate without a building:

> I think the church of the future will be a mixed body for a while. I think we're going to continue to have traditional churches, and at the same time we will make more room for alternative, emergent things; they will co-exist for a while. I think we need to be open to new expressions. . . . A Lutheran bishop I know said that a church community can meet in a school for five years, but then it will fall apart. In theory I would love to see a community that said, "We don't really care about a church building, we care about the community around us, and we would rather use our resources to impact the community than build a building." But it's in our DNA, wanting a place to call our own. Sometimes when congregations build buildings the missionary impulse dissipates. It's a challenge we have to face. Even in emergent communities they have this feeling, they would like their own place that belongs to them. It's a built-in reflex, but a church is people, not a building.[1]

1. Kirk Smith, telephone interview with the author, August 26, 2014.

As a traditional church planter myself, I can tell you that the facility question will be one of the most vexing, difficult, and expensive questions many of us will face. It is easy to assert that a "church without walls" will be the wave of the future, and it is attractive to think about a church as a group of itinerant missionaries out traveling the by-ways for Christ. But even the Franciscans ended up with fixed locations. And Christopher Carlisle, the founder of Cathedral in the Night, which worships outdoors as part of its strategy to minister to homeless people, says that its leaders chose the place to gather that congregation each week because homeless people are "location-specific and territorial."[2] That craving for a sense of place seems to be deep-seated in the human psyche. There are a few congregations that gather outdoors, but even those normally meet in a consistent place each week. People do need a place to gather, whether that place belongs to them or not. Thad's in the Diocese of Los Angeles does not plan ever to own a facility, but has worshiped in four different rented facilities, moving each time the congregation grows large enough to need more space. This model provides flexibility while still allowing the congregation to count on a consistent place to gather.

However we find and pay for consistent, dependable facilities, the challenge, as Smith points out above, will be to find a place to gather and yet not lose the missionary impulse. There are indeed times when a congregation locates in a fixed facility and settles down, believing it has arrived home and need do no further work. Leaders of churches that do find a fixed location need to work hard to keep the evangelistic vision alive.

Some churches will be able to adopt creative solutions like sharing space with another Episcopal congregation. This approach works very well if the new congregation being started is quite different from the one that is already there; worship in a language other than English, for instance, or a Fresh Expressions church appealing to a nontraditional population. In Phoenix, three congregations share the building of St. Mary's Episcopal Church: the traditional Anglo-Catholic congregation that has been there for many years; Iglesia Santa Maria, (Guerrero's Spanish-speaking congregation); and St. Jude's, a congregation aimed at urban youth. Multiple congregations sharing one space will inevitably have challenges allocating that space between them, and will have to work with the danger that the congregations might see each

2. Carlisle, interview.

other as outsiders, rather than sisters and brothers in Christ. But this solution is a natural approach for many dioceses that have some declining traditional congregations, and not enough congregations reaching out to new populations. It offers a way to make creative use of an existing capital asset for a new initiative that can answer God's call to new generations of Episcopalians. It is also a natural approach for many cathedrals, which are often located in downtown areas with very diverse populations. The Crossing in Boston, for instance, was born out of the Cathedral Church of St. Paul.

For many church plants, however, such a creative solution will not be available. This is especially true for traditional church plants that are intentionally located in areas that do not already have an Episcopal church.

Nativity, during its eight years of existence, has worshiped in three different places. We began by worshiping in an elementary school in our neighborhood, an ideal location. It was centrally located, easy to find, and had the facilities we needed: a large cafeteria for worship; a teacher's lounge, which we used as a combination sacristy, nursery, and adult education classroom; and a portable classroom building, which we used for Sunday school. We had access to the school restrooms and were required to pay a school janitor to open up, lock up, and clean up after us each Sunday. He also helped us set up and take down, out of his own kindness. (We hired him as our part-time sexton when we moved out of the school.) The parking was adequate. While the school cafeteria was not beautiful, with its white linoleum floors and fluorescent lights, it was large and welcoming, and we brought in altars and banners and flowers to make it lovely, reverent, and worshipful. Many people told us that once they stepped inside our worship area, they forgot they were in a school. The rent was extremely reasonable, and we had full access to the school all Sunday morning. We held our ministry meetings at people's houses, and we met newcomers and parishioners for coffee and lunch.

The school was an ideal place to start our church. But less than a year after we began, the school informed us that they no longer wanted to host a church, and we needed to find another place. We talked the school into letting us stay another six months while we searched for a new place, but that experience highlighted for me the danger of counting on a rented facility unless you have a dependable long-term lease. If we had not found another location (and there were not many affordable options in our area), or if the school had stuck to its original timeline and insisted that we leave before finding another place to meet, our promising, rapidly growing church would have died. Where could we have met? There were no homes large enough to hold us, and the weather outside was too undependable. People do need a place to gather.

After an extensive search failed to turn up another acceptable, affordable location for us, a miracle occurred. A member of the congregation stepped forward and offered to let us use a 5,000-square-foot suite that he owned in an office building, full-time and rent-free for five years. This amazing generosity allowed our church to survive and thrive. In our office building, we set up a sanctuary that seated about 150 people (where we soon expanded to two services per Sunday), with an overflow/narthex area that would seat another 30. We had offices, three small classrooms, a nursery, and a hospitality kitchen. We used the office building's lobby for Sunday morning hospitality, and the upstairs elevator lobby for adult education. We had access to the church facility all the time, unlike the school, and were able to hold ministry meetings, events, classes, Bible studies, and counseling sessions much more easily. But the office building was slightly outside our target neighborhood and rather difficult to find; we were hidden away. Two years after beginning to worship there, knowing that we had only three years left on our lease, we began searching for a permanent facility.

Unfortunately, real estate in our neighborhood is prohibitively expensive. Our diocese owned a piece of land they would have let us use, but it was far north of our target neighborhood, in an area where very few people lived. We searched exhaustively for an affordable alternative that would let us continue our mission, and finally found a remarkable opportunity. It was a half-built structure that was intended to be a 24,000 square foot, two-story office building, but it went into foreclosure and was abandoned mid-construction. It stood half-built, roofless and open to the sky, for several years before we bought it "as is," redesigned it, and built out the first floor only, saving the rest for later expansion. We do not own any land, only a condominium interest in the building, but we have access to an open area that we can use for outdoor events. We don't own our parking lot, but we use three hundred parking spaces on evenings and weekends that belong to the business development; on weekdays during business hours we have access to fifty parking spaces. We have a beautiful, functional facility, with a nave that can seat 250, which can be expanded later to seat 400. Every part of the building is designed to be multi-functional, and can easily be rearranged for different uses. The new building is in the center of our target area, close to many homes, down the street from an elementary school and a park, and very visible on a major street.

This building was a creative solution to a very difficult modern challenge: how to find a dependable church facility in an area of astronomical real estate prices. We paid for the building through contributions from our parishioners, a small amount of proceeds from the sale of the diocesan land, and a loan from a parishioner, more than half of which we have already been able to repay (within two years). I count the opening of this building as another miracle. Having a permanent building of our own, albeit with a decidedly nontraditional twist since we will never own any land, has allowed us to offer programs to benefit our community, such as after-school enrichment programs and community meeting spaces. Having the building has allowed us to expand our own ministry, providing Vacation Bible School and other school vacation programs for our members.

The saga of Nativity's facility searches illustrates the kinds of challenges that every planter must face. How will the church provide a space to bring people together? This is such a central question that every church planter who does not already have a space provided by the diocese should start praying about it immediately. In today's world, facilities that work for a church are expensive and hard to find. God does send remarkable answers to prayer, as Nativity's and other churches' experiences illustrate. The facility will dictate a great deal about what your church is able to become. The growth of any one worship service or gathering will be limited to the capacity of the worship area, the parking lot, the Sunday school classrooms, and the hospitality space. If any of these are 70 to 80 percent full on a regular basis, the church's growth will plateau. Choose a facility with the church's long-term vision in mind.

Any church's facilities will depend on what its diocese or sponsoring parish is willing to underwrite, what is available in its neighborhood, and what its members are able to support. In Arizona, churches can rent public school property, but this is not the case in all states. Some planters will have to look elsewhere for temporary facilities to rent: movie theaters, subdivision community rooms, private schools, existing churches or synagogues, hotel conference rooms, funeral home chapels, community centers, YMCA or Boys &

Girls Club facilities, businesses, coffee shops, bars, homes, and so on. Finding a suitable place requires creativity and persistence.

Most churches will begin in temporary, not permanent, facilities, and this is a good thing. As Griffith and Easum say, we no longer live in a "build it and they will come" culture. The planter's task in the early years of a church is to build a community, not a building. If a church's vision includes a permanent, owned facility, then that vision can be realized in time, through the efforts and contributions of the church members. But before pouring money into an expensive facility, you need to create a growing, thriving community.

No temporary facility will be absolutely ideal, but look for:

- Something as close to the center of your target neighborhood as you can find;
- Something visible, on a major street if possible;
- A facility big enough to allow for growth in the crowds you expect;
- Clean and well-maintained buildings and grounds;
- Clean and easily located restrooms;
- Classroom facilities, if you will offer children's Sunday school;
- Some way for people to gather for hospitality;
- Good, close, safe parking with enough spaces to accommodate a crowd (one parking space for every two people you expect in worship);
- Storage on site, if you can get it.

Some churches rent a large facility, like a school, for Sunday worship only, and rent an offsite meeting and office location elsewhere for weekday use. Doing so allows for more offerings of weekday Bible studies and classes. Nativity chose not to spend this money. Our staff had home offices and met in coffee shops; our classes, meetings, and Bible studies were held in homes.

Wherever you locate and however you set it up will say a great deal about who your church is and what it dreams of becoming. Look for a facility that gives you all the strategic advantages you can find. Pray for God to send you the right solution, and the money to pay for it. And work hard to keep the congregation's priorities in the right place: a church is not a building, a church is people gathered to follow Christ on a mission to the world. ❧

13

Finances and Stewardship

Now the whole group of those who believed were of one heart and soul, and no one claimed private ownership of any possessions, but everything they owned was held in common. With great power the apostles gave their testimony to the resurrection of the Lord Jesus, and great grace was upon them all. There was not a needy person among them, for as many as owned lands or houses sold them and brought the proceeds of what was sold. They laid it at the apostles' feet, and it was distributed to each as any had need. There was a Levite, a native of Cyprus, Joseph, to whom the apostles gave the name Barnabas (which means "son of encouragement"). He sold a field that belonged to him, then brought the money, and laid it at the apostles' feet. Acts 4:32–37

The point is this: the one who sows sparingly will also reap sparingly, and the one who sows bountifully will also reap bountifully. Each of you must give as you have made up your mind, not reluctantly or under compulsion, for God loves a cheerful giver. And God is able to provide you with every blessing in abundance, so that by always having enough of everything, you may share abundantly in every good work. . . . You will be enriched in every way

for your great generosity, which will produce thanksgiving to God
through us; for the rendering of this ministry not only supplies the
needs of the saints but also overflows with many thanksgivings to
God. Through the testing of this ministry you glorify God by your
obedience to the confession of the gospel of Christ and by the gener-
osity of your sharing with them and with all others, while they long
for you and pray for you because of the surpassing grace of God
that he has given you. Thanks be to God for his indescribable gift!
2 Corinthians 9:6–15

The earliest records of the Christian church show Christians exercising
remarkable generosity. Luke insists in the Acts of the Apostles that
the first Christians in Jerusalem shared all property in common, erasing
all need in the community in an astonishing way that for Luke was a sign
of the Holy Spirit's action in the church. Paul's letters show that common
ownership did not extend to the churches outside Jerusalem, but that dif-
ferences between rich and poor persisted, and even caused problems in
the church in Corinth. Nevertheless, Paul called Christians to a greater
standard than simply hoarding their wealth; he exhorted them to cheerful
generosity. He believed that Christian generosity arises out of overflowing
thanksgiving to God, and therefore it glorifies God.

Some church leaders shy away from discussing money and the Christian
discipline of giving and budgeting, but this reluctance has no basis in scripture. The Bible recognizes that money represents the fruit of our labors, and
therefore how we use our money shows, in a very real way, what our priorities are. Say what we want to about what is important to us, our check
registers tell the real story. The way we use our money reflects what we truly
believe. Some Episcopal leaders find it difficult to talk about money openly,
or to preach and teach about it as a spiritual issue. Yet the Bible addresses
the question of money repeatedly, from beginning to end, and Jesus makes
it very clear that money is indeed a spiritual issue of vital importance. We
cannot serve both God and money, and we cannot compartmentalize the two
into different spheres. Our use of our financial resources is no different from
our use of time or any other resource available to us. Learning to give more
generously is one spiritual discipline that helps us open our hearts and grow
in relationship with Christ. Yet money is a profound secret in our society;

discussing our own financial situation in public is a bigger taboo than discussing our sex lives. I believe that all church leaders need to get over their shyness about dealing with money, but addressing financial issues openly and from a Christian standpoint is absolutely essential for most church planters. As a church planter, you will have to get comfortable with talking about money, asking for money, budgeting money, writing grants for money, and giving money yourself.

As the leader of a nonprofit organization, you also need to know what each of your contributors is giving. I have spoken with a number of priests who refuse to look at members' giving because they don't trust themselves to treat the parishioners the same if they know what they give. I believe this attitude is a serious mistake, for several reasons. First, if we don't trust ourselves to give appropriate pastoral care to givers and non-givers alike, we might need to pray about our own hearts. Second, people's giving is often a substantial clue to their spiritual and emotional states of mind. A committed giver whose giving suddenly drops off may have personal issues—a lost job, a pending divorce, an illness—that you should know about, as their priest, or they may have problems with the church you should also know about as the church's leader. Third, as the leader, you need to know whom you can count on for additional fundraising in times of need. The most generous givers are often happy to help with special projects. Fourth, you should know each person's level of giving before you discern who is called into leadership. No one should be given a major leadership role, such as a vestry position, without being a committed giver, or they will simply encourage the other church members to become committed non-givers like themselves. Fifth, my experience has been, in most cases, that the biggest givers demand the least attention, and the tiniest givers are most likely to issue complaints and demands. This is because giving, in a very real way, can be a measure of someone's spiritual health. Before you let yourself be lassoed by people's demands, it helps to know their level of commitment in all ways—attendance, ministry involvement, and giving. It should go without saying in this discussion that the measure of a "big" or "small" giver should not be simply in dollar amounts, but in what they give in proportion to their income. The "widow's mite" is indeed a large and committed sacrifice that should be treated with respect and appreciation.

Another of the ten most common mistakes made by new churches according to Jim Griffith and Bill Easum is the fear of talking about money until it is too late:

> We've yet to see a church plant fail because of lack of funding. What we do see are church planters who do one or several of the following:
>
> - Create unnecessary financial crises by failing to talk about money
> - Dangerously dilute the gospel that calls for Christ's followers to place all of themselves under the authority of God
> - Greatly underestimate the cost of growing the church to where it has a positive bottom line void of subsidies
> - Display grossly inadequate money management skills
> - Have a cavalier approach toward discussions about money, bordering on arrogance, suggesting God's blessing of finances is a guarantee
> - Do not understand the meaning of "cash flow"
> - Wrongly assume that most problems can be solved by more money
> - In their zeal to be "cutting edge," find themselves at odds with Jesus' teaching on discipleship by failing to focus on teaching stewardship from day one.[1]

Churches do need money to do ministry, and the church planter should reconcile himself to the reality that it will be his responsibility not only to raise funds to support the church (and bring it to self-supporting status, in many cases), but also to teach members that generosity is one of the spiritual disciplines of the Christian life. From the beginning, planters should request their launch team members to give generously, according to their means, to the ministries of the church. People who are not invested enough in the new church's ministries to give financially have either not been converted to Christian discipleship or are not truly committed to the church. Either way, they should not be part of a launch team.

Clay Lein talks about how he made the spiritual discipline of stewardship a priority at St. Philip's Frisco:

---

1. Griffith and Easum, *Ten Most Common Mistakes*, 77.

[We did this] in a couple of ways. In our new member class, it was dinner at my house for the first five years, and we would probably get about twenty-five people every month. We would have dinner, share some of the gospel story, and then communicate our five values. They've changed since then, but [it was based on the five fingers on the hand, and they were] worship, learning, serving or impact, and fellowship, and then there was always the thumb, and that last one was giving. From the beginning I would always emphasize giving with people as a way of growing faith and impacting the world for Christ. From the beginning, I talked about giving as something *they* needed, not something *we* needed. I would even tell people, "I don't even care if you give to the church, what I want you to learn to do is to become more generous in giving to God somewhere." We always got a lot of feedback on that. People would say, "That's the first time I've ever heard a pastor say I don't have to give to their church." And that was part of what we were trying to do, we were trying to create a different paradigm. It's not about supporting the budget of this institution; it was about growing faith and testing that God will provide for us.

So we would start there. . . . We always would have a sermon series in the fall, and I actually really enjoyed preaching about giving, because my life was changed because of giving, my faith grew because of being in seminary and tithing our food stamps. When you got nothing you can still trust God by tithing. So we would do sermon series, about four to five weeks. We would address the issue head-on right out of the scriptures. We would give practical examples out of that. I would share stories of myself, other people would share stories, so they knew normal people were wrestling with this stuff too. We've always had pledges. We would have a season of prayer, often twenty-one days of prayer, whenever financially we began to struggle, so we were always connecting it to our faith. And people after several years began to get that. I guess the other thing I would say is that I had to lead that. I had to not just tithe but every year that I would challenge people to grow their generosity, I would have to bump up 1%, until for Jill and I, our largest check, period, was our giving. And I think that is an essential invisible thing that helps create inside our congregation a sense of stewardship.

Giving with generous hearts is not something that is limited to suburban congregations. In Guerrero's Latino congregation, giving is very important. Many of the members of Iglesia Santa Maria are first- or second-generation immigrants, living on the fringes of society. For these folks, it is too difficult to pledge because they don't know whether they will be employed next week. If they made a pledge and then lost their job and were unable to fulfill the pledge, Guerrero says, they would be ashamed, and would simply stop coming to church, no matter how much she tried to reassure them that they could change their pledge. So she does not ask for pledges. But that doesn't mean that the members do not give. It is a matter of pride to them to be able to contribute to the church. When each family joins, she gives them a set of offering envelopes, and each week every member of the family puts the dollars they have been able to put aside in the offering envelope. Together, they offer the envelope proudly at the time of the offertory. New worshipers, she says, see other families offering their envelopes, and they ask her for their envelopes, too. The members of the church take pride in the church, and pride in the fact that their offerings are important to God.

Mary MacGregor speaks about the importance of teaching stewardship in the church:

> We do a lousy job of stewardship [in the Episcopal Church]. Two percent of the average Episcopalian's income goes to the church. There are plenty of resources there. The other emphasis has to be on stewardship education, raising awareness, planned giving, annual giving, how we teach about money and stewardship. [We need to] work through the culture of fear around money and scarcity. [If we gave in a way that was] born out of generosity and thankfulness, we would have the money to do what we need to do.[2]

Much of the discussion of money in the twenty-first century church revolves around tight budgets and declining revenues. The God we serve is generous, giving us everything we need for life. We live in a nation of abundant resources. Yet at every level of the church, discussing how to allocate scarce resources produces more anxiety than almost any other conversation. Many parishes have seen their revenues decline as the church has shrunk in

---

2. MacGregor, interview.

size, and this contraction of financial resources has in turn reduced the money available for mission at the diocesan and church-wide levels. I would not be surprised to find that the single largest reason the Episcopal Church plants so few new congregations is that diocesan leaders feel that they just don't have the money to do it. As revenues fall, we grow more and more worried about scarcity, and are less and less likely to undertake bold new initiatives, even if those new initiatives are the very actions that could reverse the decline. If we are devoting an overwhelming majority of our resources to maintaining current ministries, and devoting very little to God's mission in our communities, the message is clear: taking care of "insiders" is the most important thing to us. Yet God's mission asks us to move away from concern with ourselves. We do this by devoting resources to ministries of service to those in need, and we do it by proclaiming the gospel to those who have not heard it.

How Much Does it Cost to Plant a Church?

How much money does it cost to plant a church? The answer, of course, varies by the vision of the church, where it ministers, and what type of congregation it can expect to gather. Depending on diocesan policies, a church can be planted on a shoestring budget, or it can cost significant amounts of money. But there are many examples of churches being planted for far less diocesan money than one might expect. Miracles do happen. Retired Bishop Claude Payne of Texas called the church "a community of miraculous expectation." Miracles happen because God is with us. God does unexpected things enough that the unexpected becomes the commonplace. Church planting is a discipline in which faith flourishes because we see the unlikely and unexpected become a reality so often.

In the case of Church of the Nativity, the diocese promised to pay my salary for the first year, two-thirds of my salary for the second year, and one-third of my salary for the third year. After that, the church was expected to (and did) take on my full salary. In addition, they promised us $10,000 a year in operating funds for those three years. As it turned out, we never drew on those funds because we were able to raise all the money we needed for operations from our congregation. The diocese also gave us a piece of land that had long ago been purchased for another failed church plant, but was not well located for us. We sold that land for $300,000 and put the money into our permanent building, which cost about $2.7 million in all. (Taking that land off the diocese's hands actually saved the diocese money, because they were paying property taxes on it.) In all, I estimate that the diocesan contribution to Nativity came to about $150,000 plus a non-productive piece of land.[3] Nativity has raised all the money for its operating budget, including taking on my salary over the course of the first three years, and raised all the money for our building from our members. We now pay over $90,000 a year in diocesan assessment, meaning the diocese broke even on Nativity years ago. A thriving congregation exists now, in a building that, if the congregation ever disappeared, would be worth many times the money the diocese originally invested.

Similarly, Thad's in the Diocese of Los Angeles was planted with very little up-front diocesan investment. According to Jimmy Bartz, the diocese contributed $20,000 the first year, out of a total budget of $360,000; Thad's has been a self-sustaining community ever since. Bartz explains that Thad's is in a fairly well-off area and reaches out to entertainment industry professionals, so it was his intention from the beginning that it be self-sustaining. He started the church with "venture capital" from several committed Christians, and the church members have supported the church from the beginning:

> I'm not saying every congregation should be financially self-sustaining, but in certain communities and certain economic contexts we should expect that. If I hear one thing from young seminarians, they say, "I would love to do that, but the bishop didn't give me any money." I say my bishop didn't give me any money either. Claude Payne told me early when shepherding me, "Money follows mission; if you get clear on mission, the resources will be there." In most of his contexts that was always true.[4]

Of course it is not true in every context that money follows mission, Bartz acknowledges. We should absolutely be planting churches in areas of high population that might not ever be self-sustaining because of economic conditions. But there are certain contexts, like Bartz's and like mine, where a church can be planted without much up-front investment, and which will

---

3. Note that the diocese did not provide my health insurance because I am covered by my spouse; the cost of the planter's salary and benefits would be higher if, as expected, the diocese provided health insurance for the planter and family.
4. Bartz, interview.

be self-supporting within a short period of time. Diocesan leaders who are interested in planting churches but are overwhelmed by the fear of having to find funds to provide several years of salary, operating expenses, and funds for a building program need to remember that the diocese will not be the one providing all of these funds. In many cases, the congregations that do not yet exist will gather together and, inspired by the power of the gospel and the vision of the church, generously give most of the money needed. What the diocese (or the sponsoring parish) must do is provide the initial seed money, the permission, prayer, and emotional support to make God's vision a reality.

St. Benedict's in the Diocese of Atlanta was a church plant that, like Nativity, quickly paid back the initial investment, and is now subsidizing the diocese's declining revenues from other congregations:

> St. Benedict's is now paying assessment equal to the decline in assessment for twenty to thirty churches. Those are churches destined to not do well in declining rural areas. The diocese put $250,000 into St. Benedict's and got more in return. St. Benedict's is now in the top five in the diocese for paying assessment. . . . It not only plugged the hole of decline, but it is paying back the initial investment. The prospects of smaller churches in rural areas aren't as good [because of] changing demographics, but when we plant successful churches, we are much better off. New product replaces old products, which would eventually die.[5]

For St. Benedict's, Lowrey found a creative solution to the facilities issue that ended up costing the diocese and the congregation very little. The church bought an unused church building for $7 million, and financed it by using the building for a school during the week. The school's rent covered the debt on the building, and the diocese did not contribute toward the church's permanent facilities.

Frank Logue (King of Peace's founder), now the Canon to the Ordinary in the Diocese of Georgia, points out that church planting is not as expensive to a diocese in the long term as people think:

> In this diocese it amazes me; we have yet to lose money on a church plant. Nobody ever talks about that. . . . Everywhere we went, even where we failed, the group bought land to bank away and that land

---

5. Lowrey, interview.

retained value. Just from a purely monetary standpoint, we have yet to lose a dollar on church planting. We should do it if we were losing every dollar we spent, but we don't. That happens everywhere. What's funny about this is people talk about church plants as if they are some sort of drain on the diocesan budget, when in our diocese even failed church plants have not drained the diocesan budget. We have failed and ended up monetarily ahead. I only say that because that's a major obstacle. That's why we don't put that money into the churches we have, because we know that new churches grow better than existing churches. . . . We know you can't buy momentum; there's no amount of money you can put into a stagnant church and make that church not stagnant.[6]

Note that Logue's point about failed church plants not costing the Diocese of Georgia money arises because that diocese has historically purchased land for its church plants, and land generally retains or increases in value. It is true, however, that some church plants can run a significant expense and still fail, and cost a significant amount of money in total, because land was never purchased. Other plants that succeed still cost the diocese money, because the congregation will likely never be wealthy enough to afford the plant-er's salary or to fully support the operations of the congregation, due to the economic status of the congregations they serve. Dioceses who plant these churches need to do it with a sincere conviction that it is God's call to them, and with a long-term, unshakeable commitment to supporting operations of the church.

A number of dioceses, in addition to Georgia, support their church plants by buying land. Generally the congregation is expected to grow to the point that it can finance the construction of its own building. The land purchase, then, becomes a strategic decision that the diocese makes very early in the church planting process, sometimes even before calling a planter. For King of Peace, the Diocese of Georgia purchased a well-located piece of land that had a small house on it. Since no other facilities were available, the church tore out some walls and used the house as a worship facility until it built its permanent building. For St. Philip's Frisco in the Diocese of Dallas, Lein says the purchase of ten acres of land on a major road was "like booster rockets"[7]

6. Logue, interview.
7. Lein, interview.

for the church's growth. St. Philip's started worship in a school, but put a sign on its land directing people to the new church, and eventually built on the land its diocese purchased. Lein says:

> Our diocese was extremely supportive. . . . They were clear that they wanted a church in Frisco, and they knew where they wanted it to be; they were going to begin by buying ten acres of land or something in that ballpark. They ended up spending about $1 million. I remember having lunch with my bishop after that had happened and I asked him what he was going to do after St. Philip's, and he kind of looked at me, smiled and he said, "Well, there isn't an 'after St. Philip's,' we're betting everything on this working." It was like, gulp, "Wow, you guys are really all-in on this," and that was really scary and encouraging at the same time. They bought the ten acres of land. . . [and] it itself is a miracle story. I can look out right now and see the tollway, which is the main artery here in Frisco. You can see us from all around (we're on a hill and it just is an amazing gift), but they gave us that. Then they gave us $200,000 in phases: $100,000 the first year, $67,000 the second year, $33,000 the third year, and then good luck. . . . I had to raise the rest, enough to pay my salary and rent our ministry center, which ended up being about $5,000 a month, to pay our part-time staff. And then an associate here (a woman priest named Katherine Thompson), found out about what we were doing. She moved to Frisco before I did and said, "I want to be on your team, I want to be your associate, I know you can't pay me, but I'll begin because I believe God is calling me." We ended up being able to pay her part-time and she was with us for the first four years. I think we were the first church plant that had an associate on staff from the beginning, but all the funding for that had to come from us, from the people right here in Frisco. That was a healthy thing for us as a way of communicating the importance of stewardship. It was key for us not to be dependent on the diocese or anyone for support. People would ask us, "Well, the diocese is supporting you, right?" And the answer was "No, we got God and us, so how are you going to help with that?"[8]

As Lein's story indicates, the Diocese of Dallas' policy of purchasing land and providing significant operational funding for its church plants means

---

8. Ibid.

that those plants get a big boost in what they are able to achieve. It also costs the diocese a significant amount of money, which means that it is able to plant a church only every few years, not keeping up with population growth in its area. But it is doing much better than it would without devoting those resources to new churches.

The Diocese of Texas is another diocese that puts significant resources into supporting church plants with land or other facilities. Bishop Andy Doyle has declared that his goal is to plant fifteen new churches in the next five years, in addition to the church plants the diocese already has underway. St. Julian of Norwich, a church plant in northwest Austin, meets in a suite in an office building that is quite lovely. The building, which also has business tenants, has southwestern, mission-style architecture, with a feature that looks like a church bell tower. The diocese helped the church locate and pay for the rent on that space, and as the church grows, will help the congregation locate other rental space as appropriate. Mary MacGregor talks about how the Diocese of Texas supports its church plants:

> To date we have purchased the land. I'm not sure we're going to do a whole lot more of that. We'll do some, but I'll share with you our vision for how we're going to move forward with planting because it's much more creative. What we've found [is] it is incredibly expensive to buy a large enough piece of land, which is usually in one of our bigger cities like Austin or Houston, [that are] really underserved. There are seven million people in the Houston metropolitan area, [and] we don't have enough churches there. We have a lot of churches there, but we don't have enough of them in the fringe areas, and we don't have enough Hispanic congregations, even though the ones we have are large. . . . We have tons of opportunity for Hispanic development in Houston, but to buy a lot of land in Houston, that's expensive.[9]

Instead of starting all its churches according to this expensive model of buying large plots of land, the Diocese of Texas' vision for the future includes various different kinds of church plants. The vision includes supporting large congregations in planting multi-site locations, and starting Fresh

9. MacGregor, interview.

Expressions gatherings, which the Diocese of Texas calls Creative Initiatives, as MacGregor explains:

> We will have Creative Initiatives, diocesan plants, and also some second campuses. . . . The Creative Initiatives thing is coming out of a generational change . . . and perhaps addresses the hopes of a younger generation to do things differently. So we hope to do a little bit of everything. We have huge hope to expand our Hispanic offerings; we are looking for people who can do Hispanic plants [because] that's really important to us. It's going to look very diverse here. People are really catching the enthusiasm and thinking because they're doing some creative things.[10]

Bishop Doyle is encouraging every congregation to think about how it can expand its reach by planting mother-daughter congregations, starting multi-site worship services, and beginning Creative Initiatives to reach underserved populations, such as young adults. The diocese's role is to provide advice and (sometimes) financial support to these parishes that are planting congregations. The bishop's role is to articulate the vision for reaching new people in intentional, creative ways, and to encourage every congregation to think about how it can start new worship ministries.

The Diocese of Arizona has planted a number of new congregations during Bishop Kirk Smith's episcopate. He talks about the expense of planting new congregations:

> I throw as much money at it as I possibly can. We have been sort of blessed recently, and have some resources to do some church planting [from a large property sale]. A lot of dioceses don't have that; they're struggling. The most important thing is having the right leader there, and that's expensive. That isn't to say you couldn't do it differently. Some of these places were on a shoestring. . . . The challenge for the Episcopal Church is to find alternative ways that are effective but less expensive.[11]

The most important resources a diocese needs to provide are not capital resources to purchase a facility, but salaries and benefits of the lead planter,

---

10. Ibid.
11. Smith, interview.

plus some support for operating costs in the first few years. While some congregations will need support for capital expenditures, others, like Nativity
and St. Benedict's, will be able to work these matters out on their own. And
others will be able to use building facilities that are already on hand—either
closed or under-utilized church buildings.

This is the case for the Latino congregation Carmen Guerrero is currently planting in Phoenix. The congregation's worship facility costs nothing
because it is shared with an older Anglo congregation. The diocese pays her
part-time salary and provides $2,500 a month for operations. The diocese
is prepared to pay her salary for the foreseeable future, because it believes
that reaching Latinos is extremely important to the future of the church. As
Smith says:

> Mission needs to take place on the fringes, because that's where growth
> usually occurs. For us in the Episcopal Church, there are two groups on
> the fringes: Hispanics and youth. Those are two groups that have been
> neglected by the Episcopal Church, at least here, so those are places we
> really need to look for possibilities for growth. Christian church history
> shows the church grows on the edges. Just look at Pope Gregory the
> Great and the mission to Anglo-Saxon England [on the edges of the civ-
> ilized world]. We ask, why is he doing that, why is it successful there?
> Those are the places we ought to be looking, areas that are underserved
> by the Episcopal Church.[12]

The Episcopal Church recognized this priority in 2012 with General
Convention legislation providing two million dollars for grants for new congregations and Mission Enterprise Zones, which give preference to congregations that serve populations who are traditionally underrepresented in the
Episcopal Church. While this is a three-year pilot program, my hope is that
it will continue and be expanded beyond 2015. Iglesia Santa Maria received
a $100,000 grant from this program, and is using it for program expenses.

St. Gabriel's in Leesburg, Virginia, is another recipient of a Mission
Enterprise Zone grant. St. Gabriel's was planted about ten years ago and is
still meeting in a school. Daniel Velez Rivera is tasked with helping the current English-speaking congregation grow and thrive, while also starting a

---

12. Smith, interview.

Latino congregation at St. Gabriel's. He talks about how his previous ministry was financially supported in Salem, Massachusetts.

> The Diocese of Massachusetts had something called the Urban Residence Program for curates: a three-year program where you were doing your curacy in a new setting under the supervision of a rector. . . . We were in a church that had Latinos in the neighborhood, but the rector did not have knowledge about doing ethnic ministry. . . . So together she, the bishop, and I met to talk about the possibility of me planting a Latino ministry at Grace Church in Salem, a three-year adventure. The holy adventure was to try it and if it worked we would see what we would do. . . . At the end of the three years it was a success. We had about one hundred people worshiping on Sundays, but the contract was over. The church couldn't afford to pay me because the church didn't come up with [any of the money for my salary during those three years], which was [a mistake], because they had no skin in the game.[13]

This story points out the sad fact that often ethnic or Fresh Expressions ministries are started without firm diocesan commitment to keep them going once the funding falls through, or the original planter has left. Sometimes a ministry is in operation only for a time, and then the time passes, and the ministry achieved what it needed to for that time. But I believe that given the demographics, Latino ministry is important enough to our church that we need to commit the financial resources it requires on a long-term basis. In generations to come, the Latino population in the U.S. will double, and as Latinos mature and move away from first-generation immigrant status, they will have increasing financial resources to support their congregations. We need to be investing now in the congregations we will need in the future. Already, according to Anthony Guillén, two-thirds of Latinos currently in the U.S. were born here, and about the same number speak English at home. Many Episcopalians now attend churches that long-ago generations sacrificed and labored to build; it is our turn to do the same for future generations.

Another congregation that received a Mission Enterprise Grant is The Abbey in Birmingham, which will minister to Millennial adults. Of the two leaders, Katie Nakamura Rengers, the priest, is paid by a large nearby

---

13. Velez Rivera and Derritt, interview.

congregation to be an associate on its staff, and she serves there on Sundays. The deacon, Kellie Hudlow, works as an attorney full-time and does not receive a church salary. The diocese has helped with some startup expenses for the coffeehouse, and the Mission Enterprise Zone grant will help fix up the storefront and get it ready for opening. The creative financial model of that ministry contemplates that eventually profits from the coffeehouse will cover the cost of operations. Rengers points out that running a business to support the religious operations is completely in keeping with the historic monastic model. One of the pillars of the Benedictine life is work, and monastics traditionally work at a business—beer making, wine making, cheese making, and so on—to support their religious communities. The Abbey's financial model gives this ancient tradition a very modern twist. Even without the coffeehouse model, it is encouraging to see a large congregation contributing to the salary of a Fresh Expressions church planter like Rengers. Helping to start a nontraditional congregation full of people who would never attend a traditional Episcopal church is one way that large, established congregations can increase their evangelistic outreach to underserved populations.

The many different stories of how church plants are financed and supported demonstrate the variety of ways a diocese can go about this work. Some well-resourced dioceses, like Texas and Dallas, support church plants with significant land purchases. Others simply provide salaries and operating expenses; such as we received at Nativity. Some church plants return the initial investment to the diocese and more, in the form of diocesan assessment. Some cost the diocese money and still do not last more than a few years, one good reason that church planters should be carefully selected and should work hard to follow good church planting principles. At a minimum, a diocese that is interested in planting new congregations should plan to pay a planter's salary and benefits for three to seven years, on a diminishing scale, while the congregation works to take on this responsibility and become self-supporting. A diocese or parish that is interested in adding a new ethnic congregation or Fresh Expressions community should also plan to support the salary of the leader. If a parish starts a second location to minister to people who will not come to the main campus, that parish may have to provide resources to acquire a location elsewhere, but, as Clay Lein points out, such a congregation could be lay-led by a bi-vocational minister.

Many dioceses do not have money to pour large sums into new property purchases, and in fact may already have more underutilized buildings than they know what to do with. Even so, there are great opportunities to use these older, underutilized buildings for ethnic church plants for a significant new ethnic group in the neighborhood or for creative, nontraditional new congregations. A diocese does not have to have major population growth in its territory to plant new churches. All it needs to have is significant numbers of people who are untouched by the good news of Christ. These are people Christ loves, and wants to reach, and they are in every part of our country. ❧

PART THREE

Where Do We Go From Here?

I believe that planting new churches is one of the most important actions the Episcopal Church can take in order to accomplish its mission in the decades to come. We have spent too long in conflict and in decline; it is time to start thinking strategically about how to reach new people with the good news of Christ. In this section, we will talk about how diocesan and denominational leaders can empower new church planting.

∼ 14

Church Planting
for Diocesan Leaders

Y ou and I are Christians today because someone, sometime, decided to take a risk to spread the gospel. It might have been a Sunday school teacher long ago or a stranger in a bar who started talking about theology. More than likely, it wasn't just one person, but a community of people over a long period of time who helped us learn about Jesus. That's one of the missions of the church: to help people come to know Jesus, and to grow in discipleship as they learn to follow him.

How do we make sure that future generations learn about Jesus too? How do we help them grow in discipleship and service to others? How do we invite them into communities of faith that will model Christ's love, becoming the Body of Christ to new believers? Someone once cared enough to plant all the Episcopal churches we now attend, not so long ago. Planting new churches is in our DNA; it is the lifeblood of our denomination.

But it's been years since the Episcopal Church planted new worshiping communities on a widespread basis, so let's start recovering some of those memories. How are diocesan leaders to go about starting new churches? What are the most important things for a bishop and diocesan council to understand, if they want to support the planting of new communities of faith?

Diocesan leaders are in wildly different circumstances across the country. Bishops in fast-growing Sunbelt cities can't find enough money to plant all the traditional churches that are needed in new developments that are exploding with growth. Bishops in declining northern cities can't figure out what to do with all the decaying buildings and tiny congregations they have. Church planting, however, offers different opportunities to dioceses in very different circumstances. There are many different ways to reach new people with the gospel:

- Using a building with a tiny traditional congregation in an older neighborhood, surrounded by neighbors who are of a different demographic or ethnic group than the few stalwarts who still attend the church, to plant a new congregation that touches a completely different population;
- Identifying a group of people—university students, urban youth, homeless street people, prisoners, nursing home residents, Hollywood studio executives—who have not been touched by the gospel or who simply cannot attend church, and starting a church without walls;
- Starting a community of faith led by an entrepreneurial layperson who brings in retired priests for sacraments, or who works under the aegis of a visionary established church that will give occasional sacramental support;
- Identifying a fast-growing new community development that has few churches, and sending a missionary priest to live among them and form a community of faith;
- Creating a business, like a coffeehouse, that will host life-giving worship and discussions of faith.

The list goes on. There are many different ways to reach people, and many of them involve forming new communities that reach new people in new ways. Some of these projects will cost a lot of money, and some will not. All of them require faithful, visionary dedication to the work of the gospel, and the sincere belief that people's lives are changed for the better as they come to know Christ and learn to follow him.

Andy Doyle describes his vision for the church in the Diocese of Texas:

We have to plant new communities. Planting [traditional] churches is one of the ways we do that, but we also need to be thinking about different kinds of communities like second sites; we need to look at it in a much broader perspective. We need a distributive system of church community; there is a lot of planting, a lot to be done. New churches are a keystone: they can model and be hubs for other work. It is essential to have new communities, new things to reach new people. New churches have more freedom to try new things. We need new congregations because congregations have an ebb and flow to their life. We think we have one and we will have it forever, but that is not viable or realistic or true. For me it's both a theological perspective but also the perspective of the church as an organism, with health and vitality.

If the vision is to create new Christian communities, if that's the driving vision, we have to find any way we can to do this. My vision in Texas is this: in the next fifteen years, we will have at least fifty-one new communities. That can be all kinds. I don't think that's enough. I think we will build momentum. My shorter vision is three to five a year, and in fifteen years I'm shooting for fifty-one.[1]

We might say that is a great vision for the Diocese of Texas, which is blessed with abundant financial resources. How is that vision relevant to struggling dioceses in the rest of the church? Bishop Doyle explains that those fifty-one communities will include a few traditional new churches, but many more nontraditional ones:

We have a church where in a three-mile radius there are three nursing homes. They could assign three bi-vocational priests or deacons to go to those places. They could say, "We will provide you a church service every Sunday for free," and let them know that they will be provided pastoral care for anyone who doesn't have someone to do it. They can say, "We will provide all that and we will be glad to come do Eucharist once a month." They won't necessarily get money from it, but it is a Christian community. Also there are a lot of ways to create new communities for people who can't get to church, who are locked in. There's a lot of different kind of stuff, there's a whole world of people. We can do different things, some edgy stuff, some regular stuff, weekday churches, all kinds of stuff. Not on Sunday necessarily; what about people who have to work on Sunday, when do they go to church?[2]

---

1. Andy Doyle, telephone interview with the author, September 8, 2014.
2. Ibid.

That broad vision of the church is what the Episcopal Church should be encouraging and engendering across the country. Even in areas of declining population, there are people who have not been touched by the gospel, and people who have no access to a church community. We need to plant new churches because there are people who need to hear about Jesus.

Casting a Vision

For diocesan leaders who are interested in planting new church communities, you are heading into an exciting new adventure. You will find yourself inspired and rewarded by what you witness as you empower people and provide support for this vital work of the Great Commission. Here are some suggestions for diocesan leaders who would like to plant churches.

First, we should broaden our vision of what the church is. Many Episcopalians, I think, can't even imagine planting new communities because of the expense that might be involved, or because they already have many small and declining churches in buildings that are far too large for them. Doyle suggests that in decaying cities, we can see evidence of revitalization, and we should be part of it:

> Because we have bought into the separation of secular and sacred in our work as church, we are missing a whole suburban and urban revitalization that is going on in cities: people are turning brown sites into green sites, old malls into community colleges, there is a whole movement of people looking at revitalizing areas of communities. We separate ourselves out because we think those are secular things; we don't even see new vitality happening in older parts of cities, we just say we need to get out of there. No, we need to be there with new visions, new eyes, we can envision what needs to be there.[3]

That vision of what needs to happen in our communities does not all need to come from the diocese. It takes people on the ground, relating with others, discerning their needs, becoming very familiar with their culture, to understand how best to touch unreached people with the good news of Jesus. Leaders need to empower ministers to be our eyes and ears on the ground, to be immersed in our communities, and to create new forms of Christian

---

3. Ibid.

gathering. That process of empowering others begins, however, with the diocese creating a vision, a vision that sees obeying the Great Commission as the
imperative for any kind of Christian leadership.

"The bishop has to lead," says Mary MacGregor:

> . . . . and has to cast a vision for growth with new congregations and
> new initiatives and whatever form it takes, and begin to really make
> that message really clear. People should know when he/she walks in the
> door, he or she is going to talk about these things, because you know
> that the resources are there. The resources are in our congregations. . . .
> What I have learned by being in this office since 1997 is that there is huge
> power in the bishop and huge influence to change the culture, to work
> on the culture to establish a positive, forward-thinking vision. They've
> got to be courageous. When bishops spend all their time managing, it's
> nothing but decline. If you don't have that vision, you will decline. It's
> going to take vision. Dioceses, rectors, can all cast that vision. We can
> be doing so much more. We have a lot of churches that are complacent.
> That's a missional challenge—we have got to get outside of ourselves.
> It's about the Great Commission, and if we ignore the need to spread
> the gospel, we deserve what we get. . . . I don't want to be a part [of the
> church] unless we care about changing people's lives and influencing
> the world around us for the sake of the kingdom of God. It takes a lot
> of talent, courage, and vision to turn the situation around. We [in Texas]
> have a culture that says, some of you are going to fail. This is not easy,
> we are all learning, trying, and failing is not a failure. Trying is what
> we're trying to encourage our folks to do.[4]

I asked Doyle what advice he would give to a bishop who wants to plant
new worshiping communities. He responded:

> I think that one of the things that planting churches challenges is the
> business-as-usual model of church. So bishops, especially new bishops,
> are just like everybody else, me included. We like to get comfortable;
> we like to create policies that will help us be comfortable. I think for the
> future of church planting, creativity and willingness to allow people to
> color outside lines and do things that make us uncomfortable is essential.

---

4. MacGregor, interview.

What a bishop needs to consider carefully is the importance of allowing people to be creative and let people do church in ways that doesn't fit their models that they know. You can do that wherever you are. I actually think that bishops who want to take on church planting need to become open-minded self-learners. You don't need to know anything to do it; you just need to start doing it. I don't believe that the professor-student "here's the information, now you've got your research, so go do it" model is the right one. Especially with the need for new models, new communities, the most important thing a new bishop can do is actually start doing it, and send people to do it.[5]

Selecting Leaders for the Twenty-First-Century Church

One of the biggest problems that diocesan executives face when planting churches is the scarcity of trained leaders. Episcopal seminaries, for the most part, do not teach church planting, and most planters either learn from the evangelical world or make it up as they go along, or both. This lack of training is a problem in itself, but an even deeper problem is that our ordination process favors leaders who look familiar: established church leaders who specialize in teaching and pastoral care, rather than entrepreneurial leaders who do community organizing, tell people about Jesus, and build something out of nothing. In chapter 6, I told the story of an aspirant for holy orders whose bishop and Commission on Ministry sent her for psychological and spiritual counseling when she said she wanted to be a church planter, to find out why she didn't want to be a "normal" priest. Such an attitude by Commissions on Ministry is unfortunately rather common. We ordain what looks familiar to us and consider the unfamiliar, entrepreneurial leader to be the exception. But what we need for the new, post-Christendom era is leaders who are willing to work outside the established norms, who are willing to make personal contact with people who have not heard the gospel, who are willing to take risks with their careers and their hearts for the sake of creating a new community. How do we find such leaders?

"Here's an example," says Doyle. "I've told our COM [that] I don't want to take anyone into seminary that hasn't started a gospel ministry with twenty-five people or more, that is sustainable after they leave. We are not

---

5. Doyle, interview.

taking those people who have that experience. There are probably plenty of clergy who haven't done that, but those are the people we need."[6] The bishop should set the vision for the type of leaders the Commission on Ministry should be looking for.

Frank Logue adds:

Commissions on Ministry aren't sending entrepreneurial leaders to seminary. Entrepreneurial leaders talk in ways that scare Commissions on Ministry. What we have to do is share as broadly as we can this need that we have and the kind of person that fills this need, so that when people see it they're less scared of it, and they say, "Oh, I have a place for this." Honestly, when I read diocesan journals, I think, we used to have the evangelical and missionary zeal we need in this diocese; we certainly had it in the 1920s and we had it again in the 1950s. I don't know when we lost it, but somehow in the therapeutic model, in the '60s, '70s, and '80s, we lost it. Our longest serving bishop from the 1920s to the '50s said that Christianity is either a missionary religion or it's not true to Jesus Christ. He planted churches in all sorts of ways and found people to do it. And I believe he was looking for entrepreneurial ability, because he was sending them off with little money to places that had no idea what an Episcopalian was and asking them to start a church. So we had it, we had this skill, and we just lost the muscle memory. Every diocese has that to tap into, and I believe every church has it, because at some point they got started. So we already have it in our history, it's in our DNA. So what we have to do is (everywhere that people will listen), to remind them of what it takes to do this stuff, and that you need some people who can act in risky ways, because the gospel involves risk. . . . I had two ideas about what I wanted to do when I went to Kingsland, I knew them well. One was that my wife, and daughter, and I . . . wanted to go do something for God that was so big, that if God wasn't in it we would fall flat on our faces. Either a miracle would happen or we would look like idiots. There would be no room for anything else. No one would be able to look back and say Frank did this on Frank's abilities, the Logues did this on the Logues' abilities. Absolutely there would be something more, more would be risked, and there would be points that later we

---

6. Ibid.

would be able to look at and say, that's a point where we took a big risk. The other one was that I wanted to start a church that if it has to close its door in ten years, that there would be people who never attended the church who miss it and wish it was back.[7]

We need to be looking for ordained leaders who are willing to take that kind of risk for the gospel, to do something so big that either it will change the community or they will fall flat on their faces and look like idiots, as Frank puts it. We need to be looking for people who have started ministries and businesses and organizations, who know how to inspire others to follow them into an improbable future.

Once we have found such entrepreneurial leaders, we must make sure they get the kind of training they need. Knowing that our seminaries generally do a terrific job of transmitting the knowledge of the past (very valuable and crucial knowledge for any priest), but don't concentrate very hard on the entrepreneurial leadership skills of the future, new priests should be given the opportunity to intern with entrepreneurial ministries. Tom Brackett suggests that potential church planters:

> Go *experience* more than anything else. Go do an internship in a new church plant before you ever go public with your desire, your sense of call. Go get a mentor for new ministry and hang out in that space. Go interview five leaders about lows, highs, joys, failures they've experienced. If you feel called to ministry in a particular context, with a particular group of people, go to that context, fall in love with those people, find a way to be embedded in that context before going public. I think a lot of times a bishop will say, "You want to do ministry, I need one over here, and I'll pay you for two years," and they are so desperate they take it. It's a huge mistake if they don't love the people they're trying to engage and the context they're trying to serve. First fall in love with the people you're called to serve, and then find a way to finance that call. Go hang out with them and let them help you tune the way you share the good news. Get real about your sense of good news and your way of telling it. Get clear about your sense of belovedness and have a community set aside that you can go to that reminds you of your belovedness.

---

7. Logue, interview.

Have a life outside the church plant that you can run to when you need to. Find some key thread of stories in scripture that connect you to what God is doing in that world. Fall back in love with scripture.[8]

Training and Empowering Lay Leaders for Multi-Site Ministry

I do not believe that we should limit our search for entrepreneurial leaders to candidates for ordination. In fact, it is possible that the future of church planting may depend on our ability to mobilize motivated lay people to plant churches, not just as part of a launch team led by a priest, but as leaders of new communities themselves. Bishop Doyle points out:

> Maybe we're lucky to get a person who wants to plant churches [who is interested in ordination]. If a person comes with a sense of call, they will talk to their rector. It will take a year of process before they get to the COM, and they're often there for a year. Then they go off to seminary for three years. Then they come back, and if they're fortunate enough they get a curacy for two years, followed by a year of transition, then the next year in a new congregation, before they can finally (maybe) make some changes they have to be there at least two years. By the time you're thinking about that, [they haven't been able to make any] change for a decade. So the problem we face as people who are calling out and recognizing gifts among our people for ministry and church planting is that typically we look through the lens of a church that no longer exists. We are looking at our own experience, but the church they're going to exist in is ten years from now. They have the ability to shape it for thirty years. Bob Johansen says we should form leaders for that time and not for today.[9]

What if we were to empower some of those lay people who have a sense of call and vision to begin communities now? What if we were to look beyond the people who present themselves for possible ordination, to gifted leaders who would never imagine such a calling? There are many talented lay people who could not imagine going away for three years, or racking up student loans, or leaving behind their current careers and community involvements. Why should they? As people who are immersed in their communities, they

8. Brackett, interview.
9. Doyle, interview.

are ideally situated to start gathering groups of people to learn about Jesus. And as leaders in their own careers, many have excellent entrepreneurial and managements skills. Clay Lein describes a model of planting communities based on lay leadership in satellite communities under the umbrella of an established parish:

> I did my D.Min. thesis on multi-site structures for the Episcopal Church in the twenty-first century. What comes after church planting, or are there other ways that we can be successful in growing communities of faith in addition to church planting? In this diocese [Dallas] we have been successful in planting one church every three years, which is not at all sufficient to keep up with population growth or the natural life processes of growth and decline in a diocese. Church planting is one approach, but the challenge of finding people who have entrepreneurial, persevering, faith, innovation, communication, preaching gifts with a collar on them in our tradition is almost impossible. It is quite disheartening.... I believe that we don't have enough church-planting clergy in the Episcopal Church. Seminaries and COM processes wean out entrepreneurial types because those people rock boats.... But if I could find a way to start a new community of faith that did not require a collar, but allowed lay people who start businesses left and right, who are teachers in schools and colleges, who have communication gifts, who are right in the trenches with real life, if I could find a way, a structure that I could mobilize some lay leaders to lay-pastor a community of faith, sure, I need a priest to do sacraments, but I can find retired priests who want an altar. To find entrepreneurial, communicative leaders, suddenly I can go from (if I really got my diocese behind that model) one church every three years, to where I could imagine doing three campuses at St. Philip's. Their boss has to be a collar. All of those little struggling shoots have their taproot connected to a larger church, with access to the staff, and our staff actually sees every one of those campuses as an integral part of their responsibility. We could have multi-site children's, youth, adult, small groups.[10]

At a visit to the Diocese of Texas clergy conference in 2013, I heard Bishop Doyle express a similar vision: urging the clergy of that diocese to

---

10. Lein, interview.

begin thinking of novel ways to extend their evangelism, and not just service or ministries, beyond their front doors. Two churches in the diocese already have second sites serving groups of people quite different from those in the main sanctuary, and others are looking at the possibility. But parishes are also being urged to consider ways to empower lay ministers to take the church's ministries to new groups of people. Doyle continues:

> We don't have to give up on the nature of the Episcopal Church as a sacramental church. We have a full range of licensing for laity. We can do new things to start communities such as licensing preachers and pastoral ministers. We say we believe in the ministry of the baptized, but sometimes we act like it's a nice thing we can float around as long as *we* can stand at the altar. We are willing in our diocese to have a layperson take a box with one or two wafers and wine to an old person who is homebound, sick, or in the hospital, but we won't let a layperson take twenty-five wafers to a nursing home and hold a service and create a community. That's a great example of a boundary. What's the difference between two people and twenty-five people? We have a tool for church planting now; you could be doing it right now with honor and reverence to the sacrament. It's doable but we don't. . . . Clergy get really nervous when I start talking about this. The truth is the way the economics of church are going right now, we won't even be able to afford full-time clergy. We must have new ways to have new communities. We only will get there with a variety of ways in which the economy of church is building, growing, thriving. Big churches have more resources and can do more, but it is just as easy for a small church. We have ways of training people, we have a ton of resources to help people be prepared, we have everything we need; we just have to go out. We have service to share, the gospel to share; we have to start reaching new communities.[11]

I asked Tom Brackett for his thoughts about trends in church planting over the next ten years. He answered:

> What I wish for, but don't see it yet in the Episcopal Church, is what I see in Methodist and Presbyterian churches: the need to sponsor

---

11. Doyle, interview.

ministries with populations that are very different from their own, people they cannot engage. There could be churches with the ability and maturity in the congregation's life cycle that they would sponsor new ministries, like the cathedral model as a hub of many ministries, not just the bishop's seat, but a center for resources to bless the surrounding community. The trend is more mother-daughter churches, more multiplying churches, so that we would have regional networks for Latino or Filipino or Hmong congregations.[12]

Encouraging existing congregations to find ways to create new worshiping communities that reach out to different populations that would not feel welcome in or attracted to the traditional church (or simply are unable to get there) has huge potential for expanding the reach of our Episcopal mission.

Liturgical Innovation

Diocesan leaders who want to plant new faith communities may need to think hard about what kinds of liturgical innovation they are willing to allow. They may need to stretch and allow departures from standard Episcopal worship. Thad's in Santa Monica does not regularly celebrate the Eucharist or follow the lectionary. This approach is appropriate for the community that that congregation wishes to reach—people involved in the entertainment industry who have never been to any kind of church. Innovation may require bishops to allow this kind of nontraditional liturgical gathering. Innovation may also involve allowing lay leaders more leadership responsibility. It may include doing things that are culturally appropriate for the congregation, though unfamiliar to many Episcopalians. As Doyle says:

> [It is] essential, as the church tries to do church plants, new starts, new sites with different cultures and ethnicities, the church has to be culturally humble. I was visiting recently a service of immigrants from the Church of South India who might be interested in uniting with us. Are we willing to allow them to do their worship? It is Anglican but not very Episcopal. You are challenged, are you willing to do a blessing of all the people when the bishop comes? The Hispanic church loves that.

---

12. Brackett, interview.

Are we willing to get outside of ourselves a bit and do things outside 1979 BCP because that's the culture? Secular culture is just as foreign.[13]

Liturgical innovation may be dramatic or not so dramatic. It may be as simple as a church not wishing to say the Nicene Creed every Sunday because the congregation includes a significant number of people who haven't worked through their thoughts about it, and aren't comfortable saying it (though they may be baptized). It may involve music that is unusual for Episcopalians, but culturally appropriate for the congregation. Bishops will need to think about how much innovation they are comfortable with, and may need to stretch their comfort zones for the sake of the gospel.

Providing Connection and Support for Church Planters

One of the most important roles the diocese can play with a new church community is that of emotional and prayer support, and helping connect the planter with a wider community of planting. Church planting can be a lonely task; surrounding churches may be unhappy to have a new church, or may simply not understand the value of the work. Priests in established parishes usually do not have any idea of the struggles that church planters face. Clergy gatherings are famous for providing opportunities for competition rather than support. Sometimes, the best thing a diocese can do is to make sure that church planters are connected with others who can pray for them and provide an understanding, caring community. If there are other planters in the diocese, making sure that they have an opportunity to connect with each other is essential. And the diocesan staff can also provide spiritual and emotional support. Doyle says:

> I believe that the first way of helping them is with relationship. Church planting is not sending someone into the wilderness by him- or herself. Bishop and staff, or in a smaller diocese executive board members, and leadership of the diocese, needs to recognize that they have a duty and requirement to support the people we send out. Jesus sent them out two by two, and looking at the first couple of centuries, people were supported by a network. Don't just send them out by themselves; they

---

13. Doyle, interview.

feel alone. Just simple pastoral support and the ability to celebrate small wins are important; even know what the wins are.

The other thing is, the bishops have to guide with a tender and caring hand, and not an adjudicatory or policy hand. I'm remembering in Mark, Jesus looks at the people who were like sheep without a shepherd and he was moved in his gut, disturbed. A bishop has to believe that so much in order for them to be willing to give up on something they thought was important in the first place to give latitude to a church planter who is trying to make connection with people in the real world.[14]

Church planting is a different and difficult enough vocation that most people don't understand what it involves. A diocese should make sure that planters are connected with other people who know what it takes to plant a church, who will give friendship and support, and who will pray. The bishop and diocesan staff should commit to praying for the planter and the project every day, as well.

Defending the New Plant against Established Churches

One of the sad truths of planting new Episcopal churches is that often, one of the biggest battles a planter has to face is with other Episcopal churches that are threatened by the presence of a new church. A bishop who wants to plant churches needs to be prepared to establish church planting as an essential vision for the diocese, and then defend that vision against churches who think it's a good idea, as long as it's not anywhere close to them. Established churches often think of geographic areas as their territory, whether they have made great inroads into that territory or not. Without the unyielding support of the bishop, the church plant might fail, not because it does not have the potential to reach new people, but because of what I call the "auto-immune reaction" from other Episcopal churches. Kirk Smith talks about this issue:

It's a shortsighted understanding . . . I've been accused of undercutting, not supporting them, establishing a new church eleven-and-a-half miles away. It's a total failure to understand that the harvest is plentiful. It is not a matter of competing for a tiny, shrinking group of people

---

14. Doyle, interview.

that want to be Episcopalians. That isn't to say their own church can't do things to grow, but sometimes you have to change your strategy to reach different people. If we were being effective, there would be people there. If you were in fact meeting the needs of people you'd be full, so what are you not doing that needs to be done? Just repeating the same old things and expecting different results is the definition of insanity. You can't just do the same things but work harder; sometimes you have to be innovative, and sometimes you will fail.[15]

I described to Andy Doyle the question one priest asked me when I was first called to plant a church: "Why should we plant new churches? The ones we have aren't full." He responded:

Those are two separate questions. I still don't really understand why those two things are connected. That comes out of a sense of scarcity. People feel anxious about planting churches nearby. I had rectors in Austin who complained about a church plant in a different city thirty minutes away. I didn't know there were so few people out there. It comes out of our sense of scarcity and fear that there are not enough people to go around. For people in those churches that are not full, it's a way of creating a diversion from the real issues affecting their churches. The real question is, how come your church isn't full? That's really hard to say. The other piece is that you can do it without shaming people, but you have to have a realistic view as the bishop or staff member charged with this. We are looking for realistic results based upon their local potential. If you're in a small town and you have a small church and you're doing really well, you're healthy, people are coming, you're reaching out, you have service ministries, and your church isn't full, there's no shame in that. You can even have that in a downtown area, an industrial wasteland. If we can begin to say, what's really going on now here in a suburban area with lots of people, but the church is half full, why is that? [We can't] allow people to deflect us from church planting and evangelism. We have to do both. It's not just about church planting; it's about congregational health and vitality.[16]

---

15. Smith, interview.
16. Doyle, interview.

It is sometimes argued that in order to plant new churches, we need to have the courage to close older ones that have outlived their life spans. While I believe the question of closing older churches is an important one for many dioceses to address in bold and courageous ways, I don't believe that it is a necessary precondition for planting new communities of faith. The economy of God is boundless; there is room for our beloved established churches *and* for new congregations. And in some cases, there are good reasons to use the buildings of older congregations to reach out to new populations nearby. This conversation may require some hard thinking about how best to use the assets the church has available. But I do not believe that church planting is always a trade-off between the old and the new.

Support for Tentmaker Church Planters

Dioceses may want to consider ways of offering support for lay or ordained church planters who are willing to work at other part-time jobs to support themselves while working to plant a church. To be clear, I think that planting a church involves a great deal of time, stress, and commitment, and if at all possible, the diocese should pay for it as a full-time job. But there are planters who are committed enough to their evangelistic work that they are willing to do it while supporting themselves elsewhere, and their life outside the church may even help them meet other people who could be touched by the church. For these "tentmaker" leaders, the diocese may want to offer support, such as health insurance for those whose part-time jobs don't provide it, or at least a part-time stipend. As fewer full-time stipendiary clergy positions become available in the years to come, many dioceses should be thinking about tent-maker approaches to ministry anyway.

Consistency

A diocese needs to be able to commit to a new church plant for a period of time. It should be very clear up front about what that commitment involves, in money and other support as well as accountability, and it should live up to its promises. There have been cases when a diocese, anxious to see its invest-ment pay off, has pulled the plug on a church plant too soon, or has simply stopped supporting it unexpectedly and left it to its own devices. It is impera-tive that if we are sending our planters out to do courageous work for the gospel, we must back them up with a clear, consistent commitment. That doesn't mean a permanent commitment; my diocese was clear up front that its commitment to me was for three years only, with a possible renewal at the end of that time. But it should not be an uncertain, year-by-year kind of support that depends on the vagaries of the economy and the diocesan budget, either. A planter needs to know exactly what she or he can count on from the diocese, and trust the diocese to live up to its promises.

Willingness to Make Mistakes

If a diocese is serious about reaching new people in new ways, it will need to try a number of different experiments. Some of these experiments will never take off. Some will prosper for a season and then fade. Others will become long-term contributors to diocesan life. A diocese that enters into this adventure should understand that not every experiment will work. There will be failures, and the challenge will be to learn from the failures and put that learning to work in other new experiments. A diocese should be careful not to shame church planters whose experiments did not succeed. There are all kinds of reasons for failures, and many of them involve reasons other than leadership. A church planter who tries should be praised for having the courage to do something very few ordained or lay Episcopalians are willing to do. Paul failed sometimes too, but it was his dogged persistence, over many different attempts, that helped the church of Christ prosper in the long term. Today, it will take many Pauls trying many different experiments to spread the kingdom in a post-Christian world.

Money?

Money is often the one issue that prevents dioceses from trying new church plants. But as chapter 13 makes clear, diocesan financial commitments to new plants vary widely. Some, like Dallas, adopt the classic model of buying land in a strategic location and supporting a planter's salary for a number of years. Others support the salary only and trust the new congregation to work out its own facility issues. Others provide the use of an already-existing facility for a new community, and pay a planter's salary plus operating expenses. And some plants are supported by a mother church, an established parish in the diocese, rather than by the diocesan budget.

The truth is that for the twenty-first century, it is imperative that we plant churches in many different ways, according to many different economic models. Even in a diocese like Texas, which has a $130 million foundation devoted to church planting resulting from the sale of St. Luke's Hospital, that money is not enough for the kingdom work that needs to be done. Doyle says:

> If we really empower the laity, we've got to create a local vision, a local army of church planters. That is the only way we can turn this ship. [In Texas] we can do some of that, but even that [money] will not keep up with growth, where there is growth. When you have money you realize [that] we cannot keep up, even with that amount of money. There is no economic model that imagines a full-time priest, land, and a building that will keep up with shifts in this country. We would need a billion dollars. Nobody has that. The reality is that we need a multitude of models. Church planters have to do it all differently. . . . It's good to have money, but in the long term that is not an economically viable model for the health and well-being of the church unless we have billions of dollars. If the vision is to create new Christian communities, if that's the driving vision, we have to find any way we can to do this. . . . Even if you don't have a lot of money, help them meet people who can bring money. The diocese usually knows who has money in the diocese, some people interested in funding something unique; bring those resources.[17]

Chapter 13 contains a more detailed discussion of finances and stewardship. The diocese will need to consider its economic model for each church plant carefully, and commit to it up front for a number of years, and state its commitment clearly.

Administrative Support

One way that a diocese could really help church plants is to provide administrative support. You might provide bookkeeping services until the new church has the personnel and equipment to do it themselves, or payroll services, or member data software, or a complete set of financial and personnel policies, or secretarial services to produce bulletins and newsletters. You don't want the church planting team to get bogged down in setting up administrative systems when they should be out making contacts with new people. An ACNA (Anglican Church of North America) priest has told me about

---

17. Doyle, interview.

a small parish in one ACNA diocese that has made administrative support, including accounting systems and website design, its ministry to a number of surrounding church plants. This is a service that either a diocese or the denomination could provide.

The Will to Do It

It is easy to get caught in the study and strategizing trap, and over-think how to go about church planting. For diocesan leaders, the key is to set the vision of creating new congregations, new churches, new communities of faith, and to awaken the creativity of people in the diocese. There are many different ways that new communities can be planted; it is good to allow the vision to bubble up from the people who are on the ground in those communities, and empower them to do the work. Doyle says:

> The challenge is that everybody says we need to plant new churches, but are you willing to do it? Do you have the will as a leader to start new congregations? People say yes, we believe in it, but if there is not a will to make it a reality, it doesn't get done. Then they make excuses: they don't have money, they don't have church planters, they don't have people. If you don't have the will to do it and it's not part of your strategy, you can forget it.[18]

Planting churches takes courage, planning, and insight, but with God's help all these things are possible. We should all be looking for opportunities to create new communities to touch people with the love of Jesus Christ, and we should all be taking action, learning from our mistakes, and taking action again. That is the Great Commission imperative to the Episcopal Church in the twenty-first century. ❧

---

18. Ibid.

~ 15

Church Planting for
Denominational Leaders

This is the time for the Episcopal Church to be planting many new churches. The society around us is changing; new peoples and ethnic groups are moving into our country; we can no longer rely on social pressure to bring people to church. If people are going to be transformed by the gospel of Jesus Christ, we are going to have to move outside our existing structures and reach them through daring, bold moves—including planting many new churches.

I am writing in a time when the Episcopal Church is attempting to reimagine its church-wide structures, how we govern ourselves, how our staff and resources are used, and how the various levels of structure—church-wide, diocesan, and local—relate to each other. The Task Force for Reimagining the Episcopal Church has correctly identified evangelism and church planting as two of the most important priorities facing our church in the coming era. As we go about reimagining ourselves, here are some ways I think our Episcopal church-wide structure could take action to empower the essential ministry of creating new church communities.

Making Connections

Just like a diocese, one of the most important things our church-wide structure can do is help church planters connect with each other, support each other, and learn from each other. The Episcopal Church does not have a denominational-level church-planting program, although we currently provide some matching grants for church plants. Our true planting happens through the sponsorship of our dioceses. But our church-wide organization can, and does, take a vital and active role in helping support planters and help them learn from each other. Bishop Andy Doyle, of the Diocese of Texas, says:

> The church-wide organization needs to really take church planting seriously. Its work is to connect those people with one another so they can self-learn and share resources. Some of the work that's being done is great: gathering people for web conferences, phone conferences, gathering people who are doing similar things. That's one of the unique ways the wider church offices can do their work. It's a great example of how we can create networks for people supporting one another in the most inexpensive way possible. . . . The connections we're doing now are very hopeful; it's one of the only things the wider church can do that no one else can do. We are healthier when we are part of a wider conversation; that's a really important thing we do well right now.[1]

Getting to know other church planters across the church can be lifesaving for people involved in a ministry that can isolate them from other clergy, since the calling of a planter is so different from most other church ministries, and some established-church clergy actively oppose the planting of new churches nearby. Planters can share experiences and learning with each other, and provide support when times are tough. That community of support is essential. If money can be located to bring people together for face-to-face support gatherings, and not just web- and telephone-based conferences, that would be even better.

Training Leaders

Related to creating a community of support is providing training for leaders. A diocese that is planting churches might have one or two church plants operating at any one time, and it is quite expensive for them to bring in a church-planting trainer for so few people. As a "connecting" body across the whole church, the denomination can supply trainers to provide the kind of

---

1. Doyle, interview.

up-front support that planters need across the church. In chapter 6, I outlined the kind of training that the Episcopal Church now provides, and also the kind of training available through mainline church planting consultants. I believe that both of these kinds of training opportunities can be very valuable, and our church-wide structure could be instrumental in making them both available. Different training could be offered for different types of church plants: traditional, ethnic, and Fresh Expressions communities.

There is a particular need for training lay and ordained leaders for ethnic ministries. The Episcopal Church should be doing significant work among the rapidly growing U.S. Latino population, and increasing work among Asian groups as well. We currently do not have nearly enough Latino church planters to meet the needs that are before us, so we need to be training non-Latinos in Latino ministry, as well as offering significant lay education opportunities to help Latino lay leaders become educated in the scriptures and the Episcopal approach to the Christian faith. A few of these lay people will go on to become ordained, and many will remain as strong lay leaders in the church. Training of lay and ordained leaders for Latino ministry is such a pressing need that I believe that the church-wide organization should be providing significant funding to develop these training programs. Anthony Guillén describes his dream of what we should offer on a regular basis:

> There should be a school, academy, or seminary institution teaching courses in Latino culture, history, and spirituality. . . . We need a training school, not just for Latinos. We need to learn about Asians too, the second-largest group. Someone has to take seriously the need to form people to be missionaries: bishops, clergy, and lay people. There is a need for more education across the church. In my ministry I would like to be doing [clergy summits in all dioceses of the church to] teach people about who Latinos are, and offer stories and conversations. That's something all dioceses ought to be doing: all-day trainings to give people some knowledge to get started in the conversation. Seminaries should be sending their students to LA, Miami, New York, Chicago, Portland, Houston, Phoenix, and to communities for the summer so they can spend those months learning the language, culture, and ministry. Our seminarians graduate, and some have some Spanish, but they have had very little hands-on ministry. They don't have to go to Panama or Honduras, they can be right here and have incredibly great experiences.

People call me all the time. They feel called, but they need to learn Spanish, and they have no funds for an intensive course. We should have money set aside for language skills and training in cultural competency. It should be an intensive two-week course, not just book learning, but experiential: connecting with people, visiting congregations, eating food, getting in touch with the spirituality and struggles of people in a two-week quick course. Later there could be more in-depth strategies. I would love to partner with folks to create this piece.[2]

Such a crucial training program, aimed to develop leaders for fast-growing ethnic groups in our country, could be developed by the church-wide organization, perhaps in conjunction with a seminary or another denomination. The need for evangelism with new ethnic groups is so pressing that we should fund it and make it a priority.

Seminaries

Seminaries, who prepare the majority of our candidates for ordination, should be offering courses in missional leadership, including evangelism and church planting. Some currently do offer such practical leadership courses, but they are usually not required for graduation, and I believe they should be. Such required courses have been standard fare at evangelical seminaries for years. I believe that such courses, taught by entrepreneurial, experienced planters and evangelists from the Episcopal world and other mainline denominations, could begin to transform the church. Seminaries do immensely important and valuable work in curating the millennia of Christian tradition and scripture and helping students learn to preach, teach, and offer pastoral care. But the leaders of the future will need to do more. They will need practical tools for leadership, evangelism, and starting new communities or redeveloping older ones. The church is changing, and these skills will be essential for future lay and ordained leaders. Seminaries who are able to offer the kinds of courses that younger leaders are now interested in may well find that their programs become more attractive both to potential students and to their bishops.

Of course, it is clear to any observer that a full three-year course of residential seminary formation is more and more difficult for most leaders in

---

2. Guillén, interview.

the church. For some, the idea of having to meet such a requirement probably prevents them from even presenting themselves for ordination. Most Episcopal seminaries currently offer online and low-residency programs, and they should be commended for adjusting to the realities of a new era in this way. Other potential offerings might include training for lay leaders who might lead off-site ministries, and formation for lay Spanish speakers who need to be educated in the scriptures and Episcopal traditions. In the future, lay leadership will become increasingly important in planting new worshiping communities.

Communications

A great role for the church-wide organization to play in supporting church planting is in the area of communications. The Episcopal Church's communications office currently provides a low-cost service to help congregations create attractive websites, and this is a helpful support ministry.[3] The communications office should also do other activities to support new church communities. It should create videos and stories highlighting inspiring stories of how newly planted communities are reaching new people and putting innovative ideas into action. One of the best ways new communities can influence a denomination is as the "research and development" department for the church. But the new things that people are learning and trying don't help others unless they hear the stories. Church-wide officers should make a priority of sharing inspiring and innovative stories.

Another great role for church-wide communications would be to provide an interactive portal where people could upload their own stories and share with each other. An interactive communications hub could help people share learning and best practices across the church. I could envision a church-wide portal with different pages for leadership, church planting, worship, Christian formation, stewardship, and other resources. Church members could upload stories and resources they find or create, vastly expanding the currency and usefulness of a church-wide communications website beyond just the content that can be created by staff alone. A staff member could check each uploaded item for appropriateness and relevance

3. Information on the Episcopal Church's website program can be found at http://www
.episcopalchurch.org/page/affordable-websites-congregations-and-diocese.

before it goes live, but otherwise it would be a free, crowd-sourced way of sharing ideas and success stories. The portal could include features that allow far-flung church members to interact with each other and discuss ideas and findings.

Such a two-pronged strategy of sharing great stories and offering a portal for crowd-sourced sharing could reshape the church-wide communications office as a service to the whole church that helps support evangelism and ministry.

Counting

Our parochial reports concentrate on a small number of statistics that hearken back to the Christendom era. Average Sunday Attendance (ASA) was an important statistic in the days when (1) people who were committed to a church attended almost every week, and (2) all important worship gatherings happened on Sunday morning or Saturday evening. Membership likewise was an important statistic in the days when almost everyone was baptized as an infant, and spent the rest of their lives industriously conveying their letters of transfer from one church to the next.

If we truly want to count the number of people who are impacted by our worship ministries, we need to count more than ASA. We need to count the attendance of those for whom their major weekly attendance happens at other times than Sunday or Saturday evening. Evening pub gatherings, weekday nursing home worship services, home gatherings, all kinds of non-traditional worship needs to be counted. This does not mean counting the regular weekday Eucharist that happens in the church and attracts five to ten people who also come on Sundays. It means counting people who don't worship in the regular Sunday gathering, but whose participation at another time is their major worship community.

We might argue that it doesn't matter whether we actually count extra worship gatherings, as long as they are happening anyway. But in many cases, rectors of churches will concentrate on improving in those areas that get measured. If only Sunday attendance really "counts," churches will concentrate on growing their Sunday services. If other services become important enough to count, churches will be motivated to become creative about reaching out in new ways, to people who would never darken the doors of a regular Sunday worship service.

"Membership" in a church plant is almost a meaningless concept. A church that grows rapidly, as many church plants do, has very little time to do the administrative work of keeping up with letters of transfer, and many of the people joining will not be former church-goers. Most of them won't have any idea of what a letter of transfer is. They may be leery or uncomprehending of the concept of membership, and will not present themselves as members, though they attend regularly, pledge, and participate in ministry. Many new churches will find that their attendance is higher than their official membership. If we really believe in evangelism of adults, we will downplay the concept of membership, with its institutional feel and attendant paperwork, and adopt the concept of "active participation" or some similar term.

We also must find a way to count worshiping communities that are not official mission or parish congregations filing a parochial report. For the first few years of a church's existence, it should avoid creating the kind of official structures that make it eligible to file a parochial report. Some, like Thad's in the Diocese of Los Angeles, do not ever intend to become an official mission or parish of the diocese, because that involves creating different liturgical and leadership structures. Yet that means that many new worshiping communities (not to mention many campus ministries, hospital ministries, school ministries, and street ministries) might as well not exist, as far as official statistics are concerned. Dioceses will be much more motivated to start new nontraditional communities, and delay their official organization as a mission congregation (and delaying that official organization is very important, for the health of the new church), if they get to count these non-mission, non-parish, nontraditional communities in their diocesan numbers.

The point is that people are motivated to do activities that they get credit for. Our counting system should be structured to give credit: to encourage rather than discourage nontraditional, non-Sunday, not-yet-official worshiping communities.

Administrative Support

The previous chapter on church planting for diocesan leaders included a suggestion for providing some administrative support such as accounting, finance, payroll, and secretarial services for new churches that are short-staffed. This support could happen even more efficiently at the denominational level. The Episcopal Church does currently offer a service that will design an attractive, low-cost website for a church. A similar concept could be expanded to help churches get the kind of administrative support they need. Help in acquiring basic accounting software and developing rudimentary systems could be great support for new churches, whose leaders are busy reaching new people for Christ.

Money

During the 2013–15 triennium, the Episcopal Church offered Mission Enterprise Zone grants for new worshiping communities, especially those that reach out to populations (ethnic groups, age groups, economic groups) that are historically underserved. The grants are matching grants, so dioceses must show that they have contributed to the projects; the diocese needs to be committed enough to the project to have "skin in the game." I think it is important that such a granting program continue. Though a strong argument could be made that the church-wide structure should leave as much money as possible in local hands for local ministry, and therefore should not be using money the dioceses contribute in order to make grants back to the dioceses, I believe there are good reasons to continue doing so. The existence of grants encourages dioceses to be creative in reaching out to new people in new ways. Because grants are available, the Episcopal Church officer in charge of administering them can personally contact bishops and other diocesan officials and encourage them to think about what opportunities in their diocese might qualify, spurring projects that were only conceptual to become realities. We can also use granting programs to direct support to strategic programs, such as Latino ministries, that reach groups that are essential to the future of the Episcopal Church.

Tom Brackett points out an additional benefit of providing grants:

> I think it would be a gift to the church at large if we continue to increase the funding available, but for a surprising reason. The benefit for the denomination is that it buys us into a partnership relationship with on-the-ground communities who show us what it is like to minister in new ways among new cultures. The benefit to the church-wide network is that when you fund new ministries, it gives you the opportunity to be in constant conversation with them and learn from them. For the new ministries, it invites them into a growing, widening network of people

struggling with the same realities. Creating a community of practice, a network, is a huge gift that these new ministries offer to the rest of us. Frankly, anything we do with new ministries with these emerging cultures is just basically investing in the future of the church. We are planting seeds for a harvest most of us can't even imagine, and the time to do it is now.[4]

And, although it is true that church-wide grants require taking money from the dioceses in order to put money back in the dioceses, there are some good reasons why this might be a good idea. Frank Logue points out:

> I think we need to be doing [church planting] as dioceses but also nation-ally. A good example is when Las Vegas was booming, but the Diocese of Nevada didn't have the resources to do church planting. There are times when the opportunities that exist need to be supported nationally because the diocese can't do it.[5]

The Episcopal Church's church-wide organization has great power to stimulate the church economy to mission. That's exactly what it should be doing.

Restructuring to Empower Church Planting

In a letter to the church in September 2014, the Task Force for Reimagining the Episcopal Church (TREC) said that the church-wide structure should take on the primary roles of Catalyst, Connector, Capability Builder, and Convener, as it evolves from a bureaucratic/regulatory agency to a network. TREC has correctly identified the following priorities among those the church must address in the years to come: "building capacity and capabil-ity across the church around evangelism, community leadership, and non-traditional parish formation."[6]

TREC is wise in its identification of the primary roles the church-wide structure must play, and the priorities we must address in the near future. But I believe that restructuring, or "reimagining," must go much further

---

4. Brackett, interview.
5. Logue, interview.
6. http://reimaginetec.org/letter-to-church/

than the governance structures that TREC concentrated on in the same letter. I believe that as a Body, our church must come to a common understanding that our primary mission is to form committed Christian disciples who
will carry on Christ's mission in the world—a mission that includes worship,
inclusivity, and the Anglican Five Marks of Mission:

- To proclaim the Good News of the Kingdom;
- To teach, baptize and nurture new believers;
- To respond to human need by loving service;
- To seek to transform unjust structures of society, to challenge violence
  of every kind and to pursue peace and reconciliation;
- To strive to safeguard the integrity of creation and sustain and renew
  the life of the earth.

The first two marks encompass evangelism and making disciples.
Disciples of Christ, empowered for mission, are the ones who accomplish all
five marks. As a church, we must structure ourselves so that we can empower
existing and new congregations to make these disciples who will walk in the
way of Christ.

It is tempting for us as a church to concentrate on changing simple things
that we can tweak: the powers of the Presiding Bishop, the structure of
Executive Council, the size and makeup of General Convention. These are
what Ronald Haifetz calls "technical changes." But while technical changes
may make some small improvements to systems and processes, we are entering an era that calls for far more than small improvements. We cannot simply
continue to do what we have been doing, only work harder at it and structure
it more logically in order to do it better. We are facing an era that calls for
adaptive, not technical, change. "Adaptive work is required when our deeply
held beliefs are challenged, when the values that made us successful become
less relevant, and when legitimate yet competing perspectives emerge," say
Haifetz and Donald Laurie.[7] This is the kind of work the Episcopal Church
needs to be doing in our rapidly changing world.

---

7. Ronald A. Haifetz and Donald L. Laurie, "The Work of Leadership," *Harvard Business
Review*, available at http://www.bostonsix.com/wp-content/uploads/The-Work-of-Leadership
-Heifetz.pdf.

The Episcopal Church must consider how to restructure itself in order to empower the vital work of evangelism that must be done at the local level. We must carefully and strategically use our financial and leadership resources to support the ministries of evangelism and church planting. We should leave more money in local hands so that vital local ministry can be done. At the same time, we should use much less of our church-wide money for direct ministry, instead using church-wide resources to provide the kind of support that the denomination can do better than dioceses can do on their own: connecting people, providing training, helping people learn about bilingual and bi-cultural ministry, giving administrative assistance. One vital strategy for evangelism, probably the single most effective strategy that will help us reach new generations and new populations, is to plant new churches. If we can begin a new movement of starting new worshiping communities of all types—traditional, ethnic, and Fresh Expressions—we can not only change the church, we can change the lives of thousands of people who need to know the love of Christ. And that is a mission worth pouring our hearts into.   ❧

~ 16

Dilemma Flipping

The people of Israel faced a dilemma. The Philistines from the coastal areas had fought the mountain-dwelling Israelites to a draw. Saul's army of Israelites now faced the experienced Philistine warriors across a narrow valley. Neither army was willing to descend into the valley and attack the other uphill. Finally, a giant named Goliath, heavily armored and carrying formidable weapons, descended into the valley. If anyone could beat him in single combat, the Philistines would withdraw in defeat.

Malcolm Gladwell analyzes the brief but decisive battle that followed in *David and Goliath: Underdogs, Misfits, and the Art of Battling Giants*.[1] The way we have always heard the story, he says, as a story of a young, unskilled boy fighting and winning against overwhelming odds, is wrong. David was not an unskilled boy at all. He was an experienced wielder of a common, deadly weapon—the sling. The very things that made him look weak—his small size and lack of armor or heavy weapons—were in fact the source of his strength, because they allowed him to maneuver easily and attack from a distance. The very things that made Goliath look strong—his armaments and his size—actually slowed him down and made him vulnerable to a

---

1. Malcolm Gladwell, *David and Goliath: Underdogs, Misfits, and the Art of Battling Giants* (New York: Little, Brown, 2013).

long-distance weapon he didn't expect. Instead of fighting the giant up close in hand-to-hand combat with heavy armor, as Goliath expected, David fought from far away with a projectile weapon against which Goliath's close-range weapons were useless. David beat Goliath because he changed the rules of the game. Gladwell explains the theme of his book:

> I want to explore two ideas. The first is that much of what we consider valuable in our world arises out of these kinds of lopsided conflicts, because the act of facing overwhelming odds produces greatness and beauty. And second, that we consistently get these kinds of conflicts wrong. We misread them. We misinterpret them. Giants are not what we think they are. The same qualities that appear to give them strength are often the sources of great weakness. And the fact of being an underdog can change people in ways that we often fail to appreciate. It can open doors and create opportunities and educate and enlighten and make possible what might otherwise have seemed unthinkable.[2]

In chapter 1, we talked about Bob Johansen's idea that we now live in a VUCA world: a world of Volatility, Uncertainty, Complexity, and Ambiguity.[3] What David did—changing the rules of the game to favor himself by using distance combat instead of hand-to-hand combat—is a classic example of what Johansen calls "Dilemma Flipping," one of the most important skills Johansen says that leaders in the coming years will need to cultivate:

> Dilemma flipping is a skill that leaders will need in order to win in a world dominated by problems that nobody can solve. . . . Dilemmas are often embedded with hope, even if the hope is hidden. . . . Dilemma flipping is reimagining an unsolvable challenge as an opportunity, or perhaps as both a threat and an opportunity. Dilemma flipping is the ability to put together a viable strategy when faced with a challenge that cannot be solved in traditional ways.[4]

We face a dilemma in the Episcopal Church. Our attendance and membership are declining, which is a symptom of the underlying dilemma: that the traditional strengths we have relied on for years are no longer effective

---

2. Ibid., 5.
3. Johansen, *Get There Early*.
4. Ibid., 57, 59.

in helping us tell the good news of the gospel. What are those traditional strengths? We have long been a church of the powerful, the church that many presidents, signers of the Declaration of Independence, and other shapers of our country's destiny belonged to. We have owned beautiful buildings and built great strength in the great cities of the eastern seaboard. We have had a recognizable "brand" name that is associated with education, wealth, and refinement. Being an Episcopalian was traditionally associated with having high social stature.

Those strengths have now become our weaknesses. Being associated with a well educated, primarily Anglo upper class is not helpful when that group is becoming smaller as a percentage of the population and other groups that we have hardly reached at all are exploding with growth. Having beautiful buildings becomes a liability when those buildings begin to decay and we no longer have enough people or money to maintain them. Strength along the eastern seaboard becomes problematic when people start moving west and some of the cities where we have traditionally been strong begin to decline.

Indeed, perhaps these "strengths" were never helpful in actually proclaiming the good news of Christ (who made his home with the poor and the humble), but only in filling our pews and our treasuries.

As a church, we are anxious over our losses of money and membership. We are bewildered as to why we don't have people flocking to our doors who are seeking a non-evangelical, science-friendly, gay-accepting, open-minded approach to the Christian faith. We don't understand why our congregations are filled with gray-haired folks instead of the hordes of children and youth that used to flock to our worship and Sunday schools long ago. After many years of decline, we are finally being awakened to our historic weakness in evangelism.

Like David, the dilemma we face is how to change the areas of our weakness into our strength.

Perhaps our very anxiety over our loss of power can become the source of our strength in a new era. Awakened to the reality that the structures of the past will no longer sustain us in the future, perhaps we can learn to refocus on the kind of evangelism and disciple-making that Jesus called us to do. Perhaps we will begin to envision new ways of telling the good news of Christ, and not just envision them, but put our energy and our resources behind them and make them a reality.

Planting new churches, I believe, may be the single most important way we will turn this dilemma into an opportunity. Some of the new churches we plant will look a lot like our older ones, and some will look quite different. All kinds of churches are necessary, because we need to reach all kinds of people. Jesus commanded us to go into all the world, making disciples, baptizing them, and teaching them to obey everything he commanded us. Today, in America, we no longer have to go into all the world—all the world can be found right here. Those who have never heard the good news of Christ are in our own cities, our own neighborhoods. Some speak English; many speak a multitude of other languages. The Spirit who breathes fire into our hearts gives us also the strength and courage to speak the words of Jesus to our neighbors.

It is time to take a leap of faith, trusting that the Spirit will catch us, and hold us, and carry us along for a wild, joyous, careening ride of faith. ❧

Index